SOUTH CAROLINA MARRIAGES
VOLUME I 1749-1867
IMPLIED IN SOUTH CAROLINA
EQUITY REPORTS

Barbara R. Langdon

LANGDON & LANGDON
GENEALOGICAL RESEARCH
132 LANGDON ROAD
AIKEN, SC 19801-9536
(803) 643-8564

Abbeville County Marriages 1780-1879
Implied in Abbeville County, S.C.
Equity Records
ISBN 0-938741   250 pages $20.00

Barnwell County Marriages 1764-1859
Implied in Barnwell County, S.C. Deeds
ISBN 0-938741-04-7   118 pages $20.00

Barnwell County Marriages 1775-1879
Implied in Barnwell County, S.C.
Probate and Equity Records
ISBN 0-938741-01-2   188 pages $20.00

Chester County Marriages 1778-1879
Implied in Chester County, S.C.
Probate and Equity Records
ISBN 0-938741-02-0   221 pages $20.00

Edgefield County Marriages 1769-1880
Implied in Edgefield County, S.C.
Probate Records
ISBN 0-938741-05-5   245 pages $20.00

Spartanburg County Marriages 1785-1911
Implied in Spartanburg County, S.C.
Probate Records
ISBN 0-938741-07-1   317 pages $25.00

York County Marriages 1770-1869
Implied in York County, S.C.
Probate Records
ISBN 0-938741-00-4   100 pages $15.00

South Carolina Marriages Volume II
1735-1885 Implied in
South Carolina Law Reports
ISBN 0-938741-08-X   172 pages $20.00

South Carolina Marriages Volume III
1671-1791 Implied in the
Provincial and Miscellaneous Records
of South Carolina
ISBN 0-938741-09-8   224 pages $20.00

Copyright 1991 Barbara R. Langdon
Second Edition 1994
ISBN 0-938741-06-3

Special thanks to T.M.B. and D.M.G., Attorneys at Law

INTRODUCTION

Marriages were not recorded in South Carolina until the twentieth century. This book is part of a series designed as an aid to discover South Carolina marriages. This collection of 1,794 marriage references and relationships is the result of the searching of the South Carolina Equity Report Books the dates of which are from after the Revolution to 1868. The year 1749 was the date of the earliest record and 1867 was the latest record found in the volumes searched. The South Carolina Equity Report books may be found at the Coleman Karesh Law Library, University of South Carolina in Columbia. The Law Library will answer requests for specific information by mail.

These equity volumes contain court cases that were appealed in the higher courts. It is believed that the original loose papers from which these volumes of court cases were compiled at the state level no longer exist. The original cases at the county level may still be on file if the courthouse survived the War Between the States (1861-1865) and other disasters.

Please note that this book contains evidence of and in many cases only clues to marriages. It is not a collection of marriage records. Proof or verification is left to the user of this book.

Husband-wife relationships often appear in equity court transcripts in which individuals state their relationship to a deceased person whose estate is being contested in order that they might inherit. Equity records often contain other vital statistics.

This book is divided into two alphabetically ordered sections Men and Women. In each section the man's or woman's name is followed by the spouse, the volume and page numbers of the equity reports volume in which the reference is found and the year one or both were living. Usually the year is that of the document in which the couple is mentioned, not necessarily the date of marriage. The couple may have lived many years prior to the court action. For example, when a testator's daughter is deceased and only her husband's name is mentioned, the nearest possible date for this couple is the date of the document. In some cases the actual date of marriage or reference to a marriage bond, contract or settlement was found and is included.

Each entry in this book contains only the information discernable from that court case alone and possibly an additional equity court case in which instance reference to this other source is given. The other reference or references may be needed to correlate and support the evidence in the first citation.

Why are some first names of men and women left blank? The court transcripts may merely show that John Smith married a daughter of James Jones. The entry in this book will leave the first name of the woman blank. Likewise, a woman may appear among her brothers with her married name, revealing the last name of her spouse, but not his first name. Thus the man's first name is left blank.

The name of a woman's father or former husband may have been found. For the first time in this series brothers of some of the women are mentioned with the idea of leading the researcher to the woman's surname. Also dates of birth and/or death of any of the individuals. A Subindex to these persons mentioned in notations below some of the references is provided at the end of the book.

When looking through this book for clues to a marriage, it is important to check all possible variations in the spelling of names. Every attempt has been made to spell the names as they appear in the records. A couple may be referred to in more than one document with sometimes drastically different spellings and different dates. In all cases all should be searched. The user of this book will have to make his own judgement as to which of the spelling variants is correct.

Geographical clues concerning the county of residence for the couple have been included in braces to the right side of the page. In some cases no geographical locale or court house site was indicated. In many the home county was not given, but the judicial court district was. Often only the court site within a judicial district was given. The following information may assist in the determination of the area in South Carolina from which a couple originated:

"A court of chancery appears to have existed in this state, very early after the settlement of the colony. There are distinct traces of it under the proprietary government - and soon after the royal government superceded the proprietary, the court of chancery was regularly established..."[1]

"An act to establish a Court of Equity within this state. - Ratified on 19th February 1791...and whereas great inconveniences have been experienced in the remote parts of the state, on account of the court of chancery having been hitherto held in one part of the state only [Charleston]

---

[1] William Henry Desassaure, Reports of Cases Argued and Determined in the Court of Chancery of the State of South Carolina from the Revolution to December 1813 Inclusive, (4 vols.; St. Paul: West Publishing Company, 1917), I, page xxxviii.

"...Be it enacted, that all future sittings of the court of equity...shall be held...at Columbia for all causes wherein the defendant shall reside in Camden, Orangeburgh or Cheraw districts...at Cambridge for all causes wherein the defendant shall reside in the district of Ninety-six...and at Charleston for all causes wherein the defendant shall reside in either of the districts of Charleston, Beaufort or Georgetown..."[2]

"An act for the better arrangement of the sittings of the Courts of Equity; for the establishment of a Court of Appeals for the same, and for other purposes therein mentioned. - Passed the 15th December, 1808: Be it enacted...that the state shall be divided into three circuits for the court of equity, to wit: the southern, the northern and the western; that the present common pleas districts of Charleston, Colleton and Beaufort...shall form the southern circuit of the court of equity; that the present common pleas districts of Georgetown, Horry, Marion, Darlington, Marlborough, Chesterfield, Lancaster, Kershaw, Sumter, Fairfield, Richland and Lexington...shall form the northern circuit of the court of equity; and the present common pleas districts of Orangeburgh, Barnwell, Edgefield, Abbeville, Pendleton, Greenville, Spartanburgh, Union, York, Chester, Laurens and Newberry...shall form the western circuit of the court of equity."[3]

"And be it further enacted...That the districts of Charleston, Colleton and Beaufort...shall form one equity district, to be called Charleston district, the courts for which shall sit at Charleston court-house...; that the districts of Georgetown, Horry, Marion, and Williamsburgh... shall form one other equity district, to be called Georgetown district; and the districts of Orangeburgh and Barnwell... shall form one other equity district to be called Orangeburgh district; the courts of Georgetown and Orangeburgh district shall be held at Georgetown and Orangeburgh court-houses... that the district of Darlington, Marlborough and Chesterfield ...shall form one other equity district to be called Cheraw district; and the district of Edgefield, Abbeville and Pendleton...shall form one other equity district, to be called Ninety-six district; the courts of Cheraw and Ninety-six shall be held at Cheraw and Abbeville court-houses...that the districts of Lancaster, Kershaw, and Sumter...shall form one other equity district, to be called Camden district; and the districts of Greenville, Laurens and Newberry, shall form one other equity district to be called Washington district; the courts for the districts of Camden and Washington shall be held at Kershaw and Laurens court-houses...that the

---

[2] Ibid., p. 75.

[3] Ibid., p. 91.

districts of Fairfield, Richland and Lexington...shall form one other equity district, to be called Columbia district; and the districts of Spartanburgh, Union, York, and Chester, shall form one other equity district, to be called Pinckney district: the courts for Columbia and Pinckney district shall be held at Richland and Union court-houses..."[4]

"And be it further enacted..., That a court of appeal for the court of equity, shall be, and the same is established which said court shall exercise appellate jurisdiction in all cases brought up from the circuit, and shall be holden at Charleston court-house for the southern circuit...and at Richland court-house for the northern and western circuits..."[5]

"An act establishing a Court of Equity in and for the district of Beaufort and for other purposes. -Passed the 19th December 1810:...Whereas sundry inhabitants of Beaufort district, have, by their petition to the legislature, represented the great inconveniences they suffer from their remote situation from the court of equity:...Be it enacted ...that the district of Beaufort shall constitute an equity district, in the southern equity circuit...to hold a court of equity at Coosawhatchie court-house..."[6] [In Beaufort District court was also held at Gillisonville.]

"An act to establish a Court of Equity for Edgefield district. Passed 21 December 1814...[to be held] at Edgefield court-house."[7]

The courts of equity ceased to exist before the end of the nineteenth century.

Barbara R. Langdon

---

[4] Ibid., pp. 91-92.

[5] Ibid., p. 92.

[6] Ibid., p. 100.

[7] Ibid., p. 105.

KEY TO TERMS AND ABBREVIATIONS:

VOLUME = bound and printed book
common-law marriage = couple was not married by law
LIVED = usually date of document in which couple appears
n.d. = no date

KEY TO SOURCES

ABBREVIATION	VOLUME OF EQUITY BOOKS
BAILEY	Bailey's Equity Reports or

Bailey's Equity Reports or

South Carolina Equity Reports, Cases in Equity Argued and Determined in the Court of Appeals of South Carolina from January 1830 to April 1831 Inclusive, by Henry Bailey, State Reporter, Annotated Edition, West Publishing Company, St. Paul, 1917.

CHEVES   Cheves' Equity Reports or

Cases in Chancery Argued and Determined in the Court of Appeals of South Carolina, Volume I, [Note: There is no Volume II] from November, 1839 to May 1840 Both Inclusive, by L. Cheves, Jr., State Reporter, Annotated Edition, West Publishing Company, St. Paul, 1917.

1 DESA   1 Desaussure's Equity Reports or

Reports of Cases Argued and Determined in the Court of Chancery of the State of South Carolina from the Revolution to December 1813 Inclusive, by Henry William Desaussure, Volume I, Annotated Edition, West Publishing Company, St. Paul, 1917.

2 DESA   2 Desaussure's Equity Reports or

Reports of Cases Argued and Determined in the Court of Chancery of South Carolina from the Revolution to December 1813 Inclusive, by Henry William Desaussure, Volume II, Annotated Edition, West Publishing Company, St. Paul, 1917.

3 DESA   3 Desaussure's Equity Reports or

Reports of Cases Argued and Determined in the Court of Chancery of South Carolina from the Revolution to December 1813 Inclusive, by Henry William Desaussure, Volume III, Annotated Edition, West Publishing Company,

KEY TO SOURCES

ABBREVIATION   VOLUME OF EQUITY BOOKS

St. Paul, 1917.

4 DESA   4 Desaussure's Equity Reports or

Reports of Cases Argued and Determined in the Court of Chancery of the State of South Carolina and in the Court of Appeals in Equity, by Henry William Desaussure, Volume IV, Annotated Edition, West Publishing Company, St. Paul 1917.

DUDLEY   Dudley's Equity Reports or

Reports of Cases Argued and Determined in the Court of Appeals of South Carolina on Appeals from the Courst of Equity Containing Decisions From December 1837 to May 1838 Inclusive, by C. W. Dudley, State Reporter, Annotated Edition, West Publishing Company, St. Paul, 1917.

HARPER   Harper's Equity Reports or

Reports of Equity Cases Determined in the Court of Appeals of the State of South Carolina, by William Harper, State Reporter, Annotated Edition, West Publishing Company, St. Paul, 1917.

1 HILL   1 Hill's Equity Reports or

Reports of Cases in Chancery Argued and Determined in the Court of Appeals of South Carolina from January 1833 to January 1834 Both Inclusive, by W. R. Hill, State Reporter, Volume I, Annotated Edition, West Publishing Company, St. Paul, 1917.

2 HILL   2 Hill's Equity Reports or

Reports of Cases in Chancery Argued and Determined in the Court of Appeals of South

KEY TO SOURCES

ABBREVIATION   VOLUME OF EQUITY BOOKS

Carolina from March 1834 to May 1837 Both Inclusive, by W. R. Hill, State Reporter, Volume II, Annotated Edition, West Publishing Company, St. Paul, 1917.

1 McC   1 McCord's Equity Reports or

Chancery Cases Argued and Determined in the Court of Appeals of South Carolina from January 1825 to May 1826 Both Inclusive, by D. J. McCord, State Reporter, Volume I, Annotated Edition, West Publishing Company, St. Paul, 1917.

2 McC   2 McCord's Equity Reports or

Chancery Cases Argued and Determined in the Court of Appeals of South Carolina from January to May 1827 Both Inclusive, by D. J. McCord, State Reporter, Volume II, Annotated Edition, West Publishing Company, St. Paul, 1917.

McMULL   McMullan's Equity Reports or

South Carolina Equity Reports, Equity Cases Argued and Determined in the Court of Appeals of South Carolina from November 1840 to May 1842 Both Inclusive to Which Are Added Cases Omitted by Former Reporters from 1827 to 1837, by J. J. McMullan, State Reporter, Annotated Edition, West Publishing Company, St. Paul, 1917.

RICE   Rice's Equity Reports or

Reports of Cases in Chancery Argued and Determined in the Court of Appeals and Court of Errors of South Carolina from December 1838 to May 1839 Both Inclusive, by William Rice, State Reporter, Annotated Edition, West Publishing Company, St. Paul, 1917.

KEY TO SOURCES

ABBREVIATION	VOLUME OF EQUITY BOOKS
RICHEQ	Richardson's Equity Cases or
	Reports of Cases in Chancery Argued and Determined in the Court of Appeals of South Carolina from May Term 1831 to May Term 1832 Both Inclusive, by J. S. G. Richardson, State Reporter, Annotated Edition, West Publishing Company, St. Paul, 1917.
1 RIEQ	1 Richardson's Equity Reports or
	Reports of Cases in Equity Argued and Determined in the Court of Appeals in Equity and Court of Errors of South Carolina, Volume I, from December 1844 to May 1845 Both Inclusive, by J. S. G. Richardson, State Reporter, Annotated Edition, West Publishing Company, St. Paul, 1917.
2 RIEQ	2 Richardson's Equity Reports or
	Reports of Cases in Equity Argued and Determined in the Court of Appeals in Equity and Court of Errors of South Carolina, Volume II, from November 1845 to May 1846 Both Inclusive, by J. S. G. Richardson, State Reporter, Annotated Edition, West Publishing Company, St. Paul, 1917.
3 RIEQ	3 Richardson's Equity Reports or
	Reports of Cases in Equity Argued and Determined in the Court of Appeals and Court of Errors of South Carolina, Volume III, from November 1850 to May 1851 Both Inclusive, by J. S. G. Richardson, State Reporter, Annotated Edition, West Publishing Company, St. Paul, 1917.
4 RIEQ	4 Richardson's Equity Reports or
	Reports of Cases in Equity Argued and Determined in the Court of Appeals and Court

KEY TO SOURCES

ABBREVIATION   VOLUME OF EQUITY BOOKS

of Errors of South Carolina, Volume IV, from November 1851 to May 1852 Both Inclusive, by J. S. G. Richardson, State Reporter, Annotated Edition, West Publishing Company, St. Paul, 1917.

5 RIEQ   5 Richardson's Equity Reports <u>or</u>

Reports of Cases in Equity Argued and Determined in the Court of Appeals and Court of Errors of South Carolina, Volume V, from November 1852 to May 1853 Both Inclusive, by J. S. G. Richardson, State Reporter, Annotated Edition, West Publishing Company, St. Paul, 1917.

6 RIEQ   6 Richardson's Equity Reports <u>or</u>

Reports of Cases in Equity Argued and Determined in the Court of Appeals and Court of Errors of South Carolina, Volume VI, from November 1853 to May 1854 Both Inclusive, by J. S. G. Richardson, State Reporter, Annotated Edition, West Publishing Company, St. Paul, 1917.

7 RIEQ   7 Richardson's Equity Reports <u>or</u>

Reports of Cases in Equity Argued and Determined in the Court of Appeals and Court of Errors of South Carolina, Volume VII, from November 1854 to May 1855 Both Inclusive, by J. S. G. Richardson, State Reporter, Annotated Edition, West Publishing Company, St. Paul, 1917.

8 RIEQ   8 Richardson's Equity Reports <u>or</u>

Reports of Cases in Equity Argued and Determined in the Court of Appeals and Court of Errors of South Carolina, Volume VIII, from November and December Term 1855 to May Term 1856 Both Inclusive, by J. S. G. Richardson,

KEY TO SOURCES

ABBREVIATION   VOLUME OF EQUITY BOOKS

                   State Reporter, Annotated Edition, West
                   Publishing Company, St. Paul, 1917.

9 RIEQ   9 Richardson's Equity Reports of

                   Reports of Cases in Equity Argued and
                   Determined in the Court of Appeals and Court
                   of Errors of South Carolina, Volume IX, from
                   November 1856 to December 1857 Both Inclusive,
                   by J. S. G. Richardson, State Reporter,
                   Annotated Edition, West Publishing Company,
                   St. Paul, 1917.

10 RIEQ   10 Richardson's Equity Reports or

                   Reports of Cases in Equity Argued and
                   Determined in the Court of Appeals and Court
                   of Errors of South Carolina, Volume X, from
                   January Term 1858 to January Term 1859 Both
                   Inclusive, by J. S. G. Richardson, State
                   Reporter, Annotated Edition, West Publishing
                   Company, St. Paul, 1917.

11 RIEQ   11 Richardson's Equity Reports or

                   Reports of Cases in Equity Argued and
                   Determined in the Court of Appeals and Court
                   of Errors of South Carolina, Volume XI, from
                   May Term 1859 to May Term 1860, Both
                   Inclusive, by J. S. G. Richardson, State
                   Reporter, Annotated Edition, West Publishing
                   Company, St. Paul, 1917.

12 RIEQ   12 Richardson's Equity Reports or

                   Reports of Cases in Equity Argued and
                   Determined in the Court of Appeals and Court
                   of Errors of South Carolina, Volume XII, from
                   May 1860 to May 1866 Both Inclusive, by J. S.
                   G. Richardson, State Reporter, Annotated
                   Edition, West Publishing Company, St. Paul,
                   1917.

KEY TO SOURCES

ABBREVIATION   VOLUME OF EQUITY BOOKS

13 RIEQ   13 Richardson's Equity Reports or

                    Cases in Equity Argued and Determined in the
                    Court of Appeals and Court of Errors of South
                    Carolina from November and December Term 1866
                    to November and December Term 1867 Inclusive,
                    Volume XIII, by J. S. G. Richardson, State
                    Reporter, Annotated Edition, West Publishing
                    Company, St. Paul, 1917.

14 RIEQ   14 Richardson's Equity Reports or

                    Reports of Cases in Equity Argued and
                    Determined in the Court of Appeals and Court
                    of Errors of South Carolina, Volume XIV, from
                    January 1868 to May 1868 Inclusive, by J. S.
                    G. Richardson, State Reporter, Annotated
                    Edition, West Publishing Company, St. Paul,
                    1917.

RILEY   Riley's Equity Reports or

                    Reports of Cases in Equity Argued and
                    Determined at Charleston in the Equity Court
                    of Appeals of South Carolina, April Term 1836
                    to February Term 1837, by Wm. Riley,
                    Charleston, 1839, Annotated Edition, West
                    Publishing Company, St. Paul, 1917.

SPEERS   Speers' Equity Reports or

                    Equity Cases Argued and Determined in the
                    Court of Appeals of South Carolina, Volume I,
                    [Note: There is no Volume II] from November,
                    1842 to May 1844 Both Inclusive, by R. H.
                    Speers, State Reporter, Annotated Edition,
                    West Publishing Company, St. Paul, 1917.

1 STRO   1 Strobhart's Equity Reports or

                    Reports of Cases in Equity Argued and
                    Determined in the Court of Appeals and in the
                    Court of Errors of South Carolina from

vii

KEY TO SOURCES

ABBREVIATION   VOLUME OF EQUITY BOOKS

November and December 1846 to November and December 1847 Both Inclusive, by James A. Strobhart, State Reporter, Volume I, Annotated Edition, West Publishing Company, St. Paul, 1917.

2 STRO   2 Strobhart's Equity Reports or

Reports of Cases in Equity Argued and Determined in the Court of Appeals and in the Court of Errors of South Carolina During the Year 1848, by James A. Strobhart, State Reporter, Volume II, Annotated Edition, West Publishing Company, St. Paul, 1917.

3 STRO   3 Strobhart's Equity Reports or

Reports of Cases in Equity Argued and Determined in the Court of Appeals and the Court of Errors of South Carolina During the Year 1849, by James A. Strobhart, State Reporter, Volume III, Annotated Edition, West Publishing Company, St. Paul, 1917.

4 STRO   4 Strobhart's Equity Reports or

Reports of Cases in Equity Argued and Determined in the Court of Appeals of South Carolina at Charleston, January Term 1850 and at Columbia, May Term 1850, by James A. Strobhart, State Reporter, Volume IV, Annotated Edition, West Publishing Company, St. Paul, 1917.

S.C. Marriages 1749-1867 Implied in S.C. Equity Reports

MAN	WOMAN	VOLUME	PAGES	LIVED

(A)

Aaron, John J.　　　　Mary Elizabeth　　9 RIEQ　411-417　1834
　　　　　　　　　　　Kennedy (daughter of Robert Kennedy
　　who died 16 October 1834)　　　　　{Barnwell}
Abrahams, _____　　_____ Dragaud　　3 DESA　25-28　1809
　　　　　　　　　　　(widow of Pierre Dragaud)
　　　　　　　　　　　　　　　　　　　{Charleston District}
Abshier, Alfred　　　Martha Gallagher　5 RIEQ　170-185　1832
　　　　　　　　　　　(daughter of John Gallagher) {York}
Adams, _____　　　　Ann Chaplin　　　　1 HILL　265-284　1776
　　　　　　　　　　　(daughter of Benjamin Chaplin of
　　　　　　　　　　　St. Helena's Parish)
Adams, Benjamin　　　Lydia Surr　　　　11 RIEQ　264-268　1859
　　(reference to marriage settlement) (widow) {Charleston}
Adams, Godfrey　　　 Jane Hoff　　　　　9 RIEQ　247-251　1805
　　(marriage settlement 6 April 1805) (widow)
　　(he of Abbeville) (she died 1852/53) {Colleton}
Adams, James B.　　　Margaret E. McDow　14 RIEQ　304-310　1867
　　　　　　　　　　　(daughter of John J. McDow) {Lancaster}
Adams, Samuel　　　　Rebecca Kelly　　　2 DESA　214-221　1794
　　(common-law marriage) (he died October 1794)
Adams, William H.　　Mary G. Evans　　　1 STRO　72-78　1830
　　(marriage settlement 17 October 1830)
　　(widow of Cadwell Evans)　　　　　　{Edgefield}
Addison, George A.　 Rebecca Harris　　 4 RIEQ　25-38　1851
　　　　　　　　　　　　　　　　　　　　{Abbeville}
Adger, John B.　　　 Elizabeth K.　　　 3 STRO　211-224　1848
　　　　　　　　　　　Shrewsbury　　　　{Charleston}
Aigne, Verg　　　　　Hannah Jewell　　 11 RIEQ　296-322　1834
　　(daughter of Benjamin Jewell)
　　　　　　　　　　　　　　　　　　　{Charleston District}
Aiken, David　　　　 _____ Rabb　　　　2 McC　118-126　1827
　　　　　　　　　　　　　　　　　　　　{Fairfield District}
Aiken, Joseph D.　　 _____ Martin　　 11 RIEQ　205-224　1849
　　(daughter of Robert Martin)
　　　　　　　　　　　　　　　　　　{Charleston and Georgetown}
Aitken, John　　　　 _____ Thomas　　　RICE　73-79　1837
　　　　　　　　　　　　　　　　　　　　{Colleton District}
Alexander, John J.　 _____ Spierin　　BAILEY　223-225　1830
　　　　　　　　　　　　　　　　　　　　{Georgetown}
Allen, George R.　　 _____ Beard　　　SPEERS　264-268　1842
　　　　　　　　　　　　　　　　　　　　{Lancaster}
Allen, James　　　　 _____ Richardson　9 RIEQ　53-57　1837
　　(daughter of John Richardson) {Lancaster}

1

S.C. Marriages 1749-1867 Implied in S.C. Equity Reports

MAN	WOMAN	VOLUME	PAGES	LIVED
Allen, Joseph D.	Nancy Myers	2 RIEQ	321-354	1838
		{Richland and Union}		
Allen, Lydall	Mildred Downs	6 RIEQ	364-369	1818
	(daughter of Jonathan Downs) {Laurens}			
Ancrum, William W.	Harriet Dawson	DUDLEY	145-154	1835
	(daughter of Lawrence Monk Dawson)			
		{Charleston}		
Ancrum, Wm. M.	Harriet Dawson	McMULL	405-409	1842
Anderson, _____	Esther Holman	3 DESA	210-212	1811
Anderson, _____	Sarah P. Kerr	9 RIEQ	369-375	1838
		{Kershaw}		
Anderson, Benjamin A.	Rebecca Rhodus	12 RIEQ	104-113	1859
		{Clarendon}		
Anderson, George	_____ Covington	9 RIEQ	137-148	1849
		{Edgefield}		
Anderson, George	Jane Caroline Fair	5 RIEQ	55-76	1830
	(daughter of Isaac Fair)			
		{Edgefield District}		
Anderson, Henry	Charlotte Askew	5 RIEQ	162-170	1852
	(daughter of Dr. _____ Askew			
	who died 18 January 1841) {Union}			
Anderson, Dr. Joel L.	Rebecca Neely	2 STRO	262-272	1847
	{Laurens and Abbeville Districts}			
Anderson, Newton	Eunice Askew	5 RIEQ	162-170	1852
	(daughter of Dr. _____ Askew			
	who died 18 January 1841) {Union}			
Anderson, Thomas	_____ Michau	SPEERS	312-321	1843
	(daughter of Isaac Michau) {Sumter}			
Anderson, Thomas R.	Mary Miller	4 RIEQ	1-9	1836
(married 1836) (daughter of James Miller)				
(she was born about 1822)	{Edgefield}			
Anderson, W. P.	Jemima Askew	5 RIEQ	162-170	1849
	(daughter of Dr. _____ Askew			
	who died 18 January 1841) {Union}			
Andrews, James J.	Ann Catherine	4 RIEQ	349-358	1829
	Felder (widow of Henry Felder)			
(married April 1829)	{Orangeburg}			
Angel, Justus	Martha Waight	BAILEY	351-359	1814
	(also known as Tucker) (daughter of			
Isaac Waight of John's Island)	{Charleston}			
[See also 2 HILL pages 26-27]				
Ardis, Abraham	Susannah	2 McC	60-72	1794
	Schinholster (daughter of John			
Schinholster who died 1781)	{Beech Island}			
Arnett, John	Elizabeth Conyers	4 STRO	189-203	1804
(married 3 January 1804) (daughter of Straud Conyers				
of North Carolina) (Arnett died 1816) {Williamsburg				
District}				

S.C. Marriages 1749-1867 Implied in S.C. Equity Reports

MAN	WOMAN	VOLUME	PAGES	LIVED

Arnold, Cicero M.   Mary Selena Schmidt 7 RIEQ 201-218   1845
    (marriage settlement 2 July 1845) (daughter of
    Dr. John W. Schmidt)   {Charleston}
Ashby, John   Magdalene Bocket   2 DESA 221-226   1793
                    (Boquet)
    (he died 1793) (she died 1801/02) [See also pages
    210-214; 419-422]
Ashby, Stephen   _____ Thomas   7 RIEQ 430-449   1843
    Jordan   (daughter of D. Thomas)
    (to Chickasaw County, Mississippi) {Union District}
    [Must also see footnotes in 1917 Edition]
Aughtery, A. R.   _____ Sims   4 STRO 103-122   1842
                    (daughter of Col. Reuben Sims
                    who died 1844)   {Union}
Aughtry, Benj. P.   Mary Ogletree   3 STRO 149-158   1844
                    (daughter of Rev. Benjamin S.
                    Ogletree)   {Newberry}
Austin, Thomas C.   Polly T. James   4 RIEQ   80-87   1851
                    (daughter of John James)
                                         {Spartanburg District}
Avery, _____   Elizabeth A. Cook   5 RIEQ 351-355   1852
                    (daughter of Daniel Cook) {Charleston}

(B)

Bailer, John, Sr.   Catharine Curtis   3 STRO 258-262   1807
                    (daughter of Thomas Curtis)
                    (she died about 1841)
Bailey, _____   Anna Boyce Henry   5 RIEQ 187-202   1852
                    (daughter of George Henry) {Charleston}
Bailey, Henry   Jane Eliza Godard   2 STRO   1-13   1845
                    (daughter of Rene Godard of Charleston,
                    who died 3 May 1845) {Charleston}
Bailey, James   Mary Champion   3 RIEQ 156-159   1826
                    (daughter of Jacob Champion) {Kershaw}
Bailey, Nicholas V. Eliza A. H. Henry   4 STRO   84-102   1850
                    (daughter of George Henry who
                    died August 1837)   {Charleston}
Baily, Jordan   Lucy Cole   RICE   17-19   1837
                    (daughter of John Cole) {Union District}
Baird, Archibald   Winifred _____   1 DESA 219-237   1773
    (married 20 October 1773) (he died 1777)
Baker, A. M.   Laura L. Garvin   4 RIEQ 392-399   1852
                                         {Barnwell}

S.C. Marriages 1749-1867 Implied in S.C. Equity Reports

MAN	WOMAN	VOLUME	PAGES	LIVED
Baker, L. B.	Ann Findlay Query (Finley) [Must also see pages 271-272]	1 RIEQ	296-301 {Charleston District}	1844
Baker, Robert L.	Isabella Chaplin (widow)	3 RIEQ	208-218 {Beaufort District}	1844
Baker, Robert L.	Isabel C. Field	7 RIEQ	386-394 {Colleton}	1847
Baker, Robert L.	Isabella C. Field	1 STRO	129-169	1843

(marriage settlement 8 June 1843) (married Charleston) (separated) (widow) (she was born 1789-1793) {Colleton and Beaufort Districts}

Baker, Williamson	Elizabeth Userry	RICHEQ	191-197	1828

(daughter of Thomas Userry of Montgomery County, North Carolina, who died 12 May 1828) {Newberry}

Ball, _____	Caroline A. Rutledge (daughter of Edward Rutledge)	14 RIEQ	245-270	1858
Ball, _____	Jane Ann Wise	4 DESA	330-350	1800

(separation agreement 1800) (daughter of Major Samuel Wise who died 1779) (she died 1808) {Richland District}

Ball, Hugh Swinton	Ann Elizabeth Channing (married 8 March 1827, Boston)	SPEERS	48-87	1827

(daughter of Walter Channing of Boston) (Ball was born 18 October 1808) (Ball and wife died 14 June 1838) [See also pages 518-532] [See also 1 RIEQ pages 361-389; 419-426]

Ballard, _____	_____ Miller	4 RIEQ	358-370	1851

(sister of William Miller of Butts County, Georgia, who died April 1850) {Lancaster}

Ballard, John	Unity Connors	10 RIEQ	389-393	1858

(he was married before) (widow of Charles P. Connors who died 5 March 1843) {Sumter}

Ballard, Wm.	_____ _____	4 DESA	550-551	1810

(marriage settlement 15 October 1810)

Barber, John M.	Rebecca Green	DUDLEY	238-241 {Chester}	1829
Barber, John M.	Rebecca Green	5 RIEQ	38-55 {Chester}	1831
Barber, John M.	Rebecca Green	1 HILL	95-101 {Chester}	1833
Barber, Nathaniel	Comfort Perry	2 HILL	638-644	1798

(he died 1832) (widow of Zadock Perry) (she died 1829) {Lancaster}

S.C. Marriages 1749-1867 Implied in S.C. Equity Reports

MAN	WOMAN	VOLUME PAGES	LIVED
Barclay, _____	Catharine S. Channing (daughter of Walter Channing of Boston)	SPEERS 48-87	1843
Barelli, Joseph A. (may have had child only) (daughter of Capt. Phillip Messervey who died 1828) [Must also see 2 RIEQ pages 162-179]	Sophia C. Messervey	2 HILL 567-584 {Charleston}	1829
Baring, Charles	Susan Heyward (widow of James Heyward of Combahee) (she died 1845)	7 RIEQ 289-327 {Charleston}	1845
Barksdale, Allen S.	Martha A. Hall (daughter of David Hall who died 15 April 1860)	13 RIEQ 180-189 {Anderson District}	1861
Barksdale, George	_____ Ash	1 DESA 603-605	1795
Barksdale, George	_____ Bona	2 HILL 184-200 {Coosawhatchie}	1798
Barksdale, George	_____ Lefitt	2 HILL 184-200 {Coosawhatchie}	1798
Barnes, Dixon (married May 1855) (widow of John S. Cunningham) (she died 12 September 1855)	Mary Cunningham	9 RIEQ 475-482 {Lancaster}	1855
Barnes, Henry W. (he died September 1840) (daughter of Alexander Stewart who died 25 October 1824)	Martha M. Stewart	1 RIEQ 396-404 {Edgefield}	1824
Barns, _____ (Barnes) 137 in footnotes of 1917 Edition]	Elizabeth (or Tracy) Parker [See also 3 RIEQ page	4 STRO 179-186 {Edgefield}	1831
Barnup, _____	_____ Cogdell (sister of John Cogdell)	3 DESA 346-393	1807
Barnwell, John B., Senr.	Jane Hay Wigg (she died 1817)	2 HILL 228-235 {Coosawhatchie}	1798
Barret, Judah (marriage settlement 19 November 1806) (widow of Jacob Bookter)	Judith Bookter	4 DESA 447-458	1806
Barrett, _____	Mary G. Perdriau	5 RIEQ 20-31 {Sumter}	1842
Bartlett, J. S.	_____ White (daughter of Leonard White) {Sumter}	8 RIEQ 271-285	1847
Bartlett, Rev. J. L.	_____ White (daughter of Leonard White who died May 1853)	13 RIEQ 269-338 {Sumter District}	1854
Bartlett, Wm	_____ Wurtz	2 HILL 171-180 {Charleston}	1833
Bass, _____	_____ Perry (daughter of Isaac Perry of St. Paul's Parish, who died 1818) {Colleton}	8 RIEQ 136-144	1851

S.C. Marriages 1749-1867 Implied in S.C. Equity Reports

MAN	WOMAN	VOLUME	PAGES	LIVED

Bass, Thomas E.   Eliza E. Perry   5 RIEQ   202-220   1824
                   {Colleton and St. George's Parish}
Bates, John   Epsiby Bond   1 STRO   1-26   1836
(in Lexington County) (daughter of John P. Bond, Sr.
of Lexington District, who died 1823) {Edgefield}
Bates, John   Hepsebah Bond   DUDLEY   71-84   1837
(daughter of John P. Bond of
Lexington District, who died September 1823) {Edgefield}
Bath, _____   Elizabeth Wightman DUDLEY   212-224   1779
(common-law marriage)   {Charleston}
Batty, Dr. Thomas Helen Ann Whatley   2 HILL   605-611   1837
                                       {Edgefield}
Bauxbaum, _____   Eliza Ashley Smyth 1 McC   301-310   1826
Bay, W.   Ann Davis   4 DESA   505-517   1814
                                       {Richland District}
Baynard, William   Elizabeth Mikell   2 DESA   342-361   1805
(daughter of Ephraim Mikell)
Beacham, Daniel J. _____ Wright   2 McC   185-206   1825
                                       {Laurens}
Beam, Albert   Sarah Mayo   2 McC   137-143   1827
(daughter of John Mayo)
Beard, _____   Catharine Barkley   SPEERS   264-268   1842
(daughter of Robert Barkley) {Lancaster}
Beard, Wm. P.   Caroline Ogletree   3 STRO   149-158   1844
(daughter of Rev. Benjamin S. Ogletree)
                                       {Newberry}
Beasley, William   Mary Teulon   7 RIEQ   84-94   1852
                                       {Abbeville District}
Beasley, William   Mary Tewlune   6 RIEQ   408-433   1852
                                       {Abbeville}
Beazley, W. B.   Mary L. Calhoun   9 RIEQ   119-128   1835
(married 1835) (daughter of Downes Calhoun)
(she died October 1838)   {Barnwell}
Beck, Charles   Sarah Kennedy   9 RIEQ   411-417   1836
(married 1836) (widow of Robert Kennedy who died
16 October 1834) (Beck died 1855)   {Barnwell}
Beck, Josiah   Mary W. Ford   SPEERS   579-592   1837
(marriage settlement February 1837) {Colleton District}
Bee, John Simons   _____ Ladson   RICHEQ   315-320   1826
(daughter of Major James Ladson)
                                       {Charleston}
Bell, George   _____ Geiger   CHEVES   162   1840
Bell, William   _____ Bell   9 RIEQ   42-45   1856
(daughter of Thomas Bell) {Fairfield}
Bellinger, _____   Martha Morris   2 RIEQ   30-31   1845
                                       {Union District}
Benson, _____   Harriott Garden   1 DESA   521-537   1796

S.C. Marriages 1749-1867 Implied in S.C. Equity Reports

MAN	WOMAN	VOLUME	PAGES	LIVED
Benton, Lemuel	_____ Kimbrough	4 DESA	17-19	1809
	(daughter of John Kimbrough) {Cheraws}			
Beresford, Hon.	Ann Elliott	1 DESA	263-271	1792
Richard	(widow of Charles Elliott)			
[See also pages 174-183; 360-366]				
Bergamy, _____	Dorcas Birch	McMULL	279-289	1839
(to Alabama)	(widow of Michael Birch) {Sumter}			
Berrie, William J.	Elizabeth	BAILEY	304-311	1817
	Swindersine (daughter of Andrew			
Swindersine who died November 1802) {Charleston}				
Berry, Stephen N.	Sarah J. Mitchell	11 RIEQ	296-322	1855
		{Charleston District}		
Berry, Thomas	Jane Josey	9 RIEQ	369-375	1844
(married 1841-1844) (widow) (she died 1848) {Kershaw}				
Berwick, _____	Ann Ash (widow)	1 DESA	603-605	1786
	(she died 1794)			
Bethea, David W.	Sarah Jane Manning	12 RIEQ	410-429	1862
	(daughter of Mealy Manning)			
		{Marlborough District}		
Bethune, _____	Margaret Williman	4 RIEQ	475-496	1813
	(daughter of Christopher Williman)			
		{Charleston}		
Bingley, Edward	_____ Box	1 McC	333-352	1815
		{Charleston District}		
Birch, Michael	Dorcas Pearson	McMULL	279-289	1783
(he died 1808)	(widow of William Pearson who died			
	6 December 1783) {Sumter}			
Black, _____	Mary Ann Shaw	6 RIEQ	240-248	1817
	(daughter of David Shaw) {Charleston}			
Black, _____	Ellinor Whitlock	13 RIEQ	165-171	1866
		{Union}		
Black, Alexander	Eliza Shaw	6 RIEQ	240-248	1849
(he died September 1849) (widow of William D. Shaw)				
(she died May 1849)		{Charleston}		
Black, Major	Eliza Shaw	SPEERS	431-438	1825
Alexander	(widow of Wm. D. Shaw)			
Black, C. H.	Mary Ann	7 RIEQ	407-421	1854
	McClenaghan	{Darlington}		
Black, Samuel C.	_____ Mikell	13 RIEQ	34-41	1857
	(daughter of J. J. Mikell) {Charleston}			
Black, William	Rachel Nichols	RICHEQ	85-109	1791
(common-law marriage)		{Newberry and Spartanburg}		
Blackman, John, Jr.	Ann Bird	11 RIEQ	536-540	1849
	(daughter of Arthur Bird who died 1835)			
		{Marion District}		
Blake, _____	_____ Middleton	2 HILL	591-599	1814
	(daughter of Arthur Middleton)			

S.C. Marriages 1749-1867 Implied in S.C. Equity Reports

MAN	WOMAN	VOLUME PAGES	LIVED
Blake, J. H.	Eliza H. Goodwyn (daughter of Major James Goodwyn) {Fairfield}	2 HILL 629-638	1824
Blake, John H.	Eliza Goodwyn (daughter of Major James Goodwyn) {Fairfield}	BAILEY 141-148	1824
Blake, Walter (married 16 June 1837)	Ann Stead Izard	3 RIEQ 225-234 {Charleston}	1837
Blakely, _____	Venus Staggers	14 RIEQ 90-104 {Williamsburg}	1867
Blakely, John	_____ Wilson	2 McC 1-11	1827
Blankton, Thomas (married April 1850) [Referred to in another case in footnotes of 1917 Edition]	Susan Huff	6 RIEQ 388-398 {Goose Creek}	1850
Blewer, _____	Nubilia Cook (daughter of Daniel Cook) {Charleston}	5 RIEQ 351-355	1852
Blewit, Thomas G.	_____ De Graffenreid (daughter of Allen De Graffenreid who died 7 January 1821) {Chester}	2 McC 90-105	1815
Blocker, Barkley M.	Nancy Brooks (daughter of Col. Z. S. Brooks) {Edgefield}	2 STRO 113-134	1828
Bofil, _____	_____ Herbemont (daughter of Nicholas Herbemont) {Richland District}	3 RIEQ 1-9	1836
Bogan, Charles	_____ Parham	6 RIEQ 140-146 {Spartanburg}	1853
Boggs, George W.	Isabella Adger (widow of William Adger, Jun.) {Fairfield}	4 RIEQ 408-413	1851
Bondy, A.	_____ Jewell	11 RIEQ 296-322 {Charleston District}	1855
Bonneau, _____	Sarina Barksdale (daughter of Thomas Barksdale, Sr.) {Charleston}	7 RIEQ 125-135	1800
Bonneau, _____	Maria Swinton (daughter of Hugh Swinton)	2 McC 440-445	1827
Bonner, John (married 28 December 1823) (she was born 9 September 1797)	Eliza Maria Day (daughter of George Day) {Charleston}	RILEY 162-165	1823
Bookter, Jacob	Judith Frost (widow)	4 DESA 447-458	1806
Boone, Thomas	Jane Fraser (daughter of J. B. Fraser)	2 McC 105-112	1825
Boone, Thomas	Jane Baxter Fraser (daughter of John B. Fraser) {Sumter}	1 HILL 360-369	1833

S.C. Marriages 1749-1867 Implied in S.C. Equity Reports

MAN	WOMAN	VOLUME	PAGES	LIVED

Booth, Wm.	Henrietta Broxson	2 STRO	31-34	1846
  (married 8 October 1846) (daughter of Henry Broxson
  of Colleton District)	{Walterborough}
Boozer, David	Elizabeth Wallace	1 HILL	393-396	1827
  (widow of Howell Wallace who
  died 1822) (she died 1831) {Newberry}
Bossard, J. P.	Charlotte White	9 RIEQ	483-499	1829
  (daughter of Joseph B. White of Sumter
  District, who died 31 December 1852) {Sumter District}
Bossard, Joseph S.	Matilda Ann Withers	3 STRO	76-78	1849
	{Columbia}
Bostick, R.	E. Singleton	2 McC	410-419	1827
	{Beaufort District}
Bostick, Richard	_____ Robert	1 STRO	393-420	1815
  (daughter of John Robert) {Gillisonville}
Bowers, Edward	Elizabeth Jemima	10 RIEQ	551-556	1835
  Graham (widow) (married in Camden)
  (he had been married before) (he died December 1835)
	{Lancaster}
Bowles, Tobias	Susannah Drayton	1 DESA	489-497	1795
  (married 10 March 1795) (daughter of John Drayton)
Boyd, _____	Mary Mathewes	4 RIEQ	233-254	1850
	{Charleston}
Boyd, Rev. Charles	Mary Mathews	4 STRO	1-25	1848
  Leroy	(daughter of William Mathews)
  (to Alabama)	{Charleston}
Boyd, Samuel	Malinda Coleman	7 RIEQ	509-520	1837
  (daughter of Charles Coleman) {Fairfield}
Boyd, William B.	Lucinda Payne	12 RIEQ	487-497	1862
  (widow of John W. Payne) {Newberry}
Boykin, John	Charlotte Adamson	2 HILL	200-204	1814
Bracey, Merry	Alice Moore	RICE	110-132	1835
  (to Mississippi) (daughter of Isham Moore) {Clarendon
  County, Sumter District}
Brackit, _____	_____ Taylor	4 DESA	167-175	1810
  (daughter of John Taylor) {Abbeville}
Bradley, _____	_____ Kittles	6 RIEQ	155-182	1822
  (to Florida)	(daughter of Jacob C. Kittles) {Barnwell}
Bradley, John A.	Louisa Lowry	SPEERS	1-19	1836
  (daughter of James M. Lowry who died
  May 1837, Perry County, Alabama)	{Chester District}
Bradley, Robert	Martha Cave	6 RIEQ	43-57	1838
  (married 6 December 1838) (daughter of David Cave who
  died October 1834) (she was born about 1802) (she died
  29 June 1851)	{Barnwell}
Bradock, Adam	Alzira Leake	SPEERS	564-568	1834
  (daughter of George Leake) {Laurens}

9

S.C. Marriages 1749-1867 Implied in S.C. Equity Reports

MAN	WOMAN	VOLUME PAGES	LIVED
Bradshaw, James	____ Smith	1 HILL 140-142	1833
(he died 1828) (daughter of John Smith of New York)			
Brailsford, Robert	Elizabeth James	McMULL 55-62	1826
(he died 1826)		{Sumter District}	
Brailsford, William	Maria Heyward	2 DESA 18-37	1800
(daughter of Daniel Heyward who died 11 October 1777) [See also pages 92-114; 291-294]			
Brandis, ____	Elizabeth Clausen	RILEY 117-120	1819
(she died 10 February 1819, Hildeshein, Germany)			
Branford, William	Elizabeth Savage	2 DESA 115-127	1754
Breithaupt,	Mary Ingram	1 RIEQ 465-474	1838
Christian (common-law marriage)		{Edgefield}	
Brewton, Miles	Rosannah Dean	9 RIEQ 423-428	1856
(daughter of John Dean) {Spartanburg}			
Brisbane, ____	Ann F. Phaelon	2 McC 423-434	1827
Britton, ____	Eliza Woodward	5 RIEQ 187-202	1852
(widow of William T. Woodward)		{Charleston}	
Britton, Edward H.	Caroline M. Johnson	2 HILL 430-442	1835
(daughter of James Johnson who died 1815)		{Marion}	
Brockaway, ____	Mary M. Naisor	RICHEQ 449-451	1799
(daughter of Philip Naisor)		{Charleston}	
Brockington, Samuel	Eliza Elmira Arnett	4 STRO 189-203	1834
(he was born 1816) (daughter of John Arnett)			
(she was born 23 March 1813)		{Williamsburg District}	
Brockway, ____	Mary M. Nasar	3 DESA 550-553	1805
(daughter of Philip Nasar)			
Brooks, ____	Margaret S. Anderson (daughter of Silas Anderson who died March 1845)	1 STRO 344-346 {Marion}	1844
Brooks, Thomas B.	Eliza Pullam	4 RIEQ 9-14	1851
(daughter of Benjamin Pullam)		{Abbeville}	
Brown, ____	Mary E. Anderson (daughter of Silas Anderson who died March 1845) (she died about April 1845)	1 STRO 344-346 {Marion}	1844
Brown, ____	____ Cattell	1 DESA 112-113	1784
(widow of William Cattell)			
Brown, ____	Eliza Cheeseborough Porter (daughter of John Porter, Jr. who died 1828)	SPEERS 496-507	1844
Brown, ____	Ann M. Shrewsbury	3 STRO 211-224	1848
		{Charleston}	
Brown, ____	Elizabeth Teulon	7 RIEQ 84-94 {Abbeville District}	1852

10

S.C. Marriages 1749-1867 Implied in S.C. Equity Reports

MAN	WOMAN	VOLUME PAGES	LIVED
Brown, Angus P. (married October 1847)	_____ _____	6 RIEQ 155-182 {Barnwell}	1847
Brown, Benjamin W. (he died 1855)	Esther Elizabeth Sessions	10 RIEQ 408-411 {Sumter}	1855
Brown, Charles J.	Susan Carr	1 STRO 363-370 {Barnwell}	1847
Brown, Charles T.	S. E.(or A.) Smith (daughter of George Smith) {Georgetown and Charleston}	2 HILL 558-566	1824
Brown, Charles T.	Sarah E. Smith (daughter of George Smith) {Georgetown}	3 RIEQ 465-542	1819
Brown, Cornelius (married March 1787/88)	Elizabeth Greenland	1 DESA 196-201	1788
Brown, George W.	Sarah Atchison (widow of John Atchison who died April 1833) {Charleston}	2 HILL 542-548	1836
Brown, George W.	Caroline L. Gibbes	5 RIEQ 291-300 {Charleston}	1844
Brown, John	Tirza McDonald (daughter of Middleton McDonald, Sen.) {Chester}	2 HILL 457-467	1817
Brown, Joseph	Sarah Harris (daughter of John Harris) {Camden}	4 DESA 60-65	1798
Brown, Wm.	Jinny Leake (daughter of George Leake) {Laurens}	SPEERS 564-568	1834
Bruce, John	Mary Benson (widow of Joshua Benson)	4 DESA 463-465	1814
Brunson, _____	Mary Ann Rhodus (daughter of William Rhodus) {Clarendon}	12 RIEQ 104-113	1859
Brunson, Ervin	_____ Hunter (daughter of Andrew Hunter) {Darlington}	2 HILL 483-492	1835
Brunson, Peter A.	Joanna Cummings	9 RIEQ 440-458 {Sumter District}	1857
Brunson, Wesley W. 20 July 1842) (she was born 1830)	Sarah Jane Britton (daughter of Henry Britton who died {Sumter}	8 RIEQ 271-285	1856

Bruton. See Brewton

Bryan, _____	Zulina Hull (daughter of Gideon H. Hull) (she was born 1828/29) {Edgefield}	2 STRO 174-195	1845
Bryan, _____	Zulina Hull {Edgefield}	3 RIEQ 65-96	1849
Bryson, Matthew H.	Mahala Pullam (daughter of Benjamin Pullam) {Abbeville}	4 RIEQ 9-14	1851
Buchanan, _____ (he died 2 April 1827) (she died 1834-36)	Margaret McCullough (daughter of Hans McCullough) {Walterborough}	1 STRO 193-196	1822

S.C. Marriages 1749-1867 Implied in S.C. Equity Reports

MAN	WOMAN	VOLUME PAGES	LIVED
Buchanan, John	Eugenia M. Felder (daughter of Samuel J. Felder) {Orangeburg}	5 RIEQ 509-518	1852
Buckalew, Abner (to Tennessee)	Elizabeth Byrd (daughter of Joseph Byrd) {Lancaster}	6 RIEQ 129-137	1844
Buckhalter, William	_____ Canady {Barnwell}	6 RIEQ 103-110	1851
Buckner, James T.	Elizabeth M'Culloch (daughter of Hance M'Culloch) {Coosawhatchie}	2 HILL 499-504	1837
Buford, _____	_____ Michau (daughter of Paul Michau) {Georgetown}	3 RIEQ 465-542	1822
Buford, William	_____ Micheau {Georgetown}	RILEY 88-96	1822
Buist, _____	Mary Sommers {Charleston}	3 RIEQ 281-304	1848
Buist, _____ [In footnotes of 1917 Edition] [See also pages 421-445; 496-504]	Mary Sommers {Charleston}	4 RIEQ 416-420	1852
Buist, Rev. George	Mary Sommers (daughter of John Sommers) (she died 1 April 1845) {Charleston}	4 STRO 37-58	1845
Buler, _____	Elizabeth Smith (daughter of Samuel Smith who died 1815) {Beaufort}	3 RIEQ 244-256	1831
Bull, _____	_____ Beale (daughter of Othniel Beale) {Charleston District}	3 DESA 22-25	1809
Bull, John B. (he died 6 January 1855) (widow) (she died 1857)	Sarah Morrow {Abbeville District}	11 RIEQ 156-204	1843
Bull, William R. (married 2 December 1838) (he was born 10 May 1819) (she was born 24 January 1823)	Julia A. Carson {Orangeburgh}	3 STRO 86-93	1838
Bull, Wm R.	Juliana Carson (daughter of James Carson who died 1826) {Orangeburg}	8 RIEQ 259-270	1856
Bunch, Timothy	Sarah Viers (widow of Maurice Viers)	3 DESA 273-296	1795
Burgess, Robert S. (married 1817/18)	Eliza Heape {Barnwell}	1 HILL 397-405	1833
Burgoyne, Dr. William (in New York) (daughter of Philip Moser formerly of Charleston, lately of Phildelphia}	Eliza Moser	DUDLEY 133-140	1837
Burke, Dr. Michael (married 1799) (she was born 1779) (she died 1804/05)	Elizabeth Elbert {Fairfield}	McMULL 475-484	1799

S.C. Marriages 1749-1867 Implied in S.C. Equity Reports

MAN	WOMAN	VOLUME	PAGES	LIVED
Burke, John	Catharine Elbert	McMULL	475-484	1799
		{Fairfield}		
Burke, Myles	Ann Tisdale	1 McC	551-557	1826
	(widow of John Tisdale)			
Burrow, John	Amanda Fretwell	11 RIEQ	559-573	1856
	(daughter of William Fretwell			
	of Greene County, Georgia) {Anderson}			
Burrows, _____	Cynthia Foster	SPEERS	569-577	1841
		{Spartanburg}		
Burt, Armstead,	Mary Scott	9 RIEQ	358-361	1839
Sen. (he died 1839) (she died 1857) {Edgefield}				
Burton, James F.	Mary Yeldell	9 RIEQ	9-18	1854
	(daughter of James Yeldell) {Edgefield}			
Busby, Lewis	Mary Pullam	4 RIEQ	9-14	1851
	(daughter of Benjamin Pullam) {Abbeville}			
Bush, Samuel B.	Caroline A. Foreman	1 STRO	377-385	1835
(marriage settlement 12 August 1835) (daughter				
of Benjamin Foreman)		{Barnwell}		
Bush, Samuel B.	Caroline A. Foreman	3 STRO	131-136	1835
	(daughter of Benjamin Foreman of			
	Barnwell District)			
Butler, _____	Elizabeth Elliott	2 McC	435-440	1775
	(she died about 1775)			
Butler, _____	Jane Ann Wise	4 DESA	330-350	1808
	(daughter of Major Samuel Wise who died			
	1779) (she died 1808) {Richland District}			
Butler, Anthony	Anne J. M. Moore	RICE	110-132	1804
	(daughter of Isham Moore) {Clarendon			
	County, Sumter District}			
Butler, John	Sarah Sherry	2 McC	60-72	1800
(he died 1818)	(widow)	{Beech Island}		
Butler, Thomas	Mary Lupton	2 STRO	51-63	1847
	Shackelford	{Charleston District}		
Byrne, Patrick	Mary Stewart	3 DESA	135-148	1792
(married 8 March 1792) (widow of Thomas Stewart				
who died 16 September 1788) (she died 8 March 1803)				

(C)

Caborne, George   Catharine Cain   3 DESA   514-528   1797
    (married 12 January 1797) (widow)
Calder, Archibald   _____ Mikell   2 DESA   342-361   1804
    John (of Edisto Island) (daughter of Ephraim Mikell)
    (Calder died 15/20 April 1804)

S.C. Marriages 1749-1867 Implied in S.C. Equity Reports

MAN	WOMAN	VOLUME PAGES	LIVED
Caldwell, J. C.	Ann Sims	4 RIEQ 168-197 {Union}	1850
Caldwell, James	_____ Williams (daughter of Washington Williams)	BAILEY 175-179 {Laurens District}	1830
Caldwell, James P. _____ McMorries 11 RIEQ 73-82 1848 (of Newberry County) (he died October 1848) {Newberry}				
Caldwell, William	Harriet M'Dowell (daughter of Patrick M'Dowell)	2 McC 43-59 {Newberry District}	1826
Calhoun, James	Polly McLewrath	2 STRO 231-237 {Barnwell}	1831
Calhoun, James J.	Polly McLewrath	RICHEQ 36-45 {Barnwell}	1827
Calhoun, James Y.	Cynthia W. Brown (daughter of Bartlett Brown who died November 1822)	6 RIEQ 155-182 {Barnwell}	1821
Calhoun, John	Agnes Griffin (daughter of Richard Griffin) (in Lincoln County, Georgia)	2 RIEQ 99-114 {Abbevile}	1845
Calhoun, William L. _____ _____ 10 RIEQ 358-376 1857 (marriage contract 26 April 1857) {Abbeville}				
Calhoun, William L. Margaret W. Cloud 10 RIEQ 358-376 1853 (married 5 January 1853) (his first marriage) (he of Abbeville) (daughter of William Cloud of Chester) (she died 9 April 1855) {Abbeville}				
Cambridge, Thomas	Elizabeth Tamplet	7 RIEQ 358-374 {Charleston}	1789
Camlin, William (married 1817) (widow of John Arnett) {Williamsburg District}	Elizabeth Arnett	4 STRO 189-203	1817
Campbell, _____	Jane Ann Wise (daughter of Major Samuel Wise who died 1779) (she died 1808)	4 DESA 330-350 {Richland District}	1808
Campbell, A. C. _____ 7 RIEQ 54-76 1835 (marriage settlement 10 April 1835, Beaufort District) {Abbeville and Beaufort Districts}				
Canady, John	Rachael George (common-law marriage) (he died 9 April 1851)	6 RIEQ 103-110 {Barnwell}	1851
Canady, John (married October 1818)	Mary Johnson	6 RIEQ 103-110 {Barnwell}	1818
Canady, John	Agness Saunders	6 RIEQ 103-110 {Barnwell}	1804
Canady, John (common-law marriage)	_____ Stringfellow	6 RIEQ 103-110 {Barnwell}	1851

S.C. Marriages 1749-1867 Implied in S.C. Equity Reports

MAN	WOMAN	VOLUME PAGES	LIVED
Cannon, Henry	Mary Langley (daughter of Christopher Langley who died 1 March 1812) (she died 16 March 1812) {Coosawhatchie}	BAILEY 204-207	1812
Cannon, Robert R.	Elizabeth Cummings	9 RIEQ 440-458 {Sumter District}	1857
Cannon, William H.	Anna Sanders (widow of Jordan Sanders) (she died May 1854) {Darlington}	10 RIEQ 394-407	1854
Cantelou, Lewis C.	Mary Rainsford (daughter of Thomas Rainsford who died December 1837)	SPEERS 385-398	1834
Cantey, _____	Camilla F. Richardson	12 RIEQ 454-486 {Clarendon District}	1859
Cape, Thomas	Mary Jaffray (widow of J. Jaffray)	1 DESA 567-570	1797
Capehart, B. W.	_____ Blackburne (daughter of William Blackburne) {Abbeville}	1 HILL 405-412	1832
Carlisle, _____	Hannah Glenn (daughter of James Glenn of Chester)	1 HILL 357-360	1833
Carlisle, William (separated 1851)	_____ _____ (lived in Fairfield and Kershaw)	7 RIEQ 20-33	1851
Carnes, _____	Susannah Elliott (widow of Col. Barnard Elliott)	2 DESA 299-304	1805
Carney, _____	Mary Albergottie (daughter of Anthony Albergottie) {Beaufort}	2 RIEQ 136-143	1815
Carolan, Philip [Referred to in another case]	Mary Davis	2 HILL 1-6	1831
Carr, Isaac	Sarah Willson (daughter of Thomas Willson of Georgetown)	1 McC 60-91	1825
Carson, Dr. James	Ann Stewart (Stuart) (widow) (she died 18 May 1780)	1 DESA 500-515	1777
Carter, John R.	_____ Harris (daughter of John Harris) {Camden}	4 DESA 60-65	1809
Carwile, Z. W.	Margaret Griffin (daughter of Richard Griffin who died 20 November 1850) {Edgefield}	9 RIEQ 71-84	1856
Cash, _____	Elizabeth E. Ellerbe (daughter of Capt. William Ellerbe who died May 1830) {Cheraw}	SPEERS 328-342	1822
Caston, Samuel	_____ Ballard (daughter of Thomas Ballard, Senr.) {Kershaw District}	RICE 13-17	1821

15

S.C. Marriages 1749-1867 Implied in S.C. Equity Reports

MAN	WOMAN	VOLUME PAGES	LIVED
Cathcart, _____	Nancy Beaty (daughter of James Beaty) {Fairfield}	5 RIEQ 83-90	1852
Chaplin, _____	Wilhelmina Chick (daughter of Burwill Chick of Greenville, who died 1847) {Greenville, Newberry and Union Districts}	10 RIEQ 178-190	1846
Chaplin, Benjamin	_____ Albergottie (daughter of William J. Albergottie) {Beaufort}	2 RIEQ 136-143	1846
Chaplin, Benjamin	Rebecca Albergottie (daughter of William J. Albergottie) {Beaufort District}	10 RIEQ 428-434	1856
Chaplin, Randal (he died about 1831)	Elizabeth Givens (daughter of John Givens who died 1822) (she was born May 1810) {Beaufort District}	RICE 132-158	1831
Chapman, Dr. Joseph	_____ Caldwell {Newberry}	11 RIEQ 73-82	1848
Chesnut, John	_____ Maybin (daughter of Andrew Maybin) {Chester}	1 HILL 122-128	1831
Chesnut, John	_____ Maybin {Chester}	2 HILL 146-152	1833
Cheves, John R.	Rachel Susan Bee {St. Matthew's Parish}	5 RIEQ 370-403	1843
Chewning, Finsley (married 1823)	Huldah Goodman	2 McC 11-15	1823
Chick, Reuben	_____ Moorman (daughter of Thomas Moorman) {Union}	SPEERS 343-350	1840
China, John, Jr.	Ann M. Perdriau {Sumter}	5 RIEQ 20-31	1842
China, Thomas	Maria Bonneau Taylor (daughter of William Taylor) (she died April/May 1852) {Williamsburg}	5 RIEQ 426-434	1852
Chisolm, _____	Mary Edings {Charleston}	4 RIEQ 276-301	1834
Chisolm, Edward N. (marriage contract 1831) (he died 1 September 1836) (she died November 1838) {Beaufort District}	Mary E. Hazard	4 RIEQ 266-275	1831
Chisholm, George (married 14 January 1823) (daughter of William Edings who died April 1836) (she died 19 October 1834)	Sarah Edings	1 RIEQ 301-319	1823
Chisolm, George, Jr.	Sarah Edings (daughter of William Edings) {Charleston}	4 RIEQ 276-301	1834
Chisholme, S.	_____ De Graffenreid {Chester}	2 McC 90-105	1827
Chovin, A. E.	_____ McKenzie (daughter of Daniel W. McKenzie {Gillisonville}	2 STRO 40-44	1836

S.C. Marriages 1749-1867 Implied in S.C. Equity Reports

MAN	WOMAN	VOLUME	PAGES	LIVED
Chovin, Isaac A. E.	Eliza A. McKenzie	1 STRO	393-420	1828

(married September 1828) (widow of Daniel W. McKenzie who died 1826) (she died March 1843) {Gillisonville}

Ciples, Lewis   Sarah Adamson   2 HILL   200-204   1814
                     (daughter of John Adamson of Camden, who
                     died May 1816) [See also pages 235-243]
Clanton, _____   Sarah Ingram   4 STRO   171-175   1831
                                          {Lancaster}
Clark, _____   _____ McMullen   4 RIEQ   117-135   1846
                     (daughter of Hugh McMullen of
   Chester District, who died December 1841) {Chester}
Clark, _____   _____ Mikell   3 DESA   168-175   1810
   (daughter of William Joseph Mikell) {Charleston}
Clark, _____   Ann L. Perdriau   5 RIEQ   20-31   1842
                     (daughter of Peter Perdriau) {Sumter}
Clark, Eli   _____ Mosely   1 RIEQ   396-404   1845
                     (daughter of John Mosely) {Edgefield}
Clark, W. T.   Nancy Reid   SPEERS   343-350   1840
                     (daughter of Jethro L. Reid) {Union}
Clark, William M.   Abigail Jenkins   CHEVES   129-142   1815
                     Murray (daughter of Joseph James
   Murray who died 18 July 1818) (Clark married twice)
   [Must also see pages 80-93]   {Charleston}
Clarke, Caleb, Sr.   Julia B. Harrison   4 STRO   167-170   1831
                     {Chester, Fairfield, Lancaster and Union}
Clarke, Jacob   _____ Hearst   4 DESA   143-145   1810
                                          {Ninety-Six District}
Clarke, William   Judith Craddock   1 HILL   69-76   1815
                     (daughter of Edmund Craddock) {Laurens}
Clarke, William   Elizabeth Davis   1 McC   191-197   1825
Clarke, William M.   Elizabeth Mary   3 RIEQ   318-341   1831
                     Jenkins
   (his second marriage) (he died 1831) {Charleston}
Clarke, William M.   Martha Mary Murray   3 RIEQ   318-341   1821
   (married 1820/21) (his first marriage) (daughter of
   Joseph James Murray) (she died 1821) {Charleston}
Clay, Joseph   Mary Savage   2 McC   435-440   1827
Cleary, _____   _____ Graves   RILEY   232-247   1828
                     (widow of Samuel Colleton Graves)
                     [See also pages 219-231]
Cleary, N. G.   Susan Graves   1 HILL   135-138   1833
                     (widow of Samuel C. Graves)
Cleary, Nathaniel   _____ Graves   BAILEY   268-274   1829
   G.   (widow of Samuel Colleton Graves)
                                          {Charleston}

S.C. Marriages 1749-1867 Implied in S.C. Equity Reports

MAN	WOMAN	VOLUME PAGES	LIVED
Cleary, Nathaniel G.	Susan Graves (widow of Samuel Colleton Graves) (she died 19 July 1848) {Charleston}	3 RIEQ 218-225	1848
Cleary, Nathaniel G.	Susan M. Graves (widow of Samuel C. Graves) {Colleton District}	1 RIEQ 319-324	1829
Cleckley, William	Leah E. Patterson (daughter of Anthony Patterson who died 31 May 1850) {Orangeburg}	4 RIEQ 340-348	1852
Clement, _____	Elizabeth Minter (daughter of Joseph Minter) (she died in Virginia) {Ninety-Six District}	1 RIEQ 78-91	1807
Clement, William (married 1799)	Sarah Wilkinson (he was born about 1778) (he died 1820) {St. Paul's Parish, Charleston}	HARPER 72-88	1799
Clendinen, _____	_____ Myers (daughter of David Myers) {Lexington District}	2 McC 214-269	1827
Clendinen, _____	Mary Myers (daughter of Col. David Myers) {Richland and Union}	2 RIEQ 321-354	1835
Clendinen, Robert	_____ Myers (daughter of David Myers) {Columbia}	BAILEY 23-33	1830
Clifford, Loftus C.	Caroline M. Graves (daughter of Samuel Colleton Graves) {Charleston}	3 RIEQ 218-225	1850
Cobb, Edward	Julia Fretwell (daughter of William Fretwell of Greene County, Georgia) {Anderson}	11 RIEQ 559-573	1856
Cobb, Henry	Eleanor Parris (daughter of Henry Parris who was born about 1752/53 and died 27 September 1847) {Anderson}	5 RIEQ 450-472	1843
Cobb, Middleton W. (married 1833)	Malinda Leake (daughter of George Leake) (she died 1835) {Laurens}	SPEERS 564-568	1833
Cochran, Thomas	_____ Hawie (widow)	2 DESA 521-524	1807
Cockfield, Washington	Janet M. Graham {Williamsburg}	7 RIEQ 95-99	1850
Coffie, Barnaby	Catharine Carne (marriage settlement 15 June 1793) (widow) (he died 1830) (she died 1805) {Charleston}	RICHEQ 294-301	1793
Cogdell, George (his first marriage)	Hannah Screven	1 DESA 454-458	1792
Colburn, _____	Ann A. Matthews	8 RIEQ 166-184	1851
Colburn, B. P.	Ann Ashby Mathewes {Charleston}	4 RIEQ 233-254	1845

S.C. Marriages 1749-1867 Implied in S.C. Equity Reports

MAN	WOMAN	VOLUME	PAGES	LIVED

Colburn, Benjamin   Ann A. Mathews   4 STRO   1-25   1847
  P. (married about 1834) (daughter of William
  Mathews)   {Charleston}
Colburn, James   Sarah Dunn Prince   14 RIEQ 176-244   1808
  Smith (married 1808, Boston, Massachusetts)
  (his second marriage) (to Charleston 1818/19)
  (separated 1819-22) (she died 1836, Massachusetts)
  (he died 1859)   {Charleston}
Colcock, William H. Ellen Lewis   5 RIEQ 370-403   1831
  (daughter of William L. Lewis)
                                        {St. Matthew's Parish}
Cole, Henry   Elizabeth Hicklin   1 HILL 311-323   1823
                                        {Lancaster}
Cole, William   Harriet Ellerbe   SPEERS 328-342   1841
  (daughter of Capt. William Ellerbe
  who died May 1830) {Cheraw}
Coleman, Griffin,   Elizabeth Whaley   2 STRO 334-341   1837
  Jr. (married 1837) (he was born 1819) {Marion}
Coleman, James B.   _____ Blewer   2 STRO 285-289   1843
  (widow of John G. Blewer) {Lexington}
Coleman, James B.   Elizabeth M. Blewer 10 RIEQ 191-201   1838
  (marriage settlement 29 August 1838) (widower)
  (widow of John G. Blewer)   {Lexington}
Colleton, Sir James Septima Sexta   RILEY   219-247   1819
  Roupel   Colleton Graves
  (or Baronet) (married 12 December 1819 at the Hague
  and February 1820 in London) (daughter of Admiral
  Richard Graves)
Collier, Edward   _____ Robertson   1 HILL 370-375   1821
  (married 1821) (widow of George Robertson) {Abbeville}
Collins, Alexander Elizabeth A.   BAILEY   74-77   1807
                    Skinner
  (married 1807) (widow of George Skinner who died
  1801)   {Georgetown}
Collins, George W. Lucy Gillett   SPEERS 142-158   1841
  (daughter of Dr. Elijah Gillett
  who died 1818)   {Barnwell}
Collins, George W. Lucy J. Gillett   3 RIEQ 398-403   1826
  (married 1826) (daughter of Elijah Gillett)
  (Collins died 1836)   {Barnwell}
  [Must also see 5 RIEQ page 114]
Collins, George W. Lucy J. Gillett   4 RIEQ 314-317   1852
  (daughter of Elijah Gillett) {Barnwell}
Compty, Maj. John   _____ Stanley   4 DESA 486-504   1799
Connor, John   Elizabeth Rhode   2 HILL   41-45   1831
  (widow of Christian Rhode) {Orangeburgh}

S.C. Marriages 1749-1867 Implied in S.C. Equity Reports

MAN	WOMAN	VOLUME	PAGES	LIVED
Connors, _____	Nancy M'Connico	2 McC	323-343	1827
	(daughter of William M'Connico)			
Converse, Rev. Augustus L.	Videau Marion De Veaux	9 RIEQ	535-571	1849
	(marriage settlement 27 March 1849) (widow of Robert Marion De Veaux) {Sumter District}			
Cook, _____	Eliza Ann Allen	2 RIEQ	68-74	1839
	(widow of Matthew Allen who died 1834) {Georgetown District}			
Cook, _____	Vashti Canady	6 RIEQ	103-110	1853
	(daughter of John Canady) {Barnwell}			
Cook, Daniel	Hannah H. Paslay	5 RIEQ	351-355	1838
	(she died 1850) {Charleston}			
Cook, Jedediah	_____ Yeates	1 RIEQ	78-91	1807
	(daughter of Thomas Yeates) {Ninety-Six District}			
Cook, John B.	Charlotte Massey	2 HILL	492-498	1836
	(daughter of George Massey who died about 1818) {York}			
Cook, Tobias	_____ Wright	2 McC	185-206	1825
	{Laurens}			
Cooner, James	_____ May	3 STRO	185-192	1848
	(daughter of John May, Sr.) {Walterborough}			
Cooper, John M.	Nancy Hancock	1 RIEQ	26-40	1841
	(daughter of Simon Hancock, Sr.) {Edgefield}			
Copeland, John N.	_____ Garvin	RICE	69-72	1839
	(widow of James M. Garvin who died 1836) (to Calhoun County, Florida Territory) {Barnwell District}			
Corbett, Thomas	Eliza Harleston	DUDLEY	201-212	1805
	(daughter of John Harleston) {Charleston}			
Corbett, Thomas	Elizabeth Harleston	5 RIEQ	301-326	1795
	(married May 1795) (daughter of Col. John Harleston) (Corbett died July 1850) (she died 17 September 1837) {Charleston}			
Corley, Nathaniel	Sarah Etheredge	10 RIEQ	207-216	1855
	{Edgefield}			
Coslett, _____	Ann Grimke	1 DESA	366-382	1794
Cotchet, _____	_____ Hall	2 McC	269-317	1823
	(sister of Ainsley Hall of Columbia)			
Counts, Joseph	Elizabeth Fulmer	5 RIEQ	121-128	1848
	{Lexington}			
Covington, John B.	Lucilla Fair	5 RIEQ	55-76	1830
	(widow of Isaac Fair) {Edgefield District}			

S.C. Marriages 1749-1867 Implied in S.C. Equity Reports

MAN	WOMAN	VOLUME	PAGES	LIVED
Cowan, John (he died 1822) February 1841) (to Missouri)	Amelia Griffin (widow of Richard Griffin) (she died (in Lincoln County, Georgia) {Abbeville}	2 RIEQ	99-114	1803
Cox, Harmon	____ Waller	6 RIEQ {Horry}	275-283	1842
Crankfield, Allen R.	Jemima Jones	1 STRO {Fairfield}	323-333	1847
Crawford, John	Sarah Tompkins (daughter of Stephen Tompkins, Sr.) {Edgefield}	4 DESA	176-183	1800
Crenshaw, ____	____ Finch (daughter of Edward Finch) {Newberry District}	4 DESA	185-199	1811
Crenshaw, W. T.	Sarah Askew (daughter of Dr. ____ Askew who died 18 January 1841) {Union}	5 RIEQ	162-170	1852
Creyon, ____	Sarah Hicklin	1 HILL {Lancaster}	311-323	1823
Crim, George	Margaret Patterson (daughter of Anthony Patterson who died 31 May 1850) {Orangeburg}	4 RIEQ	340-348	1852
Crispin, James R. [In footnotes of 1917 Edition]	____ Sibley	2 HILL {Newberry}	430-442	1833
Crosland, David	____ Allen (widow of Matthew Allen who died 1834, Georgetown District) {Marlborough District}	3 RIEQ	23-33	1839
Crosland, David	Eliza Ann Cook (widow)	2 RIEQ {Georgetown District}	68-74	1839
Crossland, David (to Florida)	Eliza Ann Allen (widow of Mathew Allen of Georgetown District, who died 1834) {Georgetown}	6 RIEQ	255-275	1839
Cruger, Nicholas (married 1799) February 1796)	Ann Sarah Heyward (widow of Daniel Heyward who died [Must also see pages 422-431]	2 DESA	94-115	1799
Cruger, Nicholas (to Baker County, Georgia)	Elizabeth Anne Robert (daughter of John Robert) {Charleston}	2 STRO	86-90	1847
Crum, ____	Catharine Bowman (daughter of George Bowman) {Orangeburg}	14 RIEQ	271-279	1826
Cudworth, William (married February 1810) (widow of Thomas Hall)	Sarah Hall	3 DESA	256-262	1810
Cummings, Joseph	Nancy Boyd (daughter of Samuel Boyd) {Fairfield}	7 RIEQ	509-520	1851
Cunningham, ____	Sarah Campbell (she was born about 1779) (she died 28 April 1851) {Abbeville District}	5 RIEQ	405-421	1851

S.C. Marriages 1749-1867 Implied in S.C. Equity Reports

MAN	WOMAN	VOLUME	PAGES	LIVED
Cunningham, John S. (widower)	Mary Massey (daughter of James R. Massey)	9 RIEQ	475-482 {Lancaster}	1850
Cunningham, John S. (he died November 1851)	Mary Rinaldo (widow)	9 RIEQ	475-482 {Lancaster}	1850
Cunningham, Joseph (marriage settlement 20 July 1841)	Esther A. Niles (he had been married before) (he died May 1850)	4 RIEQ	135-151 {Kershaw}	1841
Cureton, _____	Mary M. Cunningham (daughter of Joseph Cunningham)	4 RIEQ	135-151 {Kershaw}	1850
Cureton, _____	Caroline Moon	2 STRO	327-334 {Greenville}	1848
Cureton, David T.	Sarah Moon	2 STRO	327-334 {Greenville}	1848
Curry, _____	_____ Dennis (daughter of John Dennis who died 10 October 1850) {York}	4 RIEQ	307-314	1818
Curry, Samuel	Margaret J. McDow (daughter of James McDow of Lancaster District)	4 STRO	37-58	1839
Cuthbert, General J.	_____ Heyward (daughter of William Heyward)	2 McC	395-403	1814
Cuthbert, James H.	Ann Wigg	2 HILL	228-235 {Coosawhatchie}	1798

(D)

Daniel, _____	Matilda Bond (daughter of John P. Bond, Sr. of Lexington District, who died 1823)	1 STRO	1-26 {Edgefield}	1836
Daniel, Seth (married 30 November 1838)	Ann A. Allen (daughter of Josiah G. Allen)	2 RIEQ	99-114 {Beaufort and Barnwell Districts}	1838
Darbey, A. B.	Mary Eugenia Thompson (daughter of William R. Thompson)	5 RIEQ	370-403 {St. Matthew's Parish}	1848
Darby, _____	Mary S. Taylor (daughter of William M. Taylor)	1 RIEQ	155-186 {Charleston District}	1832
Darby, Dr. Artemas T.	Margaret Thompson (daughter of John Linton Thompson)	5 RIEQ	370-403 {St. Matthew's Parish}	1848
Davidson, _____	Sarah Crosswhite (daughter of Jacob Crosswhite)	6 RIEQ	88-95 {Newberry}	1825

S.C. Marriages 1749-1867 Implied in S.C. Equity Reports

MAN	WOMAN	VOLUME	PAGES	LIVED
Davidson, _____	Karen Dennis (daughter of John Dennis who died 10 October 1850) {York}	4 RIEQ	307-314	1818
Davidson, Gilbert	Eliza Williman (daughter of Christopher Williman) {Charleston}	4 RIEQ	475-496	1813
Davis, _____	Eleanor Norwell	1 DESA	202-207	1791
Davis, _____	_____ Spiva (daughter of David Spiva) {Union District}	9 RIEQ	434-439	1846
Davis, _____	Nancy Vickory (daughter of William Vickory who died 1804) (she died 1825) {Abbeville}	4 RIEQ	16-22	1825
Davis, B. F.	Gracey W. Adams (daughter of James Adams) {Columbia}	3 STRO	55-59	1846
Davis, Hiram	Ann Robinson (widow of William Robinson who died 1805) {Union}	RICHEQ	390-397	1828
Davis, P. A.	Frances McJunkin (daughter of Joseph McJunkin) {Union}	11 RIEQ	527-535	1856
Davis, Samuel B.	Eliza T. Spears (she was born about 1803) (she died January 1828) {Walterboro}	RICHEQ	287-293	1828
Davis, William	Lucy Dugan (daughter of Park Dugan) {Newberry}	DUDLEY	1-14	1837
Dawson, _____	Eliz. Carr (widow of John Carr) {Walterborough}	2 STRO	105-111	1825
Dawson, Lawrence Monk	Jane Vanderhorst (he died 3 October 1823) (daughter of Arnoldus Vanderhorst) (she died 5 December 1823) {Charleston}	DUDLEY	145-154	1823
Dawson, Richard (his second marriage)	_____ Breeland	RICE	243-274	1820
		{Beaufort District}		
Dawson, Richard (his first marriage) (he died 1835)	_____ Pelham (separated 1806)	RICE	243-274	1806
		{Beaufort District}		
Day, George (married 6 February 1794) (he died 29 June 1811) (she was born about 1777) (she died 21 April 1804) {Charleston}	Elizabeth Oats	RILEY	162-165	1794
Day, James	Elizabeth Hall (widow of William Hall who died 1812) (she died September 1820)	2 McC	27-31	1820
Deas, David (he died 1822)	Mary Summers (daughter of Humphrey Summers) {Charleston}	BAILEY	283-304	1822
Deas, E. H.	Ann Ball {Charleston}	2 STRO	24-27	1845

S.C. Marriages 1749-1867 Implied in S.C. Equity Reports

MAN	WOMAN	VOLUME PAGES	LIVED
Deas, Henry	Margaret (Peggy) Horry (daughter of Elias Horry)	2 DESA 115-127	1802
Deas, Henry	Margaret Horry (daughter of Elias Horry who died 1785) {Charleston}	2 HILL 244-249	1835
Dehay, Benjamin	Jane Maria Foxworth	1 RIEQ 266-270	1845
De Hay, Robert H.	Sarah Dennis (widow of William J. Dennis) {Charleston}	14 RIEQ 27-30	1860
Dehon, _____	Sarah Russell (daughter of Nathaniel Russell of Charleston)	DUDLEY 115-123	1832
Delesseline, Francis A.	Amelia Adamson (daughter of John Adamson of Camden, who died May 1816) (she died July 1832) [See also pages 235-243]	2 HILL 200-204	1832
Dellet, James (in <u>Claibourn</u> County, Alabama)	Harriet Willison	CHEVES 213-232 {Edgefield District}	1838
DeLorme, William M.	Mary Ann White (daughter of Joseph B. White of Sumter District, who died 31 December 1852) {Sumter District}	9 RIEQ 483-499	1829
Deschamps, G. S. C.	Mary Fraser (daughter of J. B. Fraser)	2 McC 105-112	1823
De Schamps, William F.	_____ Mitchell (daughter of Benjamin Mitchell) {Sumter}	13 RIEQ 9-24	1864
Desel, Dr. Chas.	Caroline Mazyck (daughter of Stephen Mazyck) {Charleston}	RICHEQ 263-282	1831
De Treville, _____	Sarah M. Ellis	BAILEY 35-42 {Coosawhatchie}	1827
Devall, Michael (he was married before)	Harriet _____	4 DESA 79-85 {Abbeville}	1809
Deveaux, _____	E. C. Barnwell (daughter of J. J. Barnwell)	1 DESA 497-500	1795
De Veaux, _____	Videau M. Singleton	1 STRO 283-294 {Charleston}	1834
De Veaux, Robert Marion (he was born November 1812) (he died May 1843)	Videau M. De Veaux (widow?)	1 STRO 283-294 {Charleston}	1834
De Veaux, Robert Marion	Videau Marion Singleton (daughter of Richard Singelton) {Sumter District}	9 RIEQ 535-571	1849
DeWitt, Charles	_____ Bruton (widow of George Bruton) {Barnwell}	2 HILL 367-371	1835
Dewes, Bethel	_____ Oswald	RILEY 38-41 {Beaufort District}	1836
Dews, B.	Charlotte Oswald (daughter of Joseph Oswald) {Beaufort}	RICHEQ 326-352	1817

S.C. Marriages 1749-1867 Implied in S.C. Equity Reports

MAN	WOMAN	VOLUME	PAGES	LIVED
Dick, Thomas M.	_____ White	13 RIEQ	269-338	1854
	(daughter of Leonard White who died May 1853) {Sumter District}			
Dick, Thomas W.	_____ White	8 RIEQ	271-285	1847
	(daughter of Leonard White) {Sumter}			
Dickson, John	Morning Webb	5 RIEQ	121-128	1820
	(daughter of Joseph Webb of Fairfield, who died January 1820) (she died February 1848) {Lexington}			
Dill, John	Sarah Taylor (widow)	1 DESA	237-244	1791
Dinckle, _____	_____ Muckenfuss	1 DESA	109	1784
	(daughter of Michael Muckenfuss)			
Dinkins, Gilbert	_____ Harris	4 DESA	60-65	1809
	(daughter of John Harris) {Camden}			
Dinkins, John	Sarah Bowman	RICHEQ	185-191	1820
	(married June/July 1820) (he died 1825) {Sumter}			
Divine, Thomas	Margaret Dunlap	11 RIEQ	405-415	1860
	(daughter of James Dunlap) {Charleston}			
Donald, James	Elizabeth Gray	RICE	330-342	1838
	(daughter of Robert Gray) {Abbeville}			
Donald, West	Mary Ann Gray	RICE	330-342	1838
	(daughter of Robert Gray) {Abbeville}			
Donnelly, Patrick	Ann Waties Coachman	1 STRO	81-84	1818
	(daughter of James Coachman of Prince George Winyah) (she died August 1844)			
Doughty, William	_____ Cannon	2 STRO	101-104	1784
	(daughter of Daniel Cannon) {Charleston}			
Douglass, _____	Hannah Cornwell	12 RIEQ	379-392	1848
	(daughter of Eli Cornwell) {Chester District}			
Douglass, Archibald	_____ Cochran	4 DESA	143-145	1810
	{Ninety-Six District}			
Douglass, John	Jane Brice	4 RIEQ	322-329	1818
	(married about 1818) (daughter of William Brice, Sen. who died May 1849) {Fairfield}			
Drayton, Alfred R.	Martha S. Rowand	4 STRO	37-58	1849
	(daughter of Charles E. Rowand, Sr.) {Charleston}			
	[See also 4 RIEQ page 416, in footnotes of 1917 Edition]			
Drayton, Glen	_____ Elliott	HARPER	34-46	1783
	(he died June 1796) (daughter of Samuel Elliott)			
Drayton, Glen	Eliza Elliott	3 DESA	29-31	1809
	(daughter of Samuel Elliott who died 1777) {Charleston District}			
DuBose, _____	Elizabeth Sinkler	1 RIEQ	141-154	1791
	{Colleton}			

S.C. Marriages 1749-1867 Implied in S.C. Equity Reports

MAN	WOMAN	VOLUME	PAGES	LIVED
Dubose, Daniel	___ Lee	BAILEY	166-168	1819

(married 4 March 1819) (daughter of Andrew Lee)
(she died 15 November 1820)   {Darlington}

| DuBose, Theodore S. | Jane S. Porcher | McMULL | 358-369 | 1842 |

{Charleston District}

| Dugan, ___ | Frances M'Daniel | HARPER | 108-116 | 1824 |

(widow of Thomas M'Daniel)

| Dugan, James | ___ McDaniel | DUDLEY | 1-14 | 1837 |

(widow)   {Newberry}

| Duke, Abraham (Abram) | Harriet Cannon | 10 RIEQ | 380-388 | 1834 |

(daughter of Russell Cannon who died 1824)   {Pendleton and Pickens Districts}

| Duke, Thomas G. | Louisa Webb | 5 RIEQ | 121-128 | 1820 |

(married 23 June 1820, Fairfield District) (divorced October 1825, Georgia) (he went to Chambers County, Alabama and married again)   {Lexington}

| Dumont, Guillaume (William) | Marie Adelaide Rossignol | 7 RIEQ | 201-218 | 1810 |

(she died 1833) {Charleston}

| Dunlap, H. S. | Mary G. Richbourg | HARPER | 168-170 | 1824 |
| Dunlap, Rev. David Ellison | Susannah Potts Ellison | 4 DESA | 305-329 | 1804 |

(daughter of Robert Ellison)
(he and she died 10 September 1804)

| Dunn, ___ | ___ Brown | 1 DESA | 196-201 | 1789 |

(sister of Cornelius Brown)   {England}

| Dunton, Hollis | Zelime Laborde | McMULL | 448-450 | 1820 |

(daughter of Peter Laborde who died 1821)   {Edgefield}

| Dupont, ___ | Maria Hutchinson | 10 RIEQ | 1-3 | 1857 |

(daughter of Mathias Hutchinson)
{Charleston}

| Dupont, Abraham | Jane Shanks | HARPER | 5-19 | 1824 |
| Dupont, Dr. ___ | Mary Smith | 3 RIEQ | 244-256 | 1831 |

(daughter of Samuel Smith who died 1815)   {Beaufort}

| Dupree, James | Sarah Johnson | 4 DESA | 209-215 | 1785 |

(marriage agreement 2 February 1785)   {Georgetown}

| Durant, ___ | Ruth Shannon | 2 RIEQ | 404-407 | 1838 |

(widow)   {Marion}

| Durant, C. H. | ___ Murchison | 3 STRO | 159-161 | 1849 |

(widow of Kenneth Murchison)
{Orangeburgh}

| Durant, Francis B. | Mary C. Donnelly | 1 STRO | 81-83 | 1840 |

(married 1840) (daughter of Patrick Donnelly)
(she was born about 1818) (living in Savannah)   {Marion}

| Durham, ___ | Eliza Whitlock | 13 RIEQ | 165-171 | 1866 |

{Union}

26

S.C. Marriages 1749-1867 Implied in S.C. Equity Reports

MAN	WOMAN	VOLUME	PAGES	LIVED
Dwight, Isaac M.	Martha M. Porcher	McMULL	358-369	1842
		{Charleston District}		
Dyches, Seth	Esther Benson	2 STRO	343-379	1829

(daughter of Moses Duke of Barnwell District) [See also pages 353-358, in footnotes of 1917 Edition]

(E)

Eaton, William W.	Christina W. Faust	9 RIEQ	294-302	1853

(married 1 November 1853, Georgia) (she had been divorced) [See also pages 376-391] {Fairfield}

Eddings, _____	Mary Bailey	1 DESA	355-359	1794

(widow of Henry Bailey)
{Beaufort District}

Edgerton, Otis	Elizabeth Walfe	DUDLEY	179-183	1824

(married 16 December 1824) (daughter of Jacob Walfe) (Edgerton died August 1830) (she was born about 1804)
{Barnwell}

Edmonds, Jefferson L.	Dorothy Ann Cates	1 McC	252-267	1824
		{Newberry District}		
Edmonds, Jefferson L.	_____ Wadlington	HARPER	224-242	1824
Edmonds, Jefferson L.	_____ Wadlington	1 HILL	288-296	1833
		{Newberry and Union}		
Edwards, _____	Eliza Barksdale	2 HILL	184-200	1798
		{Coosawhatchie}		
Edwards, _____	Elizabeth Barksdale	3 RIEQ	271-281	1850

(daughter of Thomas Barksdale)
{Charleston}

Edwards, _____	Elizabeth Barksdale	7 RIEQ	125-135	1854

(daughter of Thomas Barksdale, Sr.)
{Charleston}

Edwards, George	Emma Julia Barksdale	7 RIEQ	125-135	1854

(daughter of Thomas Barksdale, Jr.)
{Charleston}

Egerton, _____ (Eagerton)	_____ Cogdell	3 DESA	346-393	1807

(sister of John Cogdell)

Elam, John	Mary Yeates	1 RIEQ	78-91	1780

(married 16 November 1780) (Elam widower) (widow of Thomas Yeates) (Elam died 1824) (she was born 8 June 1756) (she died 1841)
{Ninety-Six District}

Elders, John	Margaret McGrew	4 DESA	155-162	1800

(common-law marriage)

S.C. Marriages 1749-1867 Implied in S.C. Equity Reports

MAN	WOMAN	VOLUME PAGES	LIVED
Elfe, Geo.	Jane O'Hara (widow of Arthur O'Hara) {Charleston}	RICHEQ 263-282	1831
Elfe, George	Jane Mazyck	1 HILL 242-252	1833
Elgin, Robert	Cagy Lattimer (widow of Benjamin Lattimer of Maryland) {Abbeville, Ninety-Six District}	4 DESA 26-33	1809
Ellerbe, James (married 1835)	Elizabeth E. Cash (widow) {Cheraw}	SPEERS 328-342	1835
Ellerbe, Zachariah	Obedience Ellerbe (daughter of Capt. William Ellerbe who died May 1830) {Cheraw}	SPEERS 328-342	1841
Elliott, A. B.	Lucinda Collier {Charleston}	3 RIEQ 125-132	1850
Elliott, Charles (her first marriage)	Ann Ferguson (daughter of Charles Ferguson)	1 DESA 174-183	1790
Elliott, Col. Barnard	Susannah Smith (he died October 1778) (daughter of Benjamin Smith)	2 DESA 299-304	1778
Elliott, Colonel Bernard	Mary Bellinger Elliott (married April 1766) (his first marriage) (daughter of Thomas Law Elliott who died 7 December 1756) (she died 11 December 1774) (he died October 1778/88) [See also pages 263-271]	1 DESA 183-190	1766
Elms, William	Hannah Wells (he died January 1794) (widow of Matthew Wells) {Charleston}	3 DESA 155-164	1794
Enecks, ____	Lucy J. Collins (widow of George W. Collins) {Barnwell}	3 RIEQ 398-403	1851
Enicks, ____	Lucy J. Collins (widow of George W. Collins) {Barnwell}	4 RIEQ 314-317	1852
Enicks, Barnet M.	Lucy Collins (widow of George W. Collins) {Barnwell}	SPEERS 142-158	1841
Enlow, John	____ Kinard (daughter of John M. Kinard) {Newberry}	2 RIEQ 247-259	1845
Erving, James F.	Sarah Frances Sabb (widow of Thomas Sabb who died 1811) {St. Matthew's Parish}	5 RIEQ 370-403	1808
Etheredge, Burdett (common-law marriage)	Nelly Partain {Edgefield}	10 RIEQ 207-216	1855
Evans, ____	Lydia A. Perdriau (daughter of Peter Perdriau) {Sumter}	5 RIEQ 20-31	1842
Evans, C. D.	Sarah Jane Haseldon (daughter of John Haseldon) {Marion}	6 RIEQ 26-42	1853
Evans, William	Sarah Ann Godbold (daughter of General ____ Godbold of Marion District, who died 1825)	4 RIEQ 334-340	1852

S.C. Marriages 1749-1867 Implied in S.C. Equity Reports

MAN	WOMAN	VOLUME PAGES	LIVED
Evans, William	Sarah Ann Godbold (daughter of General Thomas Godbold) {Marion}	6 RIEQ 26-42	1853
Ezell, _____	Letitia Long (daughter of William Long) {Union}	1 STRO 43-53	1846
Ezell, Amasa	Caroline Long (daughter of William Long) {Union}	1 STRO 43-53	1846

(F)

Fair, _____	Elizabeth Moon	2 STRO 327-334 {Greenville}	1848
Fairlee, George M. (reference to marriage settlement)	Margaret G. Shaffer	14 RIEQ 146-149 {Marion}	1867
Falconer, William	_____ Powe	4 DESA 86-87 {Cheraws}	1805
Fant, David A.	Amanda McJunkin (daughter of Joseph McJunkin) {Union}	11 RIEQ 527-535	1856
Fant, John	Sarah J. Thomas (widow)	11 RIEQ 527-535 {Union}	1858
Farnandes, James	Elizabeth Long (daughter of William Long) {Union}	1 STRO 43-53	1846
Farr, _____	Louisa V. Chick (daughter of Burwill Chick of Greenville, who died 1847) {Greenville, Newberry and Union Districts}	10 RIEQ 178-190	1846
Farrow, James	Caroline P. Henry (daughter of James Edward Henry) {Spartanburg}	7 RIEQ 378-385	1854
Faucheraud, Gideon	Mary Villeponteaux	1 DESA 366-382	1751
Faust, Clement C.	Christina W. Bratton (married 12 April 1837) (divorced October 1852, Georgia) (daughter of Dr. William Bratton of Winnsboro, who died 1 December 1850) [See also pages 376-391] {Fairfield}	9 RIEQ 294-302	1837
Federick, _____	Louisa Felder (daughter of Samuel J. Felder) {Orangeburg}	5 RIEQ 509-518	1852
Feemster, Joseph	Araminthia McLure (daughter of William McLure who died 1859) {York}	14 RIEQ 105-120	1866
Felder, _____	Margaret Bowman (daughter of George Bowman) {Orangeburg}	14 RIEQ 271-279	1826
Felder, Abram	_____ Conlietle	2 McC 323-343	1827

S.C. Marriages 1749-1867 Implied in S.C. Equity Reports

MAN	WOMAN	VOLUME	PAGES	LIVED

Felder, Henry   Ann Catherine Hesse 4 RIEQ   349-358   1826
   (he died 28 April 1826) (daughter of Daniel Hesse
   who died 1826) (her first marriage) {Orangeburg}
Felder, Richard   Ann Coulietle   2 McC   168-171   1827
Felder, Wm. L.   Julia M. Brailsford McMULL   55-62   1840
                                          {Sumter District}
Fennel, Cullen   Susannah Kennerly   1 HILL   76-94   1810
                     (widow of Joseph Kennerly)
Ferguson, Berkly   Ann Varlin   DUDLEY   224-229   1810
   (he died about 1827) (she died 1832) {Colleton and
   Beaufort Districts}
Field, Dr. Henry   Agnes Dupont   McMULL   369-404   1828
                     (widow)   {Gillisonville}
Fields, _____   Isabella C. Chaplin 1 STRO   129-169   1843
                     (widow) {Colleton and Beaufort Districts}
Finley, Thomas   Catharine Kinder   3 STRO   78-86   1823
   (he was born 11 February 1757)   {Abbeville District}
Finley, Thomas   Catherine Kinder   2 STRO   208-220   1831
   (had child only in Virginia) (Finley died 3 December
   1831)   {Abbeville}
Firth, _____   Mary Givens   RICE   132-158   1810
                                          {Beaufort District}
Firth, _____   Mary Hutchinson   10 RIEQ   1-3   1848
                     (daughter of Mathias Hutchinson)
                                          {Charleston}
Flagg, H. C.   Rachel Allston   1 DESA   164   1789
                     (widow)
Floyd, _____   Mourning Mayo   2 McC   137-143   1816
                     (daughter of John Mayo)
Floyd, J. B.   Drucilla Williams   8 RIEQ   248-258   1850
   (married 1850)   {Newberry}
Fludd, Augustus   Mary Matilda   DUDLEY   184-201   1837
                     Richardson (daughter of James
   Burchell Richardson who died 26 April 1836)
Flurry, W.   Beatrix Sandford   RICHEQ   357-361   1817
                     (widow)   {Charleston}
Fogartie, Dutarque   Eliza Ann Sealy   BAILEY   510-514   1830
                     (widow of David Sealy) {Charleston}
Fogg, Francis B.   Mary Rutledge   2 HILL   591-599   1837
                     (daughter of Henry M. Rutledge)
Fogler, J. J.   Mary W. Owens   2 STRO   289-296   1848
                     (widow of John A. Owens of
   Beaufort District, who died 12 December 1830)
   (she died 21 March 1836)   {Barnwell}
Follin, Charles   Caroline C. Trescot 1 RIEQ   123-130   1833
                     (widow of Doctor John Sen Trescot
   who died 1820) (she died 1833, New Orleans) {Charleston}

S.C. Marriages 1749-1867 Implied in S.C. Equity Reports

MAN	WOMAN	VOLUME PAGES	LIVED

Foote, William ____ De Graffenreid 2 McC 90-105 1827
{Chester}
Footman, ____ ____ Caldwell BAILEY 397-411 1824
(daughter of John M. Caldwell of
Orangeburgh, who died June 1824) {Charleston}
Footman, William C. Mariah H. Oliver 3 RIEQ 33-60 1832
(from Orangeburg District to Bryan County, Georgia)
{Williamsburg and Orangeburg Districts}
Ford, Frederick A. Rose Drayton 7 RIEQ 328-343 1843
{Charleston}
Forrest, George Charity Lushington 2 DESA 254-263 1794
(married 14 May 1794) (widow of R. Lushington)
Fortune, William Ann McCreary 9 RIEQ 34-36 1856
{Barnwell}
Foster, Josiah Pinckey Hall 4 RIEQ 390-392 1826
(he died 1836) (daughter of Z. Hall) (she died
about 1835) {Fairfield}
Fox, William ____ Ford 5 RIEQ 349-351 1852
{Colleton}
Franklin, Benjamin Susannah Stone HARPER 243-255 1810
(he died January 1820) {Clarendon and Sumter Counties}
Franks, ____ Catharine Fable 2 HILL 378-401 1835
{Philadelphia, Pennsylvania}
Frantz. See Frautz
Fraser, ____ Mary Livingston 2 DESA 573-576 1808
Fraser, Dr. James Mary Ashe RILEY 271-282 1787
(he died 1803) {Charleston}
Fraser, Elias L. Maria Louisa Powell 2 STRO 250-258 1848
(widow of Medicus Powell) {Barnwell}
Fraser, George Maria Boone 3 DESA 88-89 1810
(daughter of John Boone) {Charleston
District}
Fraser, Major Ann L. Smith 3 DESA 393-417 1782
Thomas (marriage settlement 6 November 1782)
{Colleton District}
Frautz, ____ Margaret Theresa RILEY 117-120 1822
Clausen (she died 17 December 1826,
Halberstadt, Germany)
Fraysse, ____ ____ Verdier 12 RIEQ 138-146 1858
(sister of Simon Verdier) {Colleton
District}
Frazer, Rev. Hugh Elizabeth Clegg 2 HILL 529-542 1796
Porter (marriage settlement 1796)
(she was born about 1780) (she died 1797) {Georgetown}
Frazer, John L. Mary Perry 4 STRO 37-58 1809
(daughter of Edward Perry, Jr.)
{Charleston}

S.C. Marriages 1749-1867 Implied in S.C. Equity Reports

MAN	WOMAN	VOLUME PAGES	LIVED
Frazier, _____	_____ Hughson (sister of John Hughson) (she was born 1780)	4 DESA 87-92 {Cheraw District}	1810
Frazier, Benjamin (he died 1844)	_____ Lott	1 STRO 79-81 {Edgefield}	1833
Frazier, James W.	_____ White (daughter of William White) (in Lincoln County, Georgia) {Abbeville}	2 RIEQ 99-114	1845
Frazier, P. W.	Mary Pawley (daughter of John Pawley of Georgetown)	1 HILL 203-210	1826
Frederick, John	Maria Robinson	4 DESA 546-550 {Orangeburg}	1816
Frederick. See Federick			
Freeman, _____	Mary Oswald	RICHEQ 326-352 {Beaufort}	1831
Freeman, _____	Mary Oswald	RILEY 38-41 {Beaufort District}	1836
Freer, Charles	Mary Stanyarne (daughter of William Stanyarne who died 5 May 1783) (she died 1811) {Charleston}	2 HILL 550-553	1811
Frierson, _____	Mary T. Graham	7 RIEQ 95-99 {Williamsburg}	1850
Fripp, Hamilton	Harriet Fripp (married 4 July 1832) (widow of William P. Fripp) {Beaufort District}	RICE 84-109	1832
Fripp, John A.	Mary Edings (married 12 February 1822) (daughter of William Edings who died April 1836)	1 RIEQ 301-319	1822
Fripp, John A.	Mary Edings (daughter of William Edings) {Charleston}	4 RIEQ 276-301	1834
Fripp, William P.	Harriet Fripp (he died October 1828) (daughter of Isaac Perry Fripp who died 5/6 January 1832) {Beaufort District}	RICE 84-109	1828
Frost, _____	Judith Dougherty	4 DESA 447-458	1806
Frost, Judge Edward	_____ Horry (daughter of Elias Horry) {Charleston}	10 RIEQ 109	1835
Fry, John B.	Sarah Byrd (daughter of Joseph Byrd) {Lancaster}	6 RIEQ 129-137	1845
Fryer, Richard	Rachel Black (married 1794/95 or common-law marriage) (common-law wife of William Black) (Fryer died 1821) (she died 29 April 1831) {Spartanburg}	RICHEQ 85-109	1831
Fuller, William	Margaret L. Guerard (marriage settlement December 1828) (she died September 1848)	7 RIEQ 170-179	1828

S.C. Marriages 1749-1867 Implied in S.C. Equity Reports

MAN	WOMAN	VOLUME	PAGES	LIVED

Fulmer, William   Louisa Duke   5 RIEQ   121-128   1835
   (common-law marriage or married 1835) (she died
   October 1848)   {Lexington}
Funchess, Daniel   Eliza M. Inabinit   3 RIEQ   370-378   1849
V. V.   (daughter of James Inabinit who
                     died 7 March 1849) {Orangeburgh}
Furman, Rev. J. C.   _____ Davis   4 STRO   133-149   1846
                  (daughter of Col. Jonathan Davis)
                  {Fairfield, Newberry and Richland Districts}

(G)

Gage, John, Sr.   _____ Johnson   HARPER   197-202   1819
                (daughter of Col. Wm. Johnson)
Gaillard, Peter   Eliza Gourdin   RILEY   167-173   1834
                                           {Charleston}
Gaillard, Samuel   Mary M. Peyre   McMULL   358-369   1835
   Porcher (marriage settlement April 1835) (she died
   1839)   {Charleston District}
Gallagher, _____   Mary Fitzpatrick   1 DESA   340-346   1793
Gallagher, John   Jane Carroll   5 RIEQ   170-185   1819
   (he died 6 March 1825) (daughter of Thomas Carroll)
   (she died March 1832)   {York}
Galloway, James   Catharine McLure   14 RIEQ   105-120   1866
                  (daughter of William McLure who
                  died 1859)   {York}
Galluchat, Joseph   Rebecca _____   6 RIEQ   1-4   1846
   (marriage settlement 1846)   {Lancaster}
Galphin, Miledge   _____ Ardis   2 McC   60-72   1827
                                        {Beech Island}
Gamage, Edward   Sarah Simons   3 RIEQ   271-281   1817
   (marriage contract 18 March 1817) (widow of Charles
   Dewar Simons) (she died 30 June 1841) {Charleston}
Gamble, William J.   Martha A. McDow   4 STRO   37-58   1839
                  (daughter of James McDow of
                  Lancaster District)
Gantt, Richard A.   Mary L. Hay   3 RIEQ   384-397   1850
                  (daughter of Col. Frederick J. Hay)
                                       {Barnwell District}
Garden, Dr.   Sarah Johnson   2 HILL   277-298   1818
   Alexander W.   (daughter of Thomas N. Johnson)
   (Garden died 5 August 1820) (his first marriage)
Gardner, Henry   Rhoda Baker   1 RIEQ   392-395   1839
   (married 1839) (widow of William Baker who died 1837)
                                              {Lancaster}

S.C. Marriages 1749-1867 Implied in S.C. Equity Reports

MAN	WOMAN	VOLUME PAGES	LIVED
Garner, Melcher	Ann _____	1 DESA 437-445	1768
(marriage settlement 14 July 1768) (he died 13 June 1789)
Garrett, John H.	_____ Hall	2 McC 27-31	1821
Garrett, Robert	Elizabeth Ware	2 STRO 272-284	1801
	(daughter of Henry Ware) {Edgefield}
Garvin, Edward K.	Mary D. Ashe	2 STRO 250-258	1848
	(daughter of Richard C. Ashe, Sr.
	who died 1837) {Barnwell}
Garvin, W. W.	Caroline Patrick	10 RIEQ 130-138	1847
		{Barnwell}
Gary, William	Nancy James	4 DESA 185-199	1811
	(daughter of John James of Newberry
	District) {Washington District}
Gayle, Miles	_____ Dozier	McMULL 236-253	1832
		{Greenville}
Gee, Charles	Mary Elizabeth Hamer	4 RIEQ 413-420	1851
		{Marlboro}
Gelzer, Thomas	Sarah Lewis	BAILEY 387-389	1830
		{Charleston}
Gervais, Rev. Paul T.	_____ Jenkins	McMULL 106-114	1830
	(daughter of Micah Jenkins who
	died about 1839)
Gettys, _____	_____ McDow	4 STRO 37-58	1839
	(daughter of James McDow of
	Lancaster District)
Gibbes, _____	Ann Smith	1 McC 119-148	1825
	(daughter of Peter Smith)
Gibbes, _____	Caroline S. Thayer	10 RIEQ 484-494	1850
		{Charleston}
Gibson, Joseph, Sr.	Rose Harten	4 DESA 139-143	1796
	(a married woman, wife of Henry Harten)
(had child only) (Gibson died about 1805)
		{Fairfield District}
Giles, William	Mary Young	RICE 315-329	1827
(marriage settlement 29 April 1827/29) (she died 1833)
		{Abbeville District}
Gillon, Alexander	Sarah Brisbane	1 McC 148-155	1821
Gilmore, James H.	Harriet C. Massey	2 HILL 492-498	1831
	(daughter of George Massey who
	died about 1818) {York}
Gist, _____	Ann Tonge	4 STRO 37-58	1828
	(widow of Edward Tonge who died
	1809) {Charleston}
Gist, States	Sarah B. Porcher	RICHEQ 209-219	1814
(married about September 1815) (he died 1822)
		{Charleston}

S.C. Marriages 1749-1867 Implied in S.C. Equity Reports

MAN	WOMAN	VOLUME PAGES	LIVED
Givens, Charles	Martha Jenkins (widow)	RICHEQ 326-352 {Beaufort}	1813
Givens, Charles	Martha Jenkins (widow of Joseph John Jenkins who died 1804) (she died 1832) {Beaufort}	2 HILL 511-515	1832
Glass, Pleasant H.	___ Miller (his second marriage) (daughter of William Miller of Butts County, Georgia, who died April 1850) {Lancaster}	4 RIEQ 358-370	1851
Glen, James E.	___ Robinson	4 DESA 546-550 {Orangeburgh}	1816
Glenn, ___	Mary Ann Caldwell	11 RIEQ 73-82 {Newberry}	1848
Glenn, ___	___ Hopkins (daughter of George W. Hopkins)	1 HILL 1-10	1818
Glover, ___	___ Heyward (sister of John Heyward who died 1820)	2 McC 395-403	1814
Glover, ___	Jane Sinkler (she died 5 December 1842) {Colleton}	1 RIEQ 141-154	1791
Glover, Charles J.	Martha Frazier (married June 1833) (daughter of Benjamin Frazier) (she was born about 1816) {Edgefield}	1 STRO 79-81	1833
Glover, Joseph	Ann Webb (married April 1777) (widow of Benjamin Webb who died 18 February 1776) {St. Bartholomew's Parish}	2 DESA 482-509	1777
Glover, Wiley, Sr.	Jemima Satterwhite (he died 8 February 1806) (daughter of Bartlet Satterwhite who died 21 January 1807) {Abbeville}	4 RIEQ 25-38	1803
Glover, Col. Wilson	Margaret Heyward (widow of Daniel Heyward) (she died 1832) {Colleton District}	2 HILL 515-528	1783
Godby, Samuel	Louisa Duke (common-law marriage, eloped March 1822, Jones County, Georgia) {Lexington}	5 RIEQ 121-128	1822
Godfrey, ___	Mary V. Spencer (widow of Captain John Vesey Spencer) {Charleston}	BAILEY 468-479	1818
Godwin, Hardy B.	Margaret McCutchen (marriage settlement 26 March 1833) (he died 1855/56) {Williamsburgh}	10 RIEQ 226-231	1833
Gomillian, John	___ Frazier	2 HILL 304-318 {Edgefield}	1824
Goodhue, Joseph	Mindwell Willard (widow)	RICE 198-242 {Beaufort District}	1835
Goodwin, James (to Arkansas)	Rhydonia Hill (daughter of Jonathan Hill) {Edgefield}	3 STRO 94-105	1847
Goodwyn, Major James	___ Green (widow of Col. ___ Green) {Fairfield}	BAILEY 141-148	1824

35

S.C. Marriages 1749-1867 Implied in S.C. Equity Reports

MAN	WOMAN	VOLUME PAGES	LIVED
Goodwyn, Robert H.	Charlotte Hart (widow of Derril Hart)	5 RIEQ 370-403 {St. Matthew's Parish}	1848
Gorden, _____	Elizabeth Parris (daughter of Henry Parris who was born 1752/53 and died 27 September 1847) {Anderson}	5 RIEQ 450-472	1843
Gordon, _____	Milly McCorkle	1 RIEQ 61-66 {Lancaster}	1844
Gordon, _____	Caroline Tims (daughter of Amos Tims) {Chester}	1 HILL 51-59	1833
Gordon, Josey	_____ Sims	2 McC 151-167	1827
Goudelock, Dr. Milton	_____ Sims (daughter of Col. Reuben Sims who died 1844) {Union}	4 STRO 103-122	1842
Gracey, _____ (of Columbia)	_____ Bratton (daughter of Dr. William Bratton of Winnsboro, who died 1 December 1850) {Fairfield}	9 RIEQ 376-391	1857
Graham, _____	Elizabeth Jemima Bowers	10 RIEQ 551-556 {Lancaster}	1835
Graham, _____ [Referred to in another case]	Rebecca Cooper (widow of George Cooper)	3 STRO 261-262	n.d.
Grant, Joseph	_____ Galphin	1 McC 280-300 {Edgefield District}	1826
Graves, Samuel C.	Susan M'Pherson	1 HILL 135-138	1833
Graves, Samuel C.	Susan M. M'Pherson	1 RIEQ 319-324 {Colleton District}	1829
Graves, Samuel Colleton	_____ McPherson	BAILEY 268-274 {Charleston}	1824
Graves, Samuel Colleton	_____ McPherson	RILEY 219-247	1824
Graves, Samuel Colleton (marriage settlement 15 April 1818) {Charleston}	Susan McPherson	3 RIEQ 218-225	1818
Gray, _____	Elizabeth Jenkins (widow of John H. Jenkins who was born 3 February 1797) {Beaufort}	2 HILL 511-515	1834
Gray, Henry (he died 5 April 1831) (daughter of Dr. Reuben Flanagan of Newberry)	_____ Flanagan	2 HILL 644-653 {Newberry and Abbeville}	1829
Gray, Robert (he died about 1811) (daughter of Alexander Donald who died about 1806)	Nancy Donald	RICE 330-342 {Abbeville}	1803
Green, _____	Ann Finley	14 RIEQ 167-175 {Abbeville}	1859
Greene, _____	Mary Ann (or Mary R.) Lehre [See also pages 271-272]	1 RIEQ 296-301	1844

S.C. Marriages 1749-1867 Implied in S.C. Equity Reports

MAN	WOMAN	VOLUME	PAGES	LIVED
Gregg, Joseph	_____ James	DUDLEY	42-54	1835
	(daughter of George James) {Marion}			
Gregorie, _____	Eliza Snelgrove	4 DESA	274-304	1812
	(daughter of Henry Snelgrove)			
Grier, Robert C.	Barbara B. Moffatt	5 RIEQ	95-111	1852
	(daughter of William Moffatt who died 15 April 1851) {Chester}			
Griffin, Leroy	_____ Mobley	2 RIEQ	56-58	1841
	{Chester}			
Griffin, Richard	Amelia Sims	2 RIEQ	99-114	1784
(he died 1799)	(daughter of Nathan Sims of Abbeville)			
(to Lincoln County, Georgia)	{Abbeville}			
Grimke, _____	_____ Drayton	RICHEQ	321-325	1831
	(daughter of Thomas Drayton) {Charleston}			
Grimke, Hon. John F	_____ Smith	1 McC	119-148	1825
	(daughter of Thomas Smith)			
Grimke, John F.	Mary Smith	1 DESA	366-382	1794
	(daughter of Thomas Smith)			
Grimke, John Paul	Mary Faucheraud	1 DESA	366-382	1751
	(daughter of Gideon Faucheraud)			
Guffin, Charles B.	Jane Mathis	8 RIEQ	79-81	1855
	{Abbeville District}			
Guillemot, Jacques Magnus	Madelaine Julie Antheaume	1 RIEQ	187-221	1836
	{Paris, France}			
Guillemot, Philipe Eugene	Jeane Elvina Lacoste	1 RIEQ	187-221	1836
(marriage contract 23 May 1836, Paris, France)				
(daughter of Charles Gregorie Arnauld Lacoste)				
Gunnels, William C.	Temperance Martin	2 RIEQ	259-270	1844
(he died 17/18 December 1844) (daughter of George Martin)	{Greenville and Laurens Districts}			
Gunter, _____	_____ Adams	4 RIEQ	152-164	1851
	(daughter of Shockley Adams who died 10 October 1824) {Marlborough}			
Gurganes, David	Elizabeth Hancock	McMULL	298-303	1834
	(widow of Simon Hancock, Sr.) {Edgefield}			
Gurganus, David	Elizabeth Hancock	1 RIEQ	26-40	1829
	(widow of Simon Hancock, Sr.) {Edgefield}			
Gurganus, David	Elizabeth Hancock	McMULL	69-74	1838
	(widow of Simon Hancock, Sr.) {Edgefield}			

S.C. Marriages 1749-1867 Implied in S.C. Equity Reports

MAN	WOMAN	VOLUME PAGES	LIVED

(H)

Haigood, _____ Mary C. (or E.) 2 HILL 492-498 1836
 Massey (daughter of George Massey
 who died about 1818) {York}
Haile, _____ Mary Cureton 13 RIEQ 104-110 1858
 {Lancaster District}
Hair, Irvine R. Rebecca E. Askew 10 RIEQ 163-177 1853
 (married 13 October 1853) (daughter of Seth Askew)
 {Barnwell}
Hale, Samuel Eliza Margaret 9 RIEQ 483-499 1853
 White (daughter of Joseph B. White
 of Sumter District, who died 31 December 1852)
 {Sumter District}
Hall, _____ Sabina Toomer 2 HILL 27-34 1833
 (widow)
Hall, Ainsley Sarah C. Goodwyn 2 McC 269-317 1823
 (he died August 1823) {Columbia}
Hall, Owen Judith James 2 McC 143-150 1827
 (daughter of George James)
 {Wilkes County, North Carolina}
Hall, Thomas Sarah Howard 3 DESA 256-262 1803
 (married 1803) (he died October 1808)
Hall, Wm. E. Dorcas Jones 1 STRO 323-333 1847
 {Fairfield}
Hamilton, _____ Elizabeth M. 7 RIEQ 289-327 1852
 Heyward (daughter of Daniel Heyward)
 {Charleston}
Hamilton, Joseph A. Christiana Davis 5 RIEQ 434-441 1849
 (she died 30 December 1849)
 {Abbeville District}
Hamilton, Maj. Elizabeth Harleston 1 DESA 244-247 1791
 James (widow of John Harleston who died
 April 1781)
Hammond, _____ Mary Edwards 3 RIEQ 271-281 1850
 [See also 7 RIEQ pages 125-135] {Charleston}
Hammond, Abner Catherine M. Barsh 10 RIEQ 149-156 1834
 Lewis (marriage settlement 19 November 1834)
 (she of Columbia) {Orangeburg}
Hampton, Mary E. McCord 5 RIEQ 403 1843
 Christopher F. (she died 1848) {St. Matthew's Parish}
Hanahan, John Elizabeth Mary CHEVES 129-142 1839
 Clark (widow of William M. Clark)
 [See also pages 80-93] {Charleston}

S.C. Marriages 1749-1867 Implied in S.C. Equity Reports

MAN	WOMAN	VOLUME PAGES	LIVED
Hanahan, John	Martha Mary Murray (daughter of Joseph James Murray who died 18 July 1818)	CHEVES 80-93	1839
Hanckel, _____	Elizabeth Jenkins Clarke (daughter of William M. Clarke) {Charleston}	3 RIEQ 318-341	1841
Hanion, Henry	Elizabeth Dwight	HARPER 170-174	1824
(unrecorded marriage settlement 8 January 1814, Georgetown District)			
Hankinson, Robert	_____ Blewer (daughter of John G. Blewer) {Lexington}	2 STRO 285-289	1842
Hankinson. See Haukison			
Hannahan, John	Elizabeth Clarke (widow of William M. Clarke) {Charleston}	3 RIEQ 318-341	1839
Hannahan, John	Martha M. Murray (daughter of Joseph J. Murray) {Charleston}	McMULL 352-357	1835
Harbeson, Patrick	Jane Ballentine (daughter of Dougal Ballentine) {Chester District}	2 McC 112-118	1827
Hardee, Isaac	_____ Smith (daughter of Jesse Smith who died about 1826) {Horry District}	1 RIEQ 130-140	1845
Harden, Robert	Delia Ann Badger (daughter of Nathaniel Badger who died 1842) {Barnwell}	6 RIEQ 147-149	1842
Harden, William	Sarah Gardner (widow of Robert Gardner)	2 McC 32-36	1827
Hardin, _____	Letitia McCool (she died 1843) {Chester}	3 STRO 44-54	1837
Hardwicke, _____	Mary S. M. Skrine (she died 1837) {Georgetown}	3 RIEQ 262-271	1833
Hargroves, Thomas	Susan Wheeler (widow of William Wheeler who died July 1829) {Charleston District}	2 HILL 222-228	1834
Harlan, _____	Melissa Whitlock {Union}	13 RIEQ 165-171	1866
Harlee, James J.	Mary F. Scarborough {Marion}	9 RIEQ 100-110	1853
Harlee, Robert	Ann Jane Gourley (daughter of Joseph Gourley) (she died September 1835) {Marion}	DUDLEY 42-54	1835
Harleston, John	Elizabeth Lynch	1 DESA 244-247	1781
(he died April 1781) (her first marriage)			
Harley, _____	Almedia Brown (daughter of Colonel Tarlton Brown who died September 1845) {Barnwell}	3 RIEQ 379-384	1845

39

S.C. Marriages 1749-1867 Implied in S.C. Equity Reports

MAN	WOMAN	VOLUME	PAGES	LIVED
Harley, Jacob R.	Elizabeth Bruton (daughter of George Bruton)	2 HILL	367-371 {Barnwell}	1835
Harris, _____	Elizabeth Glover (daughter of Wiley Glover, Sen.)	4 RIEQ	25-38 {Abbeville}	1851
Harris, Amos	Mary Patterson (daughter of Anthony Patterson who died 31 May 1850) (she died 25 February 1844)	4 RIEQ	340-348 {Orangeburg}	1844
Harrison, _____	Susan McDowell	RILEY	152-155 {Charleston}	1834
Harrison, _____	Ann Perry (daughter of James Perry)	1 HILL	35-48	1806
Harrison, Wm.	E. B. Campbell	9 RIEQ	376-391 {Fairfield}	1857
Hart, Derril	Charlotte Thompson (her first marriage) (daughter of William R. Thompson)	5 RIEQ	370-403 {St. Matthew's Parish}	1839
Hart, J. B.	Mariah Collier	3 RIEQ	125-132 {Charleston}	1850
Hart, Nathan	Rachel Hart (daughter of Daniel Hart who died 1811)	3 DESA	592-595	1811
Hartley, James	_____ Ladson (daughter of Thomas Ladson)	1 DESA	500-515	1796
Harvin, _____	Hester Wells	5 RIEQ	20-31 {Sumter}	1842
Harvin, Samuel	Sarah Ann Spears (she was born about 1797) (she died March 1828)	RICHEQ	287-293 {Walterboro}	1828
Haseldon, Francis G. (married 1842)	_____ Skeen (widow)	10 RIEQ	53-63 {Charleston}	1842
Haseldon, James	Mary Godbold (daughter of General Thomas Godbold)	6 RIEQ	26-42 {Marion}	1853
Haseldon, John	Elizabeth Godbold (her first marriage) (daughter of General _____ Godbold of Marion District, who died 1825)	4 RIEQ	334-340	1844
Haseldon, John	Elizabeth Godbold (her first marriage) (daughter of General Thomas Godbold)	6 RIEQ	26-42 {Marion}	1853
Haskell, Charles T.	Sophia Cheves (daughter of Hon. Langdon Cheves who died 27 June 1857)	10 RIEQ	534-550	1854
Haskell, William E.	Susan E. (or S.) Ball	SPEERS	48-87	1843

S.C. Marriages 1749-1867 Implied in S.C. Equity Reports

MAN	WOMAN	VOLUME PAGES	LIVED
Hatcher, _____	Christiana Parker	4 STRO 179-186	1840
[See also 3 RIEQ page 136 in footnotes of 1917 Edition] {Edgefield}			
Haukison, Robert (Hankison)	_____ Blewer (daughter of John G. Blewer) {Lexington}	10 RIEQ 191-201	1842
Hay, _____	Susan Cynthia Brown (daughter of Charles J. Brown)	4 RIEQ 378-389	1852
Hay, Col. Frederick J. (he died 10 August 1849)	Susan Cynthia Brown (daughter of Charles J. Brown) {Barnwell District}	3 RIEQ 384-397	1849
Hayne, William A. (married 1837)	Susan Smith Mazyck (widow of Stephen Mazyck who died November 1832)	CHEVES 37-41	1837
Hayne, Wm	_____ Perronneau (daughter of Arthur Perronneau)	1 DESA 521-537	1796
Haynesworth, James	Susan Cox Porter	HARPER 117-124	1824
Haynsworth, Henry	Mary Elizabeth Britton Spann (she died 1 June 1846) {Sumter District}	12 RIEQ 114-123	1844
Haynsworth, James L.	McConico Gulielma Spann (daughter of William Spann) {Sumter District}	12 RIEQ 114-123	1860
Hays, William	Mary Wilson	1 McC 233-242	1826
	{Laurens District}		
Hearst, _____	Phebe Cochran (widow) {Ninety-Six District}	4 DESA 143-145	1810
Heldman, Matthew	Susan Payne (daughter of Wesley Payne) {Greenville}	8 RIEQ 9-12	1851
Hemingway, _____	Mary Clendinen (widow) {Richland and Union}	2 RIEQ 321-354	1835
Henderson, Daniel	_____ Roach (widow) (she died 1816) {York}	BAILEY 138-141	1794
Henderson, Francis	Frances Laurens (daughter of Col. John Laurens)	2 DESA 170-171	1803
Henderson, Stephen	_____ Lee {Abbeville}	4 DESA 459-462	1814
Henry, _____	Sarah Talbird (daughter of John Talbird)	BAILEY 535-566	1830
[Must also see RICHEQ pages 361-369] {Beaufort District}			
Henry, Robert	_____ Connors	2 McC 323-343	1827
Henson, John K.	Huldah Kinard	3 STRO 371-379	1842
(married 16 August 1842) (daughter of Martin Kinard) (she died 22 October 1844) {Newberry and Laurens Districts}			
Herbemont, _____	Caroline Neyle	CHEVES 21-26	1839

S.C. Marriages 1749-1867 Implied in S.C. Equity Reports

MAN	WOMAN	VOLUME PAGES	LIVED

Heriot, William   _____ Thomas   4 DESA 227-242   1792
   (marriage settlement 10 May 1792) (daughter of Edward
   Thomas) (Heriot died November 1807) {Georgetown}
Herrin, Edmund   _____ Bird   11 RIEQ 536-540   1860
                         (daughter of Arthur Bird who died 1835)
                                                {Marion District}
Herrin, Wilson   Maria Bird   11 RIEQ 536-540   1849
                         (daughter of Arthur Bird who died 1835)
                                                {Marion District}
Herron, William H.   Nancy Delk   5 RIEQ 441-450   1836
                         (daughter of Newit Delk)
                         (she died 1848)   {Darlington}
Herron, William H.   Nancy H. Delk   6 RIEQ 339-342   1830
                         (daughter of Newitt Delk)
                         (she died 1848)   {Darlington}
Hext, Lawrence   Sarah C. Porcher   1 STRO 170-172   1806
   (marriage settlement 15 December 1806)
      (daughter of Peter Porcher)   {Beaufort District}
Hext, Lawrence P.   Eliza Ann Ashe   2 STRO 250-258   1848
                         (daughter of Richard C. Ashe, Sr.
                         who died 1837)   {Barnwell}
   [Must also see 5 RIEQ pages 5, 6]
Heyward, Thomas   Elizabeth Savage   2 McC   435-440   1823
Hickey, James   Mary Parris   5 RIEQ 450-472   1850
                         (daughter of William Parris
                         of Tennessee)   {Anderson}
Hicks, Claudius P.   Ann Vernon   RICHEQ 5-23   1816
   (to Mississippi)   {Darlington}
Hicks, Samuel   Lucy James   2 McC   143-150   1827
   (or William)   (daughter of George James)
                                {Wilkes County, North Carolina}
Higgenbottom, J.   Julia Gillett   3 RIEQ 398-403   1832
                                                {Barnwell}
Higginbottom, James   Julia Gillett   SPEERS 142-158   1829
                         (daughter of Dr. Elijah Gillett
                         who died 1818)   {Barnwell}
   [See also 4 RIEQ pages 314-316]
Hiles, Adam   _____ Ardis   2 McC   60-72   1786
   (he died 1785/86)   {Beech Island}
Hill, _____   Nancy Cabeen   1 HILL 51-59   1833
                         (daughter of Thomas Cabeen) {Chester}
Hill, _____   Aimy Davenport   3 RIEQ 559-578   1842
                         (daughter of Jonathan Davenport)
                                                {Newberry}
Hill, Duncan   Elizabeth Butler   2 DESA 279-285   1785
   (marriage settlement 3 December 1785)

S.C. Marriages 1749-1867 Implied in S.C. Equity Reports

MAN	WOMAN	VOLUME PAGES	LIVED
Hill, Henry H.	Martha Bond	1 STRO 1-26	1836

(daughter of John P. Bond, Sr. of
Lexington District, who died 1823) {Edgefield}

Hill, Henry H.	Martha Bond	DUDLEY 71-84	1837

(daughter of John P. Bond of
Lexington District, who died September 1823) {Edgefield}

Hill, Jonathan	Lucinda Bond	3 STRO 94-105	1844

(he went to Texas) (she died 7 October 1847) {Edgefield}

Hill, Jonathan M.	Lucinda Bond	1 STRO 1-26	1834

(in Alabama 1834) (daughter of John P. Bond, Sr.
of Lexington District, who died 1823) {Edgefield}

Hill, Jonathan M.	Lucinda Bond	DUDLEY 71-84	1837

(daughter of John P. Bond of
Lexington District, who died September 1823) {Edgefield}

Hill, Samuel	Mary Mathis	8 RIEQ 79-81	1855
		{Abbeville District}	
Hinson, Elijah	Jane Caroline	1 HILL 35-48	1829

Starke (married January 1829)
(daughter of Philemon Starke)
[See also 2 HILL pages 351-360]

Hodge, Benjamin B.	Harriet B. Dinkins	SPEERS 268-280	1838

(daughter of Gilbert Dinkins)
{Sumter District}

Hodge, Benjamin D.	Emily E. Dinkins	SPEERS 268-280	1838

(daughter of Gilbert Dinkins)
{Sumter District}

Hodge, John M.	Mary Dinkins	SPEERS 268-280	1838

(daughter of Gilbert Dinkins)
{Sumter District}

Hodges, _____	Caroline T. Chick	10 RIEQ 178-190	1846

(daughter of Burwill Chick of
Greenville, who died 1847)   {Greenville, Newberry
and Union Districts}

Hodges, Absalom T.	Julia S. Ioor	SPEERS 593-603	1837

(of Abbeville) (marriage settlement 9 March 1837)
{Edgefield District}

Hoell, Joseph H.	Ann Bonds	4 DESA 21-26	1809

(widow of William Bonds who died 1804)
{Camden}

Holbrook, Daniel	Mary Edwards	2 HILL 184-200	1835
		{Coosawhatchie}	
Holbrook, Silas E.	Esther Gourdin	RILEY 167-173	1834
		{Charleston}	
Holcombe, G. W.	_____ Evans	HARPER 202-204	1824

(daughter of John Evans)

S.C. Marriages 1749-1867 Implied in S.C. Equity Reports

MAN	WOMAN	VOLUME	PAGES	LIVED
Holeman, William W.	Sarah Hoof (daughter of James D. Hoof) {Orangeburg District}	3 STRO	66-75	1848
Holladay, William (he died 1819)	Elizabeth Birch Kingdom {Sumter}	McMULL	279-289	1819
Holland, Parker J.	Susan C. Colburn (daughter of James B. Colburn) {Boston and Charleston}	14 RIEQ	176-244	1856
Holley, John C.	Susannah Priester (daughter of William Priester) {Barnwell}	12 RIEQ	361-378	1863
Holloway, George	Rebecca Adams {Edgefield}	1 STRO	114-128	1846
Holloway, Lewis	Rachel Williams	5 RIEQ	531-579	1787

(married December 1787) (widow of Thomas Williams of Brunswick County, Virginia, who died January 1787 (Holloway died 1814) (she died 10 December 1847)
{Edgefield District}

Holmes, _____	M. E. Simons {Charleston}	3 DESA	149-154	1810
Holmes, _____	Anna Maria Thayer {Charleston}	10 RIEQ	484-494	1850
Holmes, C. R.	Mary Deas {Charleston}	7 RIEQ	328-343	1843
Holt, Thomas T. (in Georgia)	Elizabeth Ellen Burke (daughter of Dr. Michael Burke) {Fairfield}	McMULL	475-484	1831
Hood, _____	Narcissa Harris	9 RIEQ	311-330	1846

(daughter of John Harris, Sr. who died 1840, Mecklenburgh County, North Carolina) {Lancaster}

Hood, Thomas O.	_____ Alexander {Lancaster}	9 RIEQ	311-330	1845
Hoof, James D.	Ann Jackson	3 STRO	66-75	1813

(married April 1813) (daughter of Thomas Jackson) (Hoof was born about 1796) (to Edgefield) {Orangeburg District}

Hopkins, George W. (he died 1805)	Martha Booker (daughter of Bird Booker)	1 HILL	1-10	1799
Hopkins, James S.	Margaret Mazyck	1 HILL	242-252	1824

(marriage settlement 24 February 1824)

Hopkins, James S.	Margaret M. Mazyck	RICHEQ	263-282	1824

(marriage settlement 24 February 1824) (daughter of Samuel Mazyck) {Charleston}

Horlbeck, Edward	Ainsley Rives {Charleston}	7 RIEQ	353-357	1850
Horn, _____	Elizabeth Robertson	3 RIEQ	136	1840

[In footnotes of 1917 Edition] {Edgefield}

S.C. Marriages 1749-1867 Implied in S.C. Equity Reports

MAN	WOMAN	VOLUME PAGES	LIVED
Hornsby, William	Rebecca Smith	10 RIEQ 475-483	1838

(he died September 1855) (in Wayne County, Georgia)
{Beaufort}

| Horry, Elias | Elizabeth Branford | 2 DESA 115-127 | 1770 |

(married 1770) (daughter of William Branford)
(Horry died 11 February 1785) (she died 1785)

| Horry, Elias | Harriet Vanderhorst DUDLEY | 145-154 | 1810 |

(daughter of Arnoldus Vanderhorst)
{Charleston}

| Horry, Peter | Margaret Guignard | 4 DESA 614-616 | 1793 |

(marriage settlement 9 February 1793)

| Horry, Thomas | Ann Branford | 2 DESA 115-127 | 1771 |

(married 1771) (daughter of William Branford)

| House, James | Lavinia Falconer | 4 DESA 86-87 | 1810 |

(widow of William Falconer who died June 1805) {Cheraws}

| Houseal, _____ | Margaret McRa | 3 RIEQ 96-111 | 1848 |

{Kershaw}

| Houseal, Dr. J. G. | _____ Phaelon | 2 McC 423-434 | 1815 |

(married 1815) (widow of Major Edward Phaelon who died 1810) (she died 1816)

| Houston, Alexander | Jane Postell | 9 RIEQ 85-99 | 1826 |

(he was married before) (she died 26 November 1843)
{Abbeville}

| Houston, John A. | Amy Garrett | 1 STRO 96-103 | 1843 |

{Edgefield}

| Houston, John A. | Amy Garrett | 2 STRO 272-284 | 1843 |

{Edgefield}

| Howe, Captain M. S. | Ann Timothy Cleland | 4 RIEQ 254-260 | 1849 |

{Charleston}

| Huey, John | Lydia Blackburne | 1 HILL 405-412 | 1830 |

(he died 1830) (widow of William Blackburne) {Abbeville}

| Huger, Benjamin | Celestine Pinckney | 2 RIEQ 218-245 | 1842 |

(daughter of Thomas Pinckney)

| Huger, John | Esther Gabriella De Veaux | 1 STRO 283-294 | 1843 |

(daughter of Stephen Gabriel De Veaux) {Charleston}

| Huger, John | _____ Glover | 2 HILL 515-528 | 1832 |

(daughter of Col. Wilson Glover)
{Colleton District}

| Huger, T. Pinckney | Anna Cheves | 10 RIEQ 534-550 | 1854 |

(daughter of Hon. Langdon Cheves who died 27 June 1857)

| Huggins, George A. | Ellen Blakely | 9 RIEQ 408-410 | 1857 |

{Sumter}

| Hughes, _____ | Mary Eddings (widow) | 5 RIEQ 274-289 | 1852 |

45

S.C. Marriages 1749-1867 Implied in S.C. Equity Reports

MAN	WOMAN	VOLUME	PAGES	LIVED
Hughes, ____	Beulah Lawton (daughter of Winborn Lawton)	3 DESA	199-203	1811
Hughes, Arthur	Hannah Elms (widow of William Elms) {Charleston}	3 DESA	155-164	1810
Huguenin, C. C.	Adelaide Barksdale (daughter of Thomas Barksdale, Jr.) {Charleston}	7 RIEQ	125-135	1854
Hull, Gideon H.	Ann ____	2 STRO	174-195	1828

(common-law marriage) (he died October 1840, Hamburg, S.C.) {Edgefield}

| Hull, Gideon H. | Currency Osborne | 2 STRO | 174-195 | 1820 |

(divorced February 1830, Connecticut)

Hume, ____	Catharine Lucas	5 RIEQ	270-274	1840
			{Charleston}	
Hunt, ____	Susan B. Mathewes (daughter of Wm. Mathewes) {Charleston}	4 RIEQ	233-254	1852
Hunt, Alfred M.	Martha Lane	9 RIEQ	459-473	1838

(married 15 March 1838) (widow of William S. Lane) {Richland}

| Hunt, Col. Benjamin F. | Susan B. Mathews (daughter of William Mathews) {Charleston} | 4 STRO | 1-25 | 1848 |
| Hunt, Col. Benjamin F., Jr. | Susan B. Matthews (daughter of William Matthews who died 22 July 1848) {Charleston and | 6 RIEQ | 183-199 | 1826 |

Georgetown District} [See also 8 RIEQ pages 166-184]

| Hunt, Col. Benjamin Faneul, Sr. | ____ Mathews (daughter of William Mathews) | 11 RIEQ | 205-224 | 1849 |

(Hunt died 1854/55) {Charleston and Georgetown District} [Must also see pages 269-281; 296-322]

Hunt, John	Ann Ball	1 DESA	137-142	1769
Hunt, William G.	____ Heath (daughter of Frederick Heath who died 1816) {Orangeburg}	2 HILL	100-107	1816
Hunter, ____	Ruth Vickory (daughter of William Vickory who died 1804) {Abbeville}	4 RIEQ	16-22	1825
Hunter, Alexander D.	____ Tate (daughter of Enos Tate) {Abbeville}	3 STRO	136-149	1842
Hunter, Andrew	Mary Andrews	2 HILL	483-492	1819

(marriage settlement 10 February 1819) {Darlington}

| Hunter, John | Sarah Bowler (daughter of J. H. Bowler who died 1804) | HARPER | 69-71 | 1824 |
| Hunter, W. M. | Harriet Priester (daughter of William Priester) {Barnwell} | 12 RIEQ | 361-378 | 1863 |

S.C. Marriages 1749-1867 Implied in S.C. Equity Reports

MAN	WOMAN	VOLUME PAGES	LIVED
Huson, Peter M.	___ Lewis (daughter of John Lewis) (she died 1836)	1 RIEQ 1-25 {Union}	1836
Hutchinson, Capt. Hugh	Ann (Nancy) Peyton	2 DESA 313-320	1805
Hyde, Ezekiel F.	Nancy A. Hunter	13 RIEQ 250-258 {Laurens}	1864
Hyrne, P.	___ Youngblood	2 DESA 294-299	1790

(I)

Iley, John	___ Hodges (daughter of Richard Hodges) {Laurens}	HARPER 295-298	1824
Iley, John	___ Hodges	1 McC 518-523	1826
Inglis, Alexander	Mary Deas	1 DESA 333-340	1785
Inglis, Alexander [Referred to in another case]	Mary Deas	10 RIEQ 137	1793
Ingraham, ___	Harriet Laurens	6 RIEQ 217-226 {Charleston}	1842
Ingraham, ___	Joanna Postell (daughter of William Postell of Charleston)	1 McC 94-99	1825
Ingraham, Benjamin F.	Lucy E. Minor	3 STRO 105-111 {Barnwell}	1847
Ingraham, D. N.	Harriet Laurens (daughter of Henry Laurens, Jr.)	14 RIEQ 139-145 {Charleston}	1866
Ingram, Benjamin F. (married 15 July 1847) (widow) (she died 19 February 1856)	Lucy E. Minor	10 RIEQ 130-138 {Barnwell}	1847
I'On, ___	Mary Ashby	2 DESA 210-214	1802
Irvine, E. S.	Ann Jemima Harris	4 RIEQ 25-38 {Abbeville}	1851
Izard, Allen Smith of Charleston, who died 21 August 1854) {Charleston}	___ Huger (daughter of Hon. Daniel Elliott Huger	9 RIEQ 217-243	1856
Izard, Henry	___ Middleton {St. James Goose Creek and Charleston}	BAILEY 228-240	1813
Izard, Henry	___ Middleton (daughter of Arthur Middleton)	2 HILL 591-599	1814
Izard, Ralph Stead	Rosetta Pinckney (daughter of Thomas Pinckney)	2 RIEQ 218-245	1842

S.C. Marriages 1749-1867 Implied in S.C. Equity Reports

MAN	WOMAN	VOLUME	PAGES	LIVED

(J)

Jacks, James   Ann Wilson   1 DESA   543-557   1797
    (widow of George Wilson)
Jackson, Green   _____ Yeates   1 RIEQ   78-91   1807
    (daughter of Thomas Yeates)
                                                                          {Ninety-Six District}
Jackson, Thomas   Sarah Hoof   3 STRO   66-75   1813
    (married about January 1813) (widower) (widow of
    James D. Hoof)   {Orangeburg District}
Jackson, William   Martha Barber   5 RIEQ   38-55   1849
    (daughter of John M. Barber) {Chester}
Jaffray, J.   Mary Adams   1 DESA   567-570   1797
    (daughter of N. Adams)
James, George   Nancy Smith   2 McC   143-150   1797
    (daughter of Samuel Smith of
    North Carolina)
James, John   Elizabeth Roten   4 DESA   185-199   1780
    (married 6 April 1780) (Routen) (he died 6 December 1807)
    (of Newberry District)   {Washington District}
James, John   Ann (Nancy) Tucker   4 DESA   185-199   1800
    (common-law marriage) {of Newberry District}
                                                                           {Washington District}
James, Philip   Susannah _____   1 HILL   76-94   1785
    (married 1785)
James, Philip   Susannah Fennell   HARPER   288-295   1817
    (Fannell) (of Lexington District)
Jaudon, Paul   _____ McDonald   RICHEQ   246-258   1826
    (daughter of Adam McDonald) {Georgetown}
Jefcoat, Elijah   Jerusha Hoover   10 RIEQ   118-129   1811
    (daughter of John Hoover who died 1832)
    (she died 1818)   {Lexington District}
Jeffries, Howell L. Sarah (Sally)   9 RIEQ   459-473   1834
                       Hamner (daughter of George B. Hamner,
    Sr. of Mecklenburg County, Virginia) {Richland}
Jelineau, Francis   Elizabeth F.   2 DESA   45-52   1800
                       La Barthe (widow?)
    (married February 1800)
Jenkins, _____   Elizabeth Grimball   3 RIEQ   318-341   1830
                       Clarke   {Charleston}
Jenkins, _____   Martha Stephens   RICHEQ   326-352   1813
    (daughter of George Stephens who died
    7 February 1817)   {Beaufort}
Jenkins,   _____ Wilkinson   HARPER   72-88   1824
    Christopher   {Charleston}

S.C. Marriages 1749-1867 Implied in S.C. Equity Reports

MAN	WOMAN	VOLUME PAGES	LIVED

Jenkins, Rolly   Laurania (Lauraney) 5 RIEQ 450-472   1843
                 Parris (daughter of Henry Parris who
   was born 1752/53 and died 27 September 1847) {Anderson}
Jervey, Thomas H.   Floride Taylor   2 DESA 221-226   1802
   (married 6 May 1802) [See also pages 419-422]
Jeter, Ary   _____ McDaniel   DUDLEY 1-14   1837
                                        {Newberry}
Jeter, James   _____ Frazier   2 HILL 304-318 1824
                                        {Edgefield}
Jeter, William   Harriet McJunkin   11 RIEQ 527-535   1858
                 (daughter of Joseph McJunkin) {Union}
Jewell, Benjamin   Sarah J. Isaacs   11 RIEQ 296-322   1813
   (married June 1813, Richmond, Virginia) (he died
   1828, Louisiana)   {Charleston District}
Jewell, Benjamin   Sophie Prevost   11 RIEQ 296-322   1795
   (from Savannah to Barnwell District about 1804,
   then to Charleston) (separated 10 December 1810)
                                       {Charleston District}
Jewell, Benjamin   Sophie Prevost   RICHEQ 112-115   1796
   (married 1796 at Savannah) (separated 1810)
   [In footnotes of 1917 Edition]   {Charleston}
Johnson, _____   _____ Clarkson   3 RIEQ 305-318 1850
                 (sister of John Clarkson)
Johnson, _____   Maria Smart   McMULL 345-348   1842
                 (daughter of James Smart) {Beaufort}
Johnson, _____   Maria Stuart   6 RIEQ 95   n.d.
                 (daughter of James Stuart)
   [Referred to in another case]
Johnson, Hugh   Jane Fowke   SPEERS 233-249   1837
   (marriage settlement 4 October 1837) {Barnwell}
Johnson, John   _____ Gilbert   13 RIEQ 42-49   1860
                 (daughter of Jesse Gilbert, Sr. of
   Darlington District, who died 20 July 1852)
                                       {Darlington District}
Johnson, Richard M. Elizabeth Garrett 2 STRO 272-284   1843
                                       {Edgefield}
Johnson, Richard W. Elizabeth Garrett 1 STRO 96-103   1843
                                       {Edgefield}
Johnson, Thomas N. Mary James   2 HILL 277-298   1818
                 (she died January 1818)
Johnson, William K. _____ Gilbert   13 RIEQ 42-49   1860
                 (daughter of Jesse Gilbert, Sr. of
   Darlington District, who died 20 July 1852)
                                       {Darlington District}
Johnston, _____   Ann Ewing   2 DESA 451-456   1806
                 (daughter of Adam Ewing who died
                 October 1796)

49

S.C. Marriages 1749-1867 Implied in S.C. Equity Reports

MAN	WOMAN	VOLUME PAGES	LIVED
Johnston, Archibald	Agnes Ewing	1 HILL 228-242	1807

Simpson (marriage contract 8 April 1807) (he died
15 September 1819) (she died 27 March 1828) {Charleston}

Johnston, R. (Johnson)	Mary Cogdell (daughter of George Cogdell)	1 DESA 454-458	1795
Jones, _____	Elizabeth Glover	1 RIEQ 141-154 {Colleton}	1845
Jones, _____	Margaret Meacham	4 STRO 203-206 {Edgefield}	1849
Jones, _____	Harriet Zimmerman (daughter of Jacob Zimmerman) {Coosawhatchie}	BAILEY 195-204	1821
Jones, George	Sarah Campbell	2 DESA 380-388 {Pendleton District}	1796
Jones, Lewis, Sen.	Elizabeth Pou (daughter of William Pou) {Edgefield}	1 RIEQ 50-52	1820
Jones, Thomas	Mercy Minter (daughter of Joseph Minter) (her first marriage) {Ninety-Six District}	1 RIEQ 78-91	1807
Jones, William	Mary Smith (daughter of Philip Smith) {Charleston}	BAILEY 244-267	1811
Jones, William	Mary Smith (stepdaughter of Philip Smith) {Charleston District}	3 DESA 165-168	1811
Jordan, A. B.	Elizabeth Ann Finklea (widow of Hugh Finklea) {Marion}	14 RIEQ 160-166	1867
Josey, _____	Jane Webb	9 RIEQ 369-375	1828

(married about 1828) (widow of John Webb, Sr.)
(Josey died about 1832) {Kershaw}

Jough, _____	Harriet D. (or E.) Williman (daughter of Christopher Williman) {Charleston}	4 RIEQ 475-496	1850
Joyce, A. J.	Maria Gunnels (daughter of William C. Gunnels) {Greenville and Laurens Districts}	2 RIEQ 259-270	1845
Joyce, John H.	Nancy Ramsey	McMULL 236-253	1832

(married 15 May 1832) (separated 1834) (widow of
John Ramsey of Edgefield District) (she went to Alabama)
{Greenville}

(K)

Kaigler, John	_____ Heath	2 HILL 100-107 {Orangeburg}	1831

S.C. Marriages 1749-1867 Implied in S.C. Equity Reports

MAN	WOMAN	VOLUME	PAGES	LIVED
Keals, Peter R.	Magdaline China	5 RIEQ	426-434	1852
	(daughter of Thomas China) {Williamsburg}			
Keckley, Edward C.	Mary Jane Moore	2 STRO	21-24	1840
	(daughter of James Moore) {Charleston}			
Keith, _____	Susannah Bullein	1 DESA	353-355	1794
Keith, John	Malinda Boyd	7 RIEQ	509-520	1838
(married 10/12 October 1838) (widow of Samuel Boyd)				
(Keith died 7 November 1842) {Fairfield}				
Keitt, George D.	Olivia Felder	4 RIEQ	349-358	1843
	(daughter of Henry Felder) {Orangeburg}			
Keitt, Wesley	Henrietta Felder	4 RIEQ	349-358	1852
	(daughter of Henry Felder) {Orangeburg}			
Kelly, _____	Rebecca Snelgrove	4 DESA	274-304	1812
	(daughter of Henry Snelgrove)			
Kelly, William H.	Nancy Fretwell	11 RIEQ	559-573	1856
	(daughter of William Fretwell			
	of Greene County, Georgia) {Anderson}			
Kennedy, Joseph	Eliza Watson	3 STRO	1-15	1837
(married 1837) (daughter of Hardaway D. Watson)				
		{Fairfield District}		
Kennedy, Joseph	Eliza A. Watson	7 RIEQ	100-105	1854
		{Fairfield}		
Kennerly, Joseph	Susannah James	1 HILL	76-94	1808
(married 1800/01) (widow of Philip James)				
(Kennerly died about 1808)				
Kerr, John	Catherine R. Burke	McMULL	475-484	1831
(in Georgia)	(daughter of Dr. Michael Burke)			
		{Fairfield}		
Ketchin, Thomas	Margaret (Peggy)	5 RIEQ	83-90	1852
	Beaty (daughter of James Beaty)			
		{Fairfield}		
Key, Henry	Mary Garrett	1 STRO	96-103	1843
		{Edgefield}		
Key, Henry	Mary Garrett	2 STRO	272-284	1843
		{Edgefield}		
Keys, John M.	Lucinda _____	6 RIEQ	388-398	1838
(common-law marriage or married 23 August 1838)				
		{Anderson}		
Kilgore, _____	Polly Moon	2 STRO	327-334	1848
		{Greenville}		
Kimbrell, _____	Sarah Cureton	13 RIEQ	104-110	1858
		{Lancaster District}		
Kinard, John P.	Catharine Wicker	1 HILL	376-382	1826
(he died 1828)	(widow of Uriah Wicker) (she died 1826)			
		{Newberry}		
King, _____	Elizabeth Bride	1 McC	399-406	1826
	(widow)			

51

S.C. Marriages 1749-1867 Implied in S.C. Equity Reports

MAN	WOMAN	VOLUME PAGES	LIVED
King, Wm.	Nancy _____	2 HILL 624-629	1806
(separated about 1806)		{Edgefield}	
King, Wm.	Mary Johnson	2 HILL 624-629	1806
(common-law marriage) (he died 1836)		{Edgefield}	
Kinloch, Frederick	_____ Lowndes	1 HILL 190-193	1833
	(daughter of Thomas Lowndes)	{Charleston}	
Kirk, Rollin H.	_____ Garth	11 RIEQ 259-263	1855
	(she went to Kentucky)	{Beaufort}	
Kirk, William John	Mary Jane Winckler	2 DESA 640-646	1808
	(widow of Nicholas Winckler, Jun. who died March 1802)	{Beaufort District}	
Kirkland, _____	Dorcas Cave	6 RIEQ 43-57	1834
	(daughter of David Cave who died October 1834)	{Barnwell}	
Kling, George	Mary Perryclear	BAILEY 42-48	1807
(he died 1807)	(daughter of Michael Perryclear) (she died 1824)	{Walterborough}	
Knox, _____	Elizabeth Haile	13 RIEQ 104-110	1858
		{Lancaster District}	
Knox, _____	Susan A. Strong	7 RIEQ 117-124	1845
	(daughter of Robert Strong who died 19 September 1845)	{Williamsburg}	
Kottman, E. D.	Julia Higginbottom	SPEERS 29-35	1839
(marriage settlement November 1838) (widow of James Higginbottom) (Kottman was born August 1818) {Barnwell} [See also pages 142-158]			

(L)

Labatut, Pierre J.	Charlotte _____	SPEERS 421-426	1797
(married 1797) (separated) (she returned to France)			
Lacoste, Charles Gregorie Arnauld	Gabrielle Emelie de Rochefort	1 RIEQ 187-221	1836
Ladson, Major James	Judith Smith	RICHEQ 315-320	1778
(married 1778)		{Charleston}	
Lamar, Robert	Judith Winfrey	4 DESA 617-645	1806
(did not marry; had child only)		{Edgefield District}	
Lamb, James	Mary S. Buist	4 STRO 37-58	1845
	(daughter of Rev. George Buist)	{Charleston}	
Lamb, Jas.	Mary S. Buist	4 RIEQ 416-420	1852
[In footnotes of 1917 Edition]			
Lancaster, Allen	_____ Barnett	6 RIEQ 111-114	1853
	(daughter of Jorial Barnett)	{Spartanburg}	

S.C. Marriages 1749-1867 Implied in S.C. Equity Reports

MAN	WOMAN	VOLUME PAGES	LIVED
Lane, William S.	Martha Hamner (daughter of George B. Hamner, Sr. of Mecklenburg County, Virginia)	9 RIEQ 459-473 {Columbia, Richland}	1835
Lanford, Lowry	Amelia B. Dean (daughter of John Dean)	9 RIEQ 423-428 {Spartanburg}	1856
Langdon, _____	Zulina Hull (daughter of Gideon H. Hull)	2 STRO 174-195 {Connecticut}	1845
Langley, _____	_____ Harley (daughter of William J. Harley)	10 RIEQ 253-275 {Barnwell}	1857
Lanham, Josiah	Martha Meacham	4 STRO 203-206 {Edgefield}	1849
Lanier, _____	Susan Haile	13 RIEQ 104-110 {Lancaster District}	1858
Larey, Peter H.	_____ Beazley (daughter of W. B. Beazley) (she was born 1838)	9 RIEQ 119-128 {Barnwell}	1856
Lark, _____	Catharine Payne	12 RIEQ 487-497 {Newberry}	1857
Lartigue, Isadore	Adela Gillison (daughter of Samuel R. Gillison who died 1847)	4 RIEQ 213-222 {Beaufort}	1847
Laurens, _____	Caroline Ball	SPEERS 48-87	1843
Laurens, _____	Margaret Harleston Corbett (daughter of Thomas Corbett) (she was born 7 June 1805)	5 RIEQ 301-326 {Charleston}	1837
Laurens, Edward R.	Margaret Horry	14 RIEQ 139-145 {Charleston}	1866
Laurens, Edward R.	Margaret H. Horry (daughter of Elias Lynch Horry who died 1831)	2 HILL 244-249 {Charleston}	1835
Laurens, John	_____ Laurens (daughter of Edward R. Laurens)	7 RIEQ 260-280 {Charleston}	1846
Laurens, John	Eliza R. Laurens (daughter of Edward R. Laurens)	14 RIEQ 139-145 {Charleston}	1866
Lawrence, David	Elizabeth Hughes	BAILEY 304-311 {Charleston}	1824
Leak, William	Eliza Gunnels (daughter of William C. Gunnels) {Greenville and Laurens Districts}	2 RIEQ 259-270	1845
Lee, Charles W. (married 1855)	_____ Nettles (daughter of Wyatt J. Nettles)	11 RIEQ 574-583 {Sumter}	1855
Lee, Simon	Ann Lee	11 RIEQ 574-583 {Sumter}	1854
Legare, Thomas	Ann Eliza Berwick	1 DESA 603-605	1794

S.C. Marriages 1749-1867 Implied in S.C. Equity Reports

MAN	WOMAN	VOLUME PAGES	LIVED
Legare, Thomas J.	Maria Louisa Wagner (daughter of Effingham Wagner)	2 STRO 1-13 {Charleston}	1845
Leland, Dr. _____	Eugenia Griffin (daughter of Richard Griffin who died 20 November 1850)	9 RIEQ 71-84 {Edgefield}	1856
Lemacks, Alfred J. (Lamacks)	Jane M. Glover	1 RIEQ 141-154 {Colleton}	1845
Lester, _____	Dolly Snelgrove (daughter of Henry Snelgrove)	4 DESA 274-304	1812
Lester, William C.	Mary Shackelford (widow of William C. Shackelford)	2 STRO 51-63 {Charleston District}	1847
Levy, Levin L. (marriage settlement 12 April 1834)	Abigail Sampson (widow)	3 STRO 197-211 {Charleston}	1834
Levy, Lewis	_____ Polock (daughter of Levi Polock who died 1848)	7 RIEQ 20-33 {Columbia, Richland}	1854
Lewis, John (he died 1822)	Elizabeth C. Brummet (daughter of Daniel Brummet who died 1816)	1 RIEQ 1-25 {Union}	1816
Lewis, John B.	Caroline Thompson (daughter of William R. Thompson)	5 RIEQ 370-403 {St. Matthew's Parish}	1843
Lewis, William L.	Ann Stewart (daughter of James Stewart) (she died 11 December 1831)	5 RIEQ 370-403 {St. Matthew's Parish}	1831
Liddle, _____	M. Sleigh	2 DESA 295-299	1805
Lide, John J.	Mary Jane Lamb (daughter of Alexander Lamb who died 1836)	SPEERS 289-302 {Marlboro District}	1843
Lide, Thomas (he died 7 November 1787) (she died February 1804) (Lide was married before)	Mehitabel Irby (widow of Charles Irby)	4 DESA 422-433 {Cheraw and Marlboro Districts}	1787
Ligon, Reuben	Patience C. Wright (widow of Samuel Wright who died 1808)	2 McC 185-206 {Laurens}	1825
Liles, _____	_____ Henderson (daughter of David Henderson)	HARPER 298-301 {Newberry District}	1824
Liles. See Lyles		{Abbeville}	
Linam, _____	Mary E. Wells	5 RIEQ 20-31 {Sumter}	1842

S.C. Marriages 1749-1867 Implied in S.C. Equity Reports

MAN	WOMAN	VOLUME	PAGES	LIVED
Lindsay, William	Rachel	RICHEQ	439-448	1836

(or Margaret) Ernest (daughter of
Henry Ernest who died 1834) {Spartanburg}

| Lindsey, John N. | _____ Coate | 2 McC | 16-22 | 1827 |

(daughter of Henry Coate)

| Lipscomb, Nathan | Jemima Glover | 4 RIEQ | 25-38 | 1808 |

(married 9 March 1808) (widow of Wiley Glover, Sen.)
(Lipscomb died 1820) (she died 29 January 1850)
{Abbeville}

| Livingston, _____ | Eliza Ashe | RICHEQ | 380-384 | 1832 |

(daughter of John Ashe) {Charleston}

| Livingston, _____ | Mary Snelgrove | 4 DESA | 274-304 | 1812 |

(daughter of Henry Snelgrove)

| Livingston, John | _____ Frazier | 2 HILL | 304-318 | 1824 |

{Edgefield}

| Lloyd, John | _____ Cannon | 2 DESA | 232-233 | 1804 |

(orphan raised by Daniel Cannon)

| Logan, _____ | Rebecca McMorries | 11 RIEQ | 73-82 | 1848 |

{Newberry}

| Logan, _____ | Rachel Perry | 1 DESA | 271-274 | 1792 |
| Logan, Maj. George J. | Sarah Snowden | RICE | 174-198 | 1820 |

(married February/March 1820) (widow of James
David Snowden) (she died August 1822) {Beaufort District}

| Long, James | Cynthia Cason | 4 RIEQ | 60-70 | 1849 |

(married 28 December 1849) (daughter of William
Cason) (she was born 6 March 1829) {Anderson}

| Loocock, Aaron | Mary Brown | 1 DESA | 471-480 | 1791 |
| Lord, Andrew | _____ Gadsden | 1 DESA | 208-219 | 1780 |

(he died 1780) (widow of Thomas Gadsden)

| Lord, Jacob N. | Mary E. Sealy | BAILEY | 510-514 | 1826 |

(stepdaughter of David Sealy)
{Charleston}

Lowndes, Thomas	_____ I'On	2 DESA	210-214	1802
Lowrey, _____	Mary Wilson	2 DESA	66-79	1783
Lowry, _____	Mary A. R. Brown	4 RIEQ	262-266	1851

(widow of William Brown who died 1815)
{Colleton}

| Lucas, John | Barbara S. Patterson | 4 RIEQ | 340-348 | 1852 |

(daughter of Anthony Patterson who died 31 May 1850) {Orangeburg}

| Lumpkin, Abram F. | Patience P. Simmons | 13 RIEQ | 366-372 | 1866 |

{Chester}

| Lyles, Col. | Susannah Fennel | 1 HILL | 76-94 | 1817 |

Aromanos (married February 1817) (widow of Cullen
Fennel) (Lyles died September 1817)

S.C. Marriages 1749-1867 Implied in S.C. Equity Reports

MAN	WOMAN	VOLUME	PAGES	LIVED

Lyles, Aromanus, Sr.   Susannah Fennell   HARPER   288-295   1817
(Fannell) (she of Lexington District)
(marriage settlement 6 February 1817) (he was married before)

(Mc)

McAfee, John T.   Hannah Douglass   12 RIEQ 379-392   1848
(married 1848)   (widow) (she died December 1855)
{Chester District}
McBee, _____   Patsey Crocker   SPEERS 20-28   1833
(daughter of Solomon Crocker)
{Spartanburgh District}
McBeth. See Macbeth
McBurney, Dr. Hugh   Elizabeth Thompson   3 RIEQ 257-262   1850
(widow of James Booth Thompson who died March 1799)   {St. Bartholomew's Parish and Colleton}
McCants, _____   Ann Rivers   3 STRO 225-245   1839
{Charleston}
M'Cants, William, Jun.   Elizabeth E. Campbell   1 McC 383-394   1826
(she was born 1804)
M'Caw, John   _____ De Graffenreid   2 McC 90-105   1821
(daughter of Allen De Graffenreid who died 7 January 1815) {Chester}
McCaw, John   _____ De Graffenreid   BAILEY 98-102   1823
(daughter of Allen De Graffenreid) {Chester}
McClellan, S. K.   Anne Jennings   13 RIEQ 172-179   1863
{Sumter}
McClenaghan, Horatio   _____ Howard   2 RIEQ 79-84   1829
(daughter of Richard Howard) {Marion}
[See also 1 STRO pages 295-323 and 2 STRO pages 227-230]
McClure, James   Mary Clifton   BAILEY 107-112   1827
(widow of James Clifton) {Chester}
McClure. See McLure
McCollough, Robert   Elizabeth Wallace   1 RIEQ 426-449   1827
(marriage settlement 23 February 1827) {Union District}
McCord, _____   Mary R. Bee   5 RIEQ 370-403   1820
(widow)   {St. Matthew's Parish}
McCord, _____   Mary R. Richardson   5 RIEQ 370-403   1820
(daughter of Col. _____ Richardson)
{St. Matthew's Parish}
McCord, David J.   Louisa Cheves   10 RIEQ 534-550   1854
(daughter of Hon. Langdon Cheves who died 27 June 1857)

S.C. Marriages 1749-1867 Implied in S.C. Equity Reports

MAN	WOMAN	VOLUME PAGES	LIVED
M'Cord, R. P.	Eliza May Hall	2 McC 269-317	1823
McCoy, Minor	Abigail Mitchell (daughter of Stephen Mitchell) {Sumter District}	12 RIEQ 263-276	1860
McCoy, William	Winney Mitchell (daughter of Stephen Mitchell) {Sumter District}	12 RIEQ 263-276	1860
McCullough, Andrew, Sen.	Jean Jeffreys	1 STRO 193-196 {Walterborough}	1795
McCullough, Dr. ____ (married 1825) (she died 1826)	____ Pickett (widow of James R. Pickett)	2 STRO 157-165 {Fairfield District}	1825
McCullough, Hans	Mary Jeffreys	1 STRO 193-196 {Walterborough}	1784

McCullough. See McCollough

McDaniel, Andrew	____ Bailey	11 RIEQ 114-134 {Chester}	1846
M'Daniel, Thomas	Frances Sims (daughter of Charles Sims)	HARPER 108-116	1785
McDonald, ____	Sarah Dupree (widow of James Dupree) {Georgetown}	4 DESA 209-215	1812
McDonald, ____	Sarah A. Rogers (daughter of William Rogers) {Spartanburg}	7 RIEQ 422-429	1854
McDonald, Wm. M.	Charlotte Harrison (widow)	4 STRO 167-170 {Chester, Fairfield, Lancaster and Union}	1812
McDow, Thomas F.	Isabella L. Cunningham (daughter of John S. Cunningham) {Lancaster}	9 RIEQ 475-482	1856
McDow, William (married about 1819) (she died about 1831)	Susan B. Sommers (widow of James D. Sommers who died 1817-19) {Charleston}	3 RIEQ 281-304	1819
McDow, William (he died 1839)	Susan B. Sommers (widow of James D. Sommers) {Charleston and Colleton Districts}	4 STRO 37-58	1820
McDowel, Thomas (married 3/4 December 1841)	Martha E. Luter {Fairfield}	1 STRO 347-349	1841
McDowell, ____	Dorcas Foster {Spartanburg}	SPEERS 569-577	1841
McElray, James	Elizabeth Ford (daughter of John Ford) {Greenville}	1 RIEQ 474-476	1843
McFeely, W. J.	Honoria Wilkes Seabrook (daughter of Thomas Wilkes Seabrook who died in Florida) {Charleston}	2 STRO 69-71	1848
M'Gillivray, ____	Mary Stanyarne (daughter of J. Stanyarne)	1 DESA 127-133	1785

S.C. Marriages 1749-1867 Implied in S.C. Equity Reports

MAN	WOMAN	VOLUME	PAGES	LIVED
M'Gowan, Henry	_____ Compty (widow of Maj. John Compty who died February 1799)	4 DESA	486-504 {Richland District}	1814
McGowen, William	_____ McWilliams (daughter of Samuel McWilliams) {Laurens}	3 RIEQ	10-13	1849
McGrath, William (married 1835) [Must see footnotes in 1917 Edition]	_____ Ashby	7 RIEQ	430-449 {Union District}	1835
McGrew, _____	Margaret McClain	4 DESA	155-162	1800
M'Guire, Peter	Rebecca Compty (daughter of Maj. John Compty who died February 1799)	4 DESA	486-504 {Richland District}	1814
McJunkin, Joseph (he died 1855) (she died 15 January 1856)	Nancy Sartor (daughter of William Sartor)	11 RIEQ	527-535 {Union}	1856
McKee. See Mackie				
McKelvy, Robert A.	Mary Elizabeth Footman (daughter of William C. Footman of Bryan County, Georgia)	2 STRO	317-324 {Williamsburg District}	1845
McKenna, William	Anna Miller (she died 26 February 1848) {Lancaster}	4 RIEQ	358-370	1848
McKenna. See Makenna				
McKensie, Samuel R.	Rebecca Ann Dawson (daughter of Richard Dawson, Sr.)	2 STRO	34-39 {Gillisonville}	1836
M'Kenzie, _____	Rebecca Ann Dawson (daughter of Richard Dawson)	CHEVES	148-157	1836
McKenzie, _____	Rebecca Ann Dawson (daughter of Richard Dawson, Sr. of St. Luke's Parish, who died 25 August 1836) (she was born September 1805)	RICE	243-274 {Beaufort District}	1836
McKenzie, Daniel W.	Eliza A. Bostick (married February 1821) (he died 1826) {Gillisonville}	1 STRO	393-420	1821
M'Kewn, Archibald (M'Kewin)	Jane Hurst (widow of Robert Hurst) (she died October 1807)	3 DESA	273-296	1795
McKinney, _____	Jane Cox	12 RIEQ	349-360 {Abbeville District}	1828
McKinney, _____	Jane Cox	1 STRO	27-43 {Abbeville}	1828
M'Kinney, B.	Ann Galphin	1 McC	280-300 {Edgefield District}	1816
McKnight, _____	Morning Webb (daughter of Joseph Webb of Fairfield, who died January 1820) {Lexington}	5 RIEQ	121-128	1820

S.C. Marriages 1749-1867 Implied in S.C. Equity Reports

MAN	WOMAN	VOLUME PAGES	LIVED
McKnight, A. Isaac	Jane J. Bradley (daughter of Dr. James Bradley)	10 RIEQ 557-572 {Williamsburg District}	1854
McKnight, Isaac (marriage settlement 18 December 1853) (daughter of Dr. _____ Bradley)	Cecilia A. Bradley	10 RIEQ 157-162 {Williamsburg}	1853
McKnight, James	Caroline McLure (daughter of William McLure who died 1859)	14 RIEQ 105-120 {York}	1866
M'Leod, _____	_____ Brailsford (daughter of Robert Brailsford)	2 HILL 277-298	1835
M'Leod, _____	_____ Hamilton (sister of Paul Hamilton who died about 1797 in England)	2 McC 354-367 {Charleston}	1827
M'Leod, Rev. Doctor Donald (he died 1820)	Elizabeth Bailey Seabrook (widow of John Seabrook)	1 RIEQ 155-186 {Charleston District}	1820
McLure, Carey	Maria Louisa Davenport (daughter of Jonathan Davenport)	3 RIEQ 559-578 {Newberry}	1842
McMeekin, Thomas (married 1825/26) (she died February 1835)	Elizabeth C. Lewis (widow of John Lewis)	1 RIEQ 1-25 {Union}	1825
McMillan, _____	Gatsey Moye (daughter of Matthew Moye)	12 RIEQ 361-378 {Barnwell}	1828
McMillan, James	Margaret Griffin (daughter of Richard Griffin) (in Lincoln County, Georgia)	2 RIEQ 99-114 {Abbeville}	1845
McMullan, Hugh (he died 1841) 3 March 1831)	Charlotte McDonald (widow of Wm. M. McDonald) (she died {Chester, Fairfield, Lancaster and Union}	4 STRO 167-170	1831
McNeil, _____	_____ Stone (widow of Daniel Stone who died 9 January 1822) (she married at least three times) {Marion}	RICHEQ 397-399	1832
McNish, John	Ann Screven (she died 1 October 1851) {Beaufort District} [See also 8 RIEQ pages 112-129]	7 RIEQ 186-200	1829
McNish, John (in Savannah, Georgia)	Ann Screven	4 STRO 66-83 {Beaufort District}	1829
McOwen, _____	_____ Lothrop (daughter of Seth Lothrop)	2 RIEQ 412-472 {Charleston}	1846
McPherson, _____	Sarah Perry (daughter of Edward Perry, Sr.)	4 STRO 37-58 {Charleston}	1809

S.C. Marriages 1749-1867 Implied in S.C. Equity Reports

MAN	WOMAN	VOLUME	PAGES	LIVED
McQueen, A. J.	Caroline Adams	4 RIEQ	152-164	1841

(married 1838/41) (daughter of Shockley Adams who died 10 October 1824) (she was born October 1824) (to Richmond County, North Carolina) {Marlborough}

| McRa, Powell | Mary Martha Singleton | 3 RIEQ | 96-111 | 1817 |

(daughter of John Singleton) (separated 6 March 1817) (McRa died 19 May 1847) {Kershaw}

| McSween, John | Susan Cummings | 9 RIEQ | 440-458 | 1857 |

{Sumter District}

(M)

| Mabray, Daniel | Mary Long | 1 STRO | 43-53 | 1846 |

(daughter of William Long) {Union}

| Macbeth, James | Mary Barksdale | 7 RIEQ | 125-135 | 1854 |

(daughter of Thomas Barksdale, Jr.) {Charleston}

| Mackie, Mungo | Elizabeth Baynard | 2 DESA | 342-361 | 1805 |

(widow of William Baynard)

| Maffitt, John N. | Caroline Read | 11 RIEQ | 285-295 | 1852 |

(married August 1852) (widow of James Withers Read) (she died March 1859) {Charleston}

| Maffitt, John W. | Caroline Laurens Read | 8 RIEQ | 145-154 | 1852 |

(married 2 August 1852) (widow of James Withers Read who died June 1851) {Charleston}

| Makenna, Wm. | _____ _____ | CHEVES | 163-166 | 1835 |

(married October 1835) {Lancaster}

| Mallory, Hamlin | Louisa Omones | McMULL | 157-200 | 1821 |

(common-law marriage?) (she died 1822) {Beaufort District}

| Mallory, Hamlin | Louisa Omones | RILEY | 102-112 | 1822 |

(she died 1822)

| Manes, Elmore | Isaballa C. Shannon | 2 RIEQ | 404-407 | 1838 |

(married September 1838) {Marion}

| Manigault, _____ | _____ Huger | 9 RIEQ | 217-243 | 1856 |

(daughter of Hon. Daniel Elliott Huger of Charleston, who died 21 August 1854) {Charleston}

| Manigault, Charles D. | Emma L. Horry | 2 HILL | 244-249 | 1835 |

(daughter of Elias Lynch Horry who died 1831) {Charleston}

| Manigault, Joseph | _____ Middleton | 2 HILL | 591-599 | 1814 |

(daughter of Arthur Middleton)

S.C. Marriages 1749-1867 Implied in S.C. Equity Reports

MAN	WOMAN	VOLUME	PAGES	LIVED
Mantz, Christopher	Mary P. Jeter	1 STRO	103-113	1826

(daughter of William Jeter who died 7 September 1820) {Edgefield}

| Marion, Hon. Robert | Esther De Veaux | 1 STRO | 283-294 | 1810 |

(widow) (she died November 1821) {Charleston}

| Markley, Wade J. | Celia Ann | 11 RIEQ | 393-404 | 1855 |

Singletary (married May 1855) (daughter of Daniel M. Singletary) (she was born about 1834) {St. James Goose Creek}

| Marsh, John | Sarah Nail | RICHEQ | 115-121 | 1826 |

(married October 1826) (widow of John Nail) {Edgefield}

| Marsh, John | Sarah Nail | 1 RIEQ | 24 | 1826 |

(married October 1826) (widow of John Nail) [Referred to in another case]

| Marshall, _____ | Mary Chandler | RICE | 373-388 | 1825 |

{Charleston District}

| Marshall, _____ | Patience McKenzie Morton | BAILEY | 395-397 | 1831 |

{Philadelphia, Pennsylvania}

| Marshall, _____ | Charlotte Neyle | CHEVES | 21-26 | 1839 |
| Marshburn, James H. | _____ Wirtemburgh | BAILEY | 334-342 | 1826 |

{Charleston}

| Martin, Edward | _____ Jeter | 1 STRO | 103-113 | 1820 |

(daughter of William Jeter who died 7 September 1820) {Edgefield}

| Martin, Robert | _____ Bobo | McMULL | 304-310 | 1840 |

(daughter of Barron Bobo)

| Martin, William M. | _____ Bell | 9 RIEQ | 42-45 | 1854 |

(daughter of Thomas Bell) {Fairfield}

| Martin, William O. | Martha (Patsey) Jefcoat | 10 RIEQ | 118-129 | 1828 |

(married about 1828) (he died November 1839) {Lexington District}

| Marvin, Samuel | _____ Dawson | CHEVES | 148-157 | 1821 |

(daughter of Richard Dawson)

| Marvin, Samuel | Mary Dawson | RICE | 243-274 | 1820 |

(daughter of Richard Dawson, Sr. of St. Luke's Parish, who died 25 August 1836) {Beaufort District}

| Mason, David M. | Harriet A. China | 5 RIEQ | 426-434 | 1852 |

(daughter of Thomas China) {Williamsburg}

| Massey, _____ | Elizabeth Cureton | 13 RIEQ | 104-110 | 1858 |

{Lancaster District}

| Massey, Benjamin Sykes | Sarah Miller | 9 RIEQ | 438 | 1855 |

[Referred to in another case] {Lancaster}

| Matheney, John | Rachel Guess | 2 HILL | 63-70 | 1834 |

(daughter of John Guess)

S.C. Marriages 1749-1867 Implied in S.C. Equity Reports

MAN	WOMAN	VOLUME PAGES	LIVED
Matheney, W. B.	Mary Askew	10 RIEQ 163-177	1858
	(widow of Seth Askew) {Barnwell}		
Matheson, C.	Catherine Haile	13 RIEQ 104-110	1858
		{Lancaster District}	
Matheuman, William	Jane H. Willard	RICE 198-242	1817
(married 1817) (widow of Prentiss Willard) (she			
died 16 September 1817)		{Beaufort District}	
Mathews, _____	Edith Stanyarne	1 DESA 127-135	1772
	(daughter of J. Stanyarne)		
Mathews, Benjamin	Sarah Sams	1 DESA 127-135	1785
Mathews, Edward	_____ Teasdale	3 DESA 25-28	1809
Mathews, J. R.	_____ Whaley	3 DESA 80-84	1805
	(widow of Thomas Whaley who died 28		
	October 1805)	{Charleston District}	
Mathews, William	Mary Barksdale	4 STRO 1-25	1793
(he died 22 July 1848) (daughter of George Barksdale)			
(she died 30 November 1843)		{Charleston}	
Matthews, Samuel P.	Eliza Ann Mouzon	13 RIEQ 142-164	1866
(widower)	(widow of James L. Mouzon) {Williamsburg}		
Mattison, Olley	Mary Clements	1 STRO 377-385	1840
(married 1840)		{Anderson}	
Mauldin, Rucker	Mary Parris	5 RIEQ 450-472	1843
	(daughter of Henry Parris who was		
born about 1752/53 and died 27 September 1847) {Anderson}			
May, Robert	_____ Hall	BAILEY 58-61	1810
(he died 1823)	(widow of Andrew Hall) {Walterborough}		
May, Robt.	Margaret Hall	1 HILL 397-405	1829
	(widow)	{Colleton District}	
[Must also see 2 HILL pages 22-24]			
Maybin, _____	Teresa Reid	SPEERS 343-350	1840
	(daughter of Jethro L. Reid) {Union}		
Maybin, Jesse	Jemima Reid	SPEERS 343-350	1840
	(widow of Jethro L. Reid) {Union}		
Mayo, James	Nancy Mayo	2 McC 137-143	1827
	(daughter of John Mayo)		
Mayrant, Capt. John	Isabella Nelson	4 DESA 591-611	1791
	(an orphan)	{Camden}	
Mayrant, John	Isabella Norwell	1 DESA 202-207	1791
Mayrant, Robert P.	Frances Ann M. H.	3 STRO 112-130	1831
(marriage settlement 12 May 1831)		{Columbia}	
Mazyck, Stephen	Mary Young	RICHEQ 263-282	1796
	(daughter of Thomas Young) {Charleston}		
Mazyck, William	_____ Shackleford	BAILEY 48-57	1828
Meggett, James	Susan Murray	CHEVES 80-93	1839
	(daughter of Joseph James Murray		
	who died 18 July 1818)		

S.C. Marriages 1749-1867 Implied in S.C. Equity Reports

MAN	WOMAN	VOLUME PAGES	LIVED
Meray, Edward	Sarah A. Evans (daughter of John Evans)	2 HILL 222-228 {Charleston District}	1835
Meray, Edward	Susan A. Evans	BAILEY 507-509 {Charleston}	1830
Mew, _____	Nancy Smith (daughter of Samuel Smith who died 1815)	3 RIEQ 244-256 {Beaufort}	1831
Meyers, Jacob	Delia Jewell (daughter of Benjamin Jewell)	11 RIEQ 296-322 {Charleston District}	1834
Micheau, Paul	Lydia Clegg	3 RIEQ 465-542 {Georgetown}	1795
Micheau, Paul	Lydia Clegg	RILEY 88-96 {Georgetown}	1795
Mickle, Jonathan B.	_____ Montgomery	11 RIEQ 114-134 {Chester}	1851
Middleton, _____	Ann Manigault	3 DESA 249-256	1811
Middleton, Arthur	Mary Izard	1 DESA 116-123	1785
Middleton, Arthur	Alicia H. Russell (daughter of Nathaniel Russell of Charleston)	DUDLEY 115-123 {Charleston}	1832
Middleton, John Izard	Sarah (Sally) Alston	4 STRO 37-58 {Charleston}	1849
Mikell, Ephraim	_____ Calder	2 DESA 342-361	1805
Mikell, Josiah	Elizabeth Crosskeys Murray (daughter of Joseph James Murray who died 18 July 1818)	CHEVES 80-93	1839
Miles, John	_____ Garden (widow of Alexander Garden, Garden's second marriage)	2 HILL 277-298	1835
Miller, _____	_____ Gervais (daughter of Rev. Paul T. Gervais)	McMULL 106-114	1841
Miller, Alvin N. (in Savannah, Georgia)	_____ McNish (widow of Charles L. McNish)	4 STRO 66-83 {Beaufort District}	1850
Miller, Alvin N.	Sarah Jane McNish (widow of Charles Lycurgus McNish who died 1844)	8 RIEQ 112-129 {Beaufort District}	1855

[See also 7 RIEQ pages 186-200]

Miller, Daniel (he died 1819)	_____ McLewrath (widow)	BAILEY 187-194 {Barnwell}	1818
Miller, James	Martha Holland (daughter of John Holland)	BAILEY 479-482 {Charleston}	1830
Miller, James (his first marriage) (he died 29 March 1847) (she died 17 January 1824)	_____ Tillman	4 RIEQ 1-9 {Edgefield}	1824

S.C. Marriages 1749-1867 Implied in S.C. Equity Reports

MAN	WOMAN	VOLUME	PAGES	LIVED
Miller, W. D.	Mary Jane McConnell	9 RIEQ	500-520 {York District}	1853
Miller, William	Susannah Clifton (daughter of James Clifton)	BAILEY	107-112 {Chester}	1827
Miller, William	Mary Ann Dean	9 RIEQ	423-428 {Spartanburg}	1857
Mims, _____	Elizabeth (Betsey) Fretwell (daughter of William Fretwell of Greene County, Georgia)	11 RIEQ	559-573 {Anderson}	1856
Mims, Britton	Mary Ann Garrett (married 15 December 1825) (daughter of Stephen Garrett)	1 STRO	66-72 {Edgefield}	1825
Mims, Dr. Edward J.	Emeline S. Addison (daughter of Allen B. Addison who died November 1854)	9 RIEQ	58-70 {Edgefield}	1849
Minis, _____	Dinah Cohen	4 DESA	215-226 {Georgetown}	1812
Minor, _____	Lucy E. Patrick (widow)	10 RIEQ	130-138 {Barnwell}	1847
Mitchell, _____	Hetty Jewell (daughter of Benjamin Jewell)	11 RIEQ	296-322 {Charleston District}	1855
Mitchell, _____	Dorothy Richardson (daughter of James Burchell Richardson who died 28 April 1836)	DUDLEY	184-201	1826
Mitchell, Clement	Sarah Stribling	2 McC	16-22	1827
Mitchell, James D.	Amelia Dorothy V. Waring (marriage settlement 27 February 1809) (daughter of Thomas Waring, Senr.)	RICE	389-409 {Charleston}	1809
Monks, _____	Jane Gilmore	DUDLEY	14-23 {York District}	1837
Monroe, David	Elizabeth Haseldon (widow of John Haseldon) (she died 1844)	4 RIEQ	334-340 {Marion}	1844
Monroe, David	Elizabeth Haseldon (widow of John Haseldon)	6 RIEQ	26-42 {Marion}	1853
Monroe. See Munro				
Montgomery, Green B., Jr.	_____ Bailey	11 RIEQ	114-134 {Chester}	1849
Moody, William	_____ Lyles (daughter of Col. Aromanos Lyles)	1 HILL	76-94	1833
Moon, John [See also pages 407-409]	Nancy T. Ligon	2 STRO	327-334 {Greenville}	1848
Moore, _____	_____ De Veaux (daughter of Robert Marion De Veaux)	9 RIEQ	535-571 {Sumter District}	1856

S.C. Marriages 1749-1867 Implied in S.C. Equity Reports

MAN	WOMAN	VOLUME	PAGES	LIVED

Moore, _____   Sarah J. C.   DUDLEY   184-201   1826
                  Richardson (daughter of James
    Burchell Richardson who died 26 April 1836)
Moore, Hugh   _____ Lowe   1 McC   243-247   1826
Moore, Isham   Ann Singleton   RICE   110-132   1784
    (he died 1803/04) (daughter of Matthew Singleton of
    St. Mark's Parish, who died 1784)   {Clarendon County,
                                         Sumter District}
Moore, John J.   Hermione Richardson DUDLEY   184-201   1837
                   (daughter of James Burchell
    Richardson who died 26 April 1836)
Moore, Moses   Sophia S. Harris   9 RIEQ   311-330   1840
                   (daughter of John Harris, Sr. who died
    1840, Mecklenburgh County, North Carolina) {Lancaster}
Moore, Thomas   _____ McWilliams   3 RIEQ   10-13   1849
                                         {Laurens}
Moore, William   _____ McDaniel   DUDLEY   1-14   1837
                                         {Newberry}
Moorer, _____   _____ Collier   3 RIEQ   555-558   1849
                   (daughter of John Collier) {Orangeburg}
Moorer, Henry M.   Sarah A. Felder   4 RIEQ   349-358   1841
                   (daughter of Henry Felder) {Orangeburg}
Moorman, Col. James _____ M'Daniel   HARPER   108-116   1824
                   (daughter of Charles M'Daniel who
                    died 1801)
Mootry, William   Jane B. Hunt   8 RIEQ   166-184   1849
    [Must also see 11 RIEQ pages 205-224] {Charleston
    District and Georgetown}
Mootry, William   Jane B. Hunt   6 RIEQ   183-199   1853
                   (daughter of Col. Benjamin F. Hunt)
                                         {Charleston}
Mordecai, Benjamin _____ Polock   7 RIEQ   20-33   1854
                   (daughter of Levi Polock who died
                    1848)   {Columbia, Richland}
Morgan, William E. Sally Puryear   9 RIEQ   459-473   1857
                   (daughter of Reuben A. Puryear)
                                         {Richland}
Morrow, Thomas M. Sarah Mathis   8 RIEQ   79-81   1855
                                         {Abbeville District}
Mosely, John   Rebecca A. Stewart 1 RIEQ   396-404   1825
                   (daughter of Alexander Stewart who died
    25 October 1824) (she died 18 November 1825) {Edgefield}
Moultrie, Dr.   Louisa Shrewsbury 3 STRO   211-224   1848
    William   {Charleston}
Mouzon, James L.   Eliza Ann Burgess 13 RIEQ   142-164   1850
    (married 10 December 1850) (widow of James A. Burgess)
    (Mouzon died 9 December 1855)   {Williamsburg}

S.C. Marriages 1749-1867 Implied in S.C. Equity Reports

MAN	WOMAN	VOLUME PAGES	LIVED
Mullins, Daniel	Jane James	4 RIEQ 80-87	1829
(married 1829)	(widow of John James)		
(Mullins died 1844)		{Spartanburg District}	
Munday, Leroy H.	Ann Sophronia	DUDLEY 34-41	1835
	Harrison (daughter of Edward Harrison		
	who died 13 April 1829) {Edgefield}		
Munro, Daniel	Lucretia Youngblood	2 DESA 294-299	1795
(married March 1795) (widow of David Youngblood)			
(she died August 1799)			
Murph, John	Mary Holman	4 RIEQ 329-334	1821
(he died 1844)	(daughter of Conrad Holman of		
St. Matthew's Parish, who died 16 August 1816)			
(she died 1848)		{Orangeburg}	
Murphy, James	Mary Tobin	DUDLEY 161-174	1829
(in County Kilkenny, Ireland)		{Barnwell}	
Murphy, Tarlton	Nancy Buzzard	3 RIEQ 20-23	1828
		{Newberry}	
Murray, James	Elizabeth Connoly	2 HILL 204-215	1829
(marriage settlement 31 December 1829) (daughter of			
Richard Connoly)		{Charleston}	
Murray, James	Margaret Dugan	DUDLEY 1-14	1822
	(daughter of Col. Thomas Dugan)		
		{Newberry}	
Murray, John M.	Jane Connoly	2 HILL 204-215	1823
(married May 1821) (daughter of Richard Connoly)			
(Murray died 1829)		{Charleston}	
Murray, Millivan	Lydia Calon Clarke	3 RIEQ 318-341	1830
		{Charleston}	
Murril, John J.	_____ Bobo	McMULL 304-310	1840
	(daughter of Barron Bobo)		
Muse, George W.	Elizabeth Edgerton	DUDLEY 179-183	1831
(married 5 May 1831)		{Barnwell}	
Muse, George W.	Elizabeth Edgerton	2 HILL 51-53	1834
	(widow of Otis Edgerton) {Barnwell}		

(N)

Nail, John	Sarah Glover	RICHEQ 115-121	1822
	(daughter of Andrew Glover who died		
3 August 1822) (Nail died 1 November 1825) {Edgefield}			
Nail, John	Sarah Glover	1 RIEQ 24	1823
(he died 1825) [Referred to in another case]			
Naily, Casper, Jun.	_____ Ardis	2 McC 60-72	1827
		{Beech Island}	

66

S.C. Marriages 1749-1867 Implied in S.C. Equity Reports

MAN	WOMAN	VOLUME	PAGES	LIVED
Naylor, James (of Maryland) 1820, Maryland)	Sarah Young (widow) (he had divorced 14 February (South Carolina marriage declared null and void)	1 HILL	383-387	1833

{Laurens}
Nesbitt, Allen ____ Taylor 4 DESA 167-175 1810
 (daughter of Walter Taylor) {Abbeville}
Nesmitte, David Sarah M. Arnett 4 STRO 189-203 1834
 (daughter of John Arnett) (she was
 born 13 October 1810) {Williamsburg District}
Newman, William ____ Wilbourne 1 HILL 10-14 1831
Nichols, George ____ Bryson 2 HILL 113-121 1835
 {Laurens}
Nichols, Rev. ____ Louisa Rutledge 14 RIEQ 245-270 1858
 (daughter of Edward Rutledge)
Nix, ____ Elizabeth Cave 6 RIEQ 43-57 1834
 (daughter of David Cave who died
 October 1834) {Barnwell}
Nix, ____ Elizabeth Phillips 3 RIEQ 543-555 1815
 (daughter of Stephen Phillips) {Barnwell}
Noble, Patrick Elizabeth Bonneau 13 RIEQ 111-122 1834
 Pickens (daughter of Ezekiel Pickens
 of St. Thomas' Parish, who died 1813) (she died 1834)
 {Anderson}
Nobles, ____ Cynthia W. Calhoun 6 RIEQ 155-182 1853
 (widow) {Barnwell}
Nopie, ____ Dorothy Frances 5 RIEQ 351-355 1852
 Cook (daughter of Daniel Cook)
 {Charleston}
Norris, Ezekiel L. ____ Keys 6 RIEQ 388-398 1850
 {Anderson}
North, Dr. ____ Martha P. Gervais McMULL 106-114 1841
 (daughter of Rev. Paul T. Gervais)
North, John L. ____ Drayton HARPER 34-46 1806
 (married December 1806) (daughter of Glen Drayton)
 (to Pendleton 1808)
Norton, William ____ Youngblood 1 STRO 122-128 1839
 (daughter of William Youngblood) {York}

(O)

O'Bannon, Augustus Henrietta Portner 7 RIEQ 219-229 1829
 Benjamin Schmidt (married April 1829)
 {Barnwell and Charleston}

S.C. Marriages 1749-1867 Implied in S.C. Equity Reports

MAN	WOMAN	VOLUME	PAGES	LIVED
Odingsell, _____	Sarah Ashe (widow) (she died November 1801) {Charleston}	RILEY	271-282	1798
Ogletree, Rev. Benjamin S. (his first marriage)	Mary Louisa Graff Brazilman (she died 1834) {Newberry}	3 STRO	149-158	1828
O'Hanlon, _____	Elizabeth Myers (daughter of Col. David Myers) {Richland and Union}	2 RIEQ	321-354	1845
O'Hanlon, James	_____ Myers (daughter of David Myers of Richland District, who died 3 March 1835) {Richland District}	12 RIEQ	196-212	1835
O'Hanlon, John C. (married 1839) of Mecklenburg County, Virginia) (she died July 1843) (O'Hanlon died 1853)	Maria Hamner (daughter of George B. Hamner, Sr. {Richland}	9 RIEQ	459-473	1839
O'Hara, Arthur	Jane Mazyck (daughter of Stephen Mazyck) (her first marriage)	RICHEQ	263-282	1831
Old, _____	Rebecca Gardner (daughter of Robert Gardner)	2 McC	32-36	1827
Oliver, Peter M.	_____ Pendergrass {Williamsburg and Orangeburg Districts}	3 RIEQ	33-60	1850
Omones, _____	Louisa Washington (she died 1822)	McMULL {Beaufort District}	157-200	1819
Omones, _____	Louisa Washington (daughter of Thomas Washington) (she died 1822)	RILEY	102-112	1822
O'Neale, William T.	Elizabeth Dunlap (daughter of James Dunlap) {Charleston}	11 RIEQ	405-415	1860
O'Quin, Daniel, Jr.	Sarah Adams (daughter of Ephraim Adams) (she died 1818) {Sumter}	1 HILL	324-325	1817
Ortner, _____	_____ Palmer (daughter of Thomas Palmer who died about 1800) {Union}	6 RIEQ	150-154	1853

[Must also see footnotes of 1917 Edition]

Oswald, _____	_____ Stevens (daughter of George Stevens) {Beaufort District}	2 HILL	504-511	1835
Oswald, Joseph	_____ Stephens (daughter of George Stephens who died 7 February 1817) {Beaufort}	RICHEQ	326-352	1813
Oswald, William (of St. Helena)	_____ Stephens (daughter of George Stephens who died 7 February 1817) {Beaufort}	RICHEQ	326-352	1813

S.C. Marriages 1749-1867 Implied in S.C. Equity Reports

MAN	WOMAN	VOLUME PAGES LIVED
Owens, _____	Mary Bird (daughter of Arthur Bird who died 1835) {Marion District}	11 RIEQ 536-540 1849
Owens, Phillip	_____ Bird (daughter of Peter Bird) {Marion District}	11 RIEQ 536-540 1860

(P)

MAN	WOMAN	VOLUME PAGES LIVED
Pace, _____	Bethana Cox	12 RIEQ 349-360 1857 {Abbeville District}
Paisley, Henry	_____ Wright	2 McC 185-206 1825 {Laurens}
Palmer, _____	Mary Bell (daughter of Thomas Bell who died 7 September 1795) (her first marriage) {Beaufort}	RICHEQ 361-369 1795
Palmer, Job	_____ Miller (widow of Samuel Miller who died 1789) (she died 1832) {Charleston}	CHEVES 62-71 1799
Palmer, William (he died November 1817) (her first marriage) {Coosawhatchie}	Mary Bell	1 HILL 142-145 1817
Parker, _____	Eliza Heyward	7 RIEQ 289-327 1852
Parker, Thomas	Maria Drayton	RICE 373-388 1793 {Charleston District}
Parkman, Henry	Mercy Jones (widow of Thomas Jones) {Ninety-Six District}	1 RIEQ 78-91 1807
Parks, Lewis G.	Augusta G. Houston (daughter of Alexander Houston) (she was born 7 May 1835) {Abbeville}	9 RIEQ 85-99 1856
Patrick, _____	Lucy E. Dunbar	10 RIEQ 130-138 1847 {Barnwell}
Patterson, James	Nancy Smyth (daughter of Robert Smyth) {Abbeville}	McMULL 459-475 1827
Patterson, Samuel (married 2 August 1836) (he died 1839)	Helena Bache	CHEVES 29-32 1836
Patton, David	Emily G. Dean (daughter of John Dean) {Spartanburg}	9 RIEQ 423-428 1856
Paul, _____ (married 1825)	Nancy Gray (widow of Robert Gray) {Abbeville}	RICE 330-342 1825
Paulling, Dr. H. H. (married 1845)	Sarah Boulware (daughter of Thomas Boulware who died 1842) (Paulling died April 1849) {Fairfield}	4 RIEQ 317-322 1845

S.C. Marriages 1749-1867 Implied in S.C. Equity Reports

MAN	WOMAN	VOLUME	PAGES	LIVED
Payne, _____	Sabina Barksdale (daughter of Thomas Barksdale) {Charleston}	3 RIEQ	271-281	1850
Payne, John W.	Sabina Bonneau (separated) (widow) (he died 6 October 1826) {Charleston} [Must also see DUDLEY pages 124-128]	RILEY	174-179	1815
Payne, John W.	Sarina Bonneau (widow) {Charleston}	7 RIEQ	125-135	1854
Payne, Wesley	Rosa Manning McDaniel (daughter of James McDaniel) (she died 1851) {Greenville}	8 RIEQ	9-12	1836
Pearson, Col. Bird M. (to Alabama)	Isabella Croft (daughter of Edward Croft who died September 1851) {Greenville}	7 RIEQ	34-53	1838
Peay, Austin F. (married December 1818)	Eliza T. _____ {Richland}	2 RIEQ	409-411	1818
Peebles, Wm.	_____ Stuckey {Sumter}	1 HILL	308-311	1833
Pell, Ferris	Mary Ann Channing (daughter of Walter Channing of Boston) [See also pages 518-532] [See also 1 RIEQ pages 361-389; 419-426]	SPEERS	48-87	1843
Pelot, William M.	Elvira Dupont {Gillisonville}	McMULL	369-404	1841
Pepper, Daniel	Sarah Scott (daughter of Thomas Scott who died 1782) (she died 1802)	HARPER	5-19	1802
Peraire, Edward	Zelmire Sasportas {Charleston District}	10 RIEQ	38-52	1857
Perdriau, _____	_____ Michau (daughter of Paul Michau) {Georgetown}	3 RIEQ	465-542	1822
Perdrieau, Samuel	_____ Micheau {Georgetown}	RILEY	88-96	1832
Perkins, _____	Henrietta Kershaw {Camden}	1 HILL	344-352	1831
Perry, James	Mary Dixon (daughter of John Dixon)	4 DESA	504-510	1814
Perry, Zadock	Comfort Brummet (daughter of William Brummet) {Lancaster}	2 HILL	638-644	1792
Peters, _____	Mary Williman (daughter of Christopher Williman) {Charleston}	4 RIEQ	475-496	1813
Peyre, _____	Floride Bocket (Boquet) [Must also see pages 210-214; 419-422]	2 DESA	221-226	1793

S.C. Marriages 1749-1867 Implied in S.C. Equity Reports

MAN	WOMAN	VOLUME	PAGES	LIVED
Peyton, Henry	____ M'Dowall	2 DESA	313-320	1805
	(daughter of Captain Alexander M'Dowall who died 1799)			
Peyton, R. H.	Ann Stobo	2 DESA	375-380	1806
	(widow of J. Stobo of St. Paul's Parish)			
Phillips, ____	Charlotte Jeter	1 STRO	103-113	1820
	(daughter of William Jeter who died 7 September 1820) {Edgefield}			
Picket, ____	Mary Eliza Conner	3 RIEQ	452-465	1843
	{Marion}			
Picket, ____	____ Starke	4 DESA	92-94	1810
	(widow of Reuben Starke)			
Pickett, James B.	____ De Graffenreid	10 RIEQ	346-355	1837
	{Chester}			
Pickett, James R.	____ Lewis	2 STRO	157-165	1822
(he died 1822)	(daughter of William Lewis) {Fairfield District}			
Pickett, James R.	Martha G. Lewis	RICE	40-50	1822
	(daughter of William Lewis) {Fairfield}			
Picton, Charles M.	Elizabeth Byers	2 DESA	592-602	1801
(married 8 May 1801) (daughter of William Byers) (she was born 1783/84) (she died 8 June 1802) {Charleston}				
Pinckney, Thomas	Eliza Izard	2 RIEQ	218-245	1803
(marriage contract 27 December 1803) (daughter of Ralph Izard) (Pinckney died 7 July 1842, Havre, France)				
Pitts, ____	Sarah Durham	2 STRO	258-262	1843
(in Indiana)		{Newberry District}		
Player, Joshua	Charlotte E. Thomson	2 DESA	264-271	1801
(marriage settlement 31 December 1801)				
Pledger, Philip	Sarah David	4 DESA	264-266	1812
	(widow of Benjamin David)			
		{Cheraw District}		
Poag, Jackson	Esther Gallagher	5 RIEQ	170-185	1832
	(daughter of John Gallagher) (she died 1839) {York}			
Poag, Leander	Matilda Gallagher	5 RIEQ	170-185	1832
	(daughter of John Gallagher) {York}			
Pogson, M.	Henrietta Wragg	2 HILL	180-184	1805
(marriage contract 6 February 1805) {Charleston}				
Pogson, Milward	____ Wragg	3 DESA	31-38	1809
		{Charleston District}		
Polk, James	Tabitha Moore	RICE	110-132	1804
	(daughter of Isham Moore) {Clarendon County, Sumter District}			

S.C. Marriages 1749-1867 Implied in S.C. Equity Reports

MAN	WOMAN	VOLUME	PAGES	LIVED
Polk, Thomas S.	Sarah Moore	RICE	110-132	1839

(daughter of Isham Moore) {Clarendon County, Sumter District}

Polony, Dr. _____	M. R. C. Menude	2 DESA	564-570	1791

(common-law marriage?) (he died 18 September 1805)
[Must also see 3 DESA pages 44-46; 74-78] {Charleston}

Poole, John	_____ Dantzler	12 RIEQ	224-228	1860

(daughter of David Dantzler) {Spartanburg}

Pooser, George	_____ Tyler	1 McC	18-22	1825
Porcher, Peter	_____ Young	1 STRO	170-172	1806

{Beaufort District}

Porter, _____	Charity Crawford	McMULL	81-86	1815

(she was born 8 June 1776) {Marion District}

Porter, Hugh Humphrey	Sarah Exum	McMULL	81-86	1836

(daughter of William Exum who died about 1821) (Porter was born January/February 1815) {Marion District}

Porter, Wm.	Ann Stewart	3 DESA	135-148	1803

(daughter of Thomas Stewart who died 16 September 1788) {Charleston}

Posey, John	_____ Screven	1 HILL	252-264	1833
Postell, _____	Hannah Coachman	1 STRO	81-83	1789

(daughter of James Coachman of Prince George Winyah)

Postell, _____	_____ Skirving	1 DESA	158-159	1780

(daughter of James Skirving)

Potts, _____	Elizabeth (Eliza) Cogdell	1 DESA	454-458	1795

(daughter of George Cogdell)

Potts, _____	Ann Cureton	13 RIEQ	104-110	1858

{Lancaster District}

Pou, Joseph	Eliza M. Felder	5 RIEQ	509-518	1852

[See also 6 RIEQ pages 58-71] {Orangeburg}

Powell, J. S.	Lavinia Gillett	3 RIEQ	398-403	1832

{Barnwell}

Powell, Jacob S. P.	Lavinia Gillett	2 STRO	196-207	1832

{Barnwell}

Powell, Rev. J. S.	Lavinia Gillett	SPEERS	142-158	1829

(daughter of Dr. Elijah Gillett who died 1818) (she died 12 November 1832) {Barnwell}

Powell, Medicus	Maria Louisa Ashe	2 STRO	250-258	1841

(daughter of Richard C. Ashe, Sr. who died 1837) {Barnwell}

Poyas, J. E.	_____ Smith	1 DESA	156-157	1780

(daughter of Henry Smith)

Poyas, John E.	_____ Smith	2 DESA	65-66	1788

S.C. Marriages 1749-1867 Implied in S.C. Equity Reports

MAN	WOMAN	VOLUME PAGES	LIVED
Prather, William	Jennet _____	4 DESA 33-44	1799
(married 1799-1801)		{Washington District}	
Prescott, Daniel	_____ Holloway	7 RIEQ 9-16	1820
		{Edgefield}	
Presley, Lewis	Martha Davis	7 RIEQ 105-111	1835
		{Union}	
Price, _____	Pheraby Cox	12 RIEQ 349-360	1857
		{Abbeville District}	
Price, Cuthbert	_____ _____	CHEVES 167-174	1832
(Bird), Jr. (he married second time 1832) {Chester}			
Price, Daniel B.	Martha Lewis	3 RIEQ 172-199	1834
(married 9 January 1834) (widow of Jesse Lewis who			
died 30 October 1832)		{Darlington District}	
Price, Joseph	_____ Turner	1 HILL 445-465	1818
		{Spartanburgh}	
Price, Thomas W.	Adele Poussin	BAILEY 458-460	1812
(common-law marriage) (he died 1827) {Charleston}			
Price, Thomas W.	Charlotte Smith	BAILEY 240-267	1791
(married 1791) (deed of separation 31 December 1812)			
(daughter of Philip Smith)		{Charleston}	
Price, Thomas W.	Charlotte Smith	3 DESA 165-168	1811
(daughter of Philip Smith) {Charleston District}			
Price, William, Jr.	Eliza Lothrop	2 RIEQ 412-472	1825
(he died May 1831) (daughter of Seth Lothrop)			
		{Charleston}	
Priester, William	Elizabeth Moye	12 RIEQ 361-378	1828
(daughter of Matthew Moye)			
(Priester's second marriage) (he died March 1856)			
		{Barnwell}	
Prince, George	Sarah Hyams	1 RIEQ 282-291	1835
(married 2 March 1835, Portsmouth, England, or			
common-law marriage)			
Prince, J. P.	Sarah Clarissa Davis (daughter of Elnathan Davis)	SPEERS 29-35	1842
		{York District}	
Pringle, James R.	Elizabeth M'Pherson (daughter of Gen. John M'Pherson of Prince William's Parish, who died 24 August 1806)	2 DESA 524-546	1807
		{Colleton District}	
Pringle, James Reid	Elizabeth Mary McPherson	3 RIEQ 342-360	1807
(marriage settlement 18 March 1807) (daughter of General John McPherson) (Pringle died 11 July 1840) (she died 14 August 1843)		{Charleston}	

73

S.C. Marriages 1749-1867 Implied in S.C. Equity Reports

MAN	WOMAN	VOLUME PAGES	LIVED
Purcell, _____	Sarah B. Blake (daughter of Edward Blake) (she died 1834)	RILEY 282-284	1795
Purcell, _____	Ann Smith	1 HILL 193-203 {Charleston}	1821
Puryear, Reuben A.	Nancy Hamner (daughter of George B. Hamner, Sr. of Mecklenburg County, Virginia)	9 RIEQ 459-473 {Virginia}	1835
Puryear, Thomas	Margaret Hamner (married 31 May 1839) (daughter of George B. Hamner, Sr. of Mecklenburg County, Virginia) (she died 12 February 1845)	9 RIEQ 459-473 {Richland}	1839
Pye, Thomas	Emeline M. E. Carr (married November 1844) (daughter of Dr. William Carr of St. George Dorchester) (she was born 1825)	2 STRO 105-111 {Walterborough}	1844
Pyron, _____	Sarah M. C. Simons	SPEERS 134-142 {Charleston}	1829

(Q)

Quarles, _____	_____ Anderson (daughter of Allen Anderson, Sr. who died 1842)	9 RIEQ 137-148 {Edgefield}	1842
Quarles, Richard	_____ Middleton (daughter of Hugh Middleton who himself was married four times)	4 DESA 145-148 {Ninety-Six District}	1810

(R)

Rabe, William	P. Stairley (married March 1839) (widow of George Stairley)	McMULL 22-26 {Greenville District}	1839
Radcliffe, _____	Sophia Louisa Graves (daughter of Admiral Richard Graves) [See also pages 233-247]	RILEY 219-232	1821
Radford, John J.	Jane Moer (widow of William Moer)	RICHEQ 469-475 {Charleston}	1828
Ragan, William	Phebe Burton (daughter of William Burton who died April 1826)	RICHEQ 146-164 {Newberry}	1812
Raiford, Hamilton (in Georgia)	Mary E. Wells	RICE 243-274 {Beaufort District}	1838

74

S.C. Marriages 1749-1867 Implied in S.C. Equity Reports

MAN	WOMAN	VOLUME PAGES	LIVED
Raines, William G.	Catharine Boulware	4 RIEQ 399-408 {Fairfield}	1828
Rainsford, James	_____ Rainsford (daughter of Thomas Rainsford) [See also McMULL pages 16-21; 335-343] {Edgefield}	DUDLEY 57-71	1833
Rainsford, James	Esther Rainsford (daughter of Thomas Rainsford) (she was born June 1815) {Edgefield}	RICE 343-371	1833
Rainsford, James (married 1833)	Esther Rainsford (daughter of Thomas Rainsford who died December 1837)	SPEERS 385-398	1833
Rainsford, John	Emily Miller (daughter of James Miller) (she was born about 1823) {Edgefield}	4 RIEQ 1-9	1846
Ramsay, Dr. John	Maria Deas (widow of John Deas, Jun. who died 20 October 1790)	2 DESA 233-239	1804
Ramsay, Dr. Paul	Martha Laurens [See also 6 RIEQ pages 217-266]	2 DESA 582-592	1806
Ramsey, _____	Hester Perdriau (daughter of Peter Perdriau) {Sumter}	5 RIEQ 20-31	1842
Ramsey, John (he died 9 June 1825) (he of Edgefield District)	Nancy Dozier	McMULL 236-253 {Greenville}	1825
Ravenel, William	Eliza Butler Pringle (daughter of James Reid Pringle) {Charleston}	3 RIEQ 342-360	1851
Read, James W.	Caroline Laurens	7 RIEQ 260-280 {Charleston}	1853
Read, James Withers (married 12 May 1842) (he died 28 June 1851) (she was born 1823/24)	Caroline Laurens	11 RIEQ 285-295 {Charleston}	1842
Read, John Harleston, Sr. (marriage settlement 18 July 1811) (she died May 1817) {Charleston and Georgetown District}	Mary Withers	8 RIEQ 145-154	1811
Read, Dr. William	Sarah Harleston (daughter of Col. John Harleston) {Charleston}	5 RIEQ 301-326	1793
Redheimer, Peter	_____ Blewer (daughter of John G. Blewer) {Lexington}	10 RIEQ 191-201	1842
Redheimer, Peter	_____ Blewer (daughter of John G. Blewer) {Lexington}	2 STRO 285-289	1842
Reed, Dr. Wm. (Read)	Sarah Harleston (daughter of John Harleston) {Charleston}	DUDLEY 201-212	1805

S.C. Marriages 1749-1867 Implied in S.C. Equity Reports

MAN	WOMAN	VOLUME PAGES	LIVED
Rees, Col. Orlando S. (he died April 1852)	Catharine Waties (she died 22 January 1855) {Sumter}	10 RIEQ 86-109	1852
Reese, James	Lucy Holloway {Edgefield}	7 RIEQ 9-16	1847
Reese, James (to Columbus, Georgia)	Lucy B. West (widow of John West) {Edgefield District}	5 RIEQ 531-579	1796
Reeves, D.	____ Tucker {Barnwell}	5 RIEQ 150-155	1852
Reid, ____	Harriet Caldwell {Newberry}	11 RIEQ 73-82	1848
Reid, Jethro L.	Jemima Moorman (widow of Thomas Moorman) {Union}	SPEERS 343-350	1840
Reid, William R. (marriage settlement 21 July 1828, Lincoln County, Georgia) (widow)	Jane McKinney {Abbeville District}	12 RIEQ 349-360	1828
Reid, William R. (marriage contract 31 July 1828) (both of Lincoln County, Georgia)	Jane McKinney {Abbeville}	1 STRO 27-43	1828
Rembert, Caleb [See also 2 RIEQ pages 285-287]	Mary M. Michau (daughter of Manassah Michau who died 1805) {Sumter}	SPEERS 312-321	1843
Retmeyer, ____	Maria Agnes Clausen (she died 28 August 1826, Paderborn, Prussia)	RILEY 117-120	1822
Reynolds, William	Sarah Bailey (daughter of Henry Bailey) (she died 1789) {Beaufort District}	1 DESA 355-359	1784
Rhame, Bradley (married July 1818) (widower) (widow)	Rebecca ____	1 McC 197-209	1818
Rhode, Christian	Elizabeth Carn (daughter of Frederick Carn) {Orangeburgh}	2 HILL 41-45	1831
Rhodes, Henry	____ Durr (widow of Jacob Durr)	2 McC 368-376	1827
Rhodus, William (he died September 1857)	Jane Hilton (she died December 1856) {Clarendon}	12 RIEQ 104-113	1829
Ricard, William	Sarah Oswald {Beaufort}	RICHEQ 326-352	1817
Rice, ____	Harriet Moye (widow of Matthew Moye) {Barnwell}	12 RIEQ 361-378	1863
Rice, William	Caroline M. Spann (daughter of Charles Spann, Jr. who died 1834) {Sumter District}	13 RIEQ 59-103	1849

S.C. Marriages 1749-1867 Implied in S.C. Equity Reports

MAN	WOMAN	VOLUME	PAGES	LIVED
Richardson, Dr. Henry (marriage settlement 27 October 1801) (daughter of Dr. James Fraser) (she died 1812) {Charleston}	Mary Fraser	RILEY	271-282	1801
Richardson, James B. (married 10 May 1791) (daughter of James Sinkler who died 20 November 1800)	Ann Cantey Sinkler	2 DESA	127-140	1791
Richardson, Valentine	Sarah Ann White (daughter of James White, Sr.) {Georgetown}	McMULL	115-125	1840
Richbourg, D. D.	Sarah Dinkins (widow of John Dinkins) {Sumter}	RICHEQ	185-191	1829
Rickard, _____	Sarah Oswald {Beaufort District}	RILEY	38-41	1836
Rickenbacker, Samuel (Charleston or Orangeburg)	Juliana Jewell (daughter of Benjamin Jewell) {Charleston District}	11 RIEQ	296-322	1855
Riddlehoover, John	_____ Wicker {Newberry}	1 HILL	376-382	1832
Riggs, Thomas	Sarah Rogers {Walterboro}	RICHEQ	287-293	1810
Riley, _____	Cornelia E. Robert (daughter of John Robert) {Charleston}	2 STRO	86-90	1833
Riley, William	_____ Tyler (widow of Henry Tyler who died 1815)	1 McC	18-22	1815
Rivers, Thomas (widower)	Elizabeth Cromwell (widow) {Charleston}	3 DESA	190-199	1811
Robertson, _____	Elizabeth Jemima Bowers (widow of Edward Bowers) {Lancaster}	10 RIEQ	551-556	1835
Robertson, _____	Patsey McBee (widow) {Spartanburgh District}	SPEERS	20-28	1833
Robertson, _____	Ann Watson (widow) {Fairfield District}	3 STRO	1-15	1837
Robertson, David	Martha McBee (widow of Elijah McBee) {Spartanburg}	McMULL	485-494	1831
Robertson, John	Ann Megrath	1 DESA	445-449	1795
Robertson, William	Elizabeth Barns (widow) {Edgefield}	4 STRO	179-186	1831
Robertson, William	_____ Freer (daughter of John Freer who died November 1787)	HARPER	56-65	1824
Robinson, _____	_____ Gervais (daughter of Rev. Paul T. Gervais)	McMULL	106-114	1841
Robinson, James E.	Martha Motte Dart {Charleston}	DUDLEY	128-132	1835

S.C. Marriages 1749-1867 Implied in S.C. Equity Reports

MAN	WOMAN	VOLUME	PAGES	LIVED
Robinson, William	Mary Ann Miscally (daughter of Daniel Miscally who died August/September 1817) (Robinson died August 1820) (she died February 1821)	BAILEY {Charleston}	304-311	1817
Robison, William T.	Margaret McLure (daughter of William McLure who died 1859)	14 RIEQ {York}	105-120	1866
Robson, _____	Sarah Cotchet	2 McC	269-317	1823
Rochell, John (married 1827)	Elizabeth Tompkins (widow of Samuel Tompkins) (she died 1842)	1 STRO {Edgefield}	114-128	1827
Roebuck, _____	Betsey Crosswhite (daughter of Jacob Crosswhite)	6 RIEQ {Newberry}	88-95	1825
Rogers, John	Ann Fincher (marriage settlement 2 June 1836) (widower) (widow) (he died July 1838) (she died February 1838)	1 STRO {Union}	370-377	1836
Roper, Benjamin D.	_____ Jenkins	McMULL	106-114	1830
Rosborough, William A.	Martha Mary Moffatt (daughter of William Moffatt who died 15 April 1851)	5 RIEQ {Chester}	95-111	1852
Rose, James L.	Mary Martha Seabrook (widow of Thomas Wilkes Seabrook who died in Florida)	2 STRO {Charleston}	69-71	1848
Ross, _____ (in Illinois)	Frances Davis	4 RIEQ {Abbeville}	16-22	1851
Roswell, Thomas (of North Carolina)	Hannah M. A. Pettus (daughter of J. D. O. K. Pettus who died 29 October 1821) (she was born 1817) {York}	4 RIEQ	92-105	1845
Rottenbury, Charles	Catharina Snell (widow)	4 DESA {Orangeburg}	268-273	1812
Rowand, _____ [In footnotes of 1917 Edition]	Henrietta Sommers	4 RIEQ {Charleston}	416-420	1852
Rowand, Charles E., Jr.	Helen R. Robertson (he died 6 January 1839)	4 STRO {Charleston}	37-58	1839
Rowand, Charles E., Sr.	Henrietta Sommers (daughter of John Sommers) (she died 1 April 1838) {Charleston}	4 STRO	37-58	1838
Rowand, Charles Edward, Sr.	Henrietta Sommers (she died April 1838) {Charleston}	3 RIEQ	281-304	1838
Rowand, Robert [See also pages 262-269]	Mary Elliott	1 DESA	183-190	1790
Rowe, Donald	Ann Sabb (widow of William Sabb)	5 RIEQ {St. Matthew's Parish}	370-403	1809
Rowland, Ezekiel	_____ Sullivan (daughter of James Sullivan)	4 DESA {Washington District}	518-522	1814

S.C. Marriages 1749-1867 Implied in S.C. Equity Reports

MAN	WOMAN	VOLUME	PAGES	LIVED
Rowland, James	_____ Hamlin (widow of E. Hamlin)	BAILEY {Charleston}	226-227	1829
Rudd, _____	Elizabeth G. Davenport (daughter of Jonathan Davenport)	3 RIEQ {Newberry}	559-578	1842
Ruff, Henry	_____ Summers	4 DESA {Washington District}	529-532	1814
Rumney, Benjamin W.	Susan Shackelford (daughter of William C. Shackelford)	2 STRO {Charleston District}	51-63	1847
Rumph, George (married 1805) (separated 1816/17) (widow of Josiah Allen who died about 1796) (she died 1828)	Janet Allen	2 HILL {Walterborough}	1-6	1805
Rutherford, William	_____ Ruff (daughter of George Ruff who died 1803)	BAILEY {Newberry}	7-13	1830
Rutledge, _____	_____ Smith (daughter of Thomas Smith)	1 McC	119-148	1806
Rutledge, Edward (marriage settlement 1793) (daughter of John Harleston) (Rutledge died 1811) (she died 11 November 1835)	Jane Harleston	DUDLEY {Charleston}	201-212	1793
Rutledge, Edward	Jane Harleston (daughter of Col. John Harleston)	5 RIEQ {Charleston}	301-326	1795
Rutledge, Henry M.	_____ Middleton (daughter of Arthur Middleton)	2 HILL	591-599	1814
Rutledge, Nicholas H. (marriage settlement 1831) (widow) (Rutledge died 1835)	Eliza L. Bryan	DUDLEY {Charleston}	201-212	1831
Ryan, Stanmore B.	Susan A. Gallman (daughter of Benjamin Gallman)	McMULL {Edgefield}	451-457	1838

(S)

Salisbury, _____	Lovey Blankton	6 RIEQ	388-398	1850
{Goose Creek Parish and Charleston District} [Referred to in another case in footnotes of 1917 Edition]					
Sams, William	Mary M'Gillivray (daughter of J. Stanyarne)	1 DESA	127-135	1785
Sanders, _____	_____ Ferguson (widow of Charles Ferguson)	3 DESA	555-556	1813

S.C. Marriages 1749-1867 Implied in S.C. Equity Reports

MAN	WOMAN	VOLUME PAGES	LIVED
Sanders, Jordan	Anna Nettles (daughter of Zachariah Nettles) (her first marriage) {Darlington}	10 RIEQ 394-407	1854
Sanders, Wm.	Rhoda Pullam (daughter of Benjamin Pullam) {Abbeville}	4 RIEQ 9-14	1851
Sandford, ____	Beatrix Edmondston {Charleston}	RICHEQ 357-361	1817
Sanford, John	Elizabeth Tyler (daughter of William Tyler)	1 McC 18-22	1825
Sarter, John P.	Patsey Sims (daughter of Reuben Sims) {Union}	2 HILL 121-140	1832
Sarter, John S. (married 1825)	____ Sims (daughter of Reuben Sims) {Union}	RICHEQ 122-141	1825
Sartor, John P.	____ Sims (daughter of Col. Reuben Sims who died 1844) {Union}	4 STRO 103-122	1842
Sasportas, Abram (married about 16 September 1778, Charleston) (he died 1823, France) (she died 1851, Bordeaux, France)	Charlotte Canter {Charleston District}	10 RIEQ 38-52	1826
Saunders, Nathaniel [In footnotes of 1917 Edition]	____ Harris (widow of John Harris who died 1826) {Edgefield}	2 STRO 370-377	1835
Savage, ____	Mary Elliott Butler	2 McC 435-440	1778
Sawyer, Samuel	Currency Hull {Connecticut}	2 STRO 174-195	1840
Saxon, B. T. (married October 1812)	Martha Barksdale (daughter of Joseph Barksdale) {Abbeville}	4 DESA 522-529	1812
Saxon, James	Anne (Nancy) Craddock (widow of Edmund Craddock) {Laurens}	1 HILL 69-76	1818
Scanlan, J.	Martha Oswald (daughter of Joseph Oswald) {Beaufort}	RICHEQ 326-352	1817
Schmidt, Dr. John W. (marriage settlement 12 January 1810) (he was married before) [daughter of Guillaume (William) Dumont] (Schmidt died 1853)	Ursule Dumont {Charleston}	7 RIEQ 201-218	1810
Schoppert, Phillip	Mary B. Waters (daughter of Philemon Berry Waters) {Newberry}	6 RIEQ 83-87	1853
Schroder, John	____ Boyer (daughter of Jacob H. Boyer who died 1817) {Charleston}	BAILEY 334-342	1817
Schroeder, Henry W.	Ann Eugenia Chitty (daughter of Charles C. Chitty) {Charleston}	McMULL 422-430	1841

S.C. Marriages 1749-1867 Implied in S.C. Equity Reports

MAN	WOMAN	VOLUME PAGES	LIVED
Schultz, Wade Hampton	Rosa Sarah D. Boyle (daughter of John Boyle, Sr. of St. Paul's Parish, who died 1827) [See also 1 RIEQ pages 280-282]	SPEERS 533-544 {Colleton District}	1834
Scott, _____	Clarissa Bowman (daughter of George Bowman)	14 RIEQ 271-279 {Orangeburg}	1826
Scott, _____	_____ Gray (daughter of John Gray)	4 RIEQ 1-9 {Edgefield}	1846
Scott, Benjamin	Sally Fretwell (daughter of William Fretwell of Greene County, Georgia)	11 RIEQ 559-573 {Anderson}	1856
Scott, John C.	_____ Houston	9 RIEQ 85-99 {Abbeville}	1856
Scriven, C.	B. Galphin	1 McC 280-300 {Edgefield District}	1826
Scurry, E. Madison (married 1852)	Mary Ann L. Ellis	9 RIEQ 19-33 {Williamsburg District}	1852
Seabrook, Gabriel	Ann Mikell (daughter of Ephraim Mikell)	2 DESA 342-361	1805
Seabrook, John	Margaret Murray	CHEVES 80-93	1839
Seabrook, W. H.	Mary Emily Rivers (daughter of George A. C. Rivers of Wadmalaw, who died 6 August 1840) (she was born 17 January 1831)	9 RIEQ 203-216 {Charleston}	1856
Seabrook, William (Seabrook was married before)	Elizabeth Emma Edings (daughter of Joseph Edings)	McMULL 201-230 {Edisto Island}	1836
Seabrook, William	Mary Ann Mikell (daughter of Ephraim Mikell)	2 DESA 342-361	1805
Sealy, _____	Beulah Ball (widow of Samuel Ball)	1 DESA 137-142	1775
Searson, Thomas E.	Elizabeth M. Blount (daughter of Stephen W. Blount of Georgia)	8 RIEQ 130-135 {Beaufort}	1844
Searson, Zachariah Z.	_____ Lewis (daughter of Samuel Lewis) (she died 1838)	1 STRO 180-184 {Beaufort District}	1836
Seay, William	_____ Barnett (daughter of Jorial Barnett)	6 RIEQ 111-114 {Spartanburg}	1853
Secrest, James F.	_____ Caston	2 RIEQ 54-56 {Lancaster}	1843
Sergeant, _____	_____ Addison (daughter of James Addison)	3 DESA 535-539 {Charleston}	1813
Sergeant, William	Mary Tamplet	7 RIEQ 358-374 {Charleston}	1789

S.C. Marriages 1749-1867 Implied in S.C. Equity Reports

MAN	WOMAN	VOLUME	PAGES	LIVED
Shackelford, William Cartwright	Sarah C. Vanderhorst (widow of Elias Vanderhorst) (she died November 1845)	2 STRO	51-63	1845
		{Charleston District}		
Shackleford, ____	Mary Collins (granddaughter of J. Collins)	1 DESA	570-573	1797
Shackleford, Richard	Mary Woodberry	BAILEY	48-57	1828
Shanks, Joseph (married 1781) (Shanks of Great Britain)	Ann Scott (daughter of Thomas Scott who died 1782) (she died June 1801 in Wales)	HARPER	5-19	1781
Shearman, ____	Elizabeth Tucker	BAILEY	351-359	1814
		{Charleston}		
Shell, Francis A.	____ Dugan (daughter of John Dugan) {Newberry}	DUDLEY	1-14	1837
Shell, Harmon	____ Dugan (daughter of John Dugan) {Newberry}	DUDLEY	1-14	1837
Shell, Stephen	Jane Ellis (daughter of John Ellis who died 1772)	4 DESA	611-613	1815
		{Washington District}		
Sheppard, ____	Anna Teulon	7 RIEQ	84-94	1852
		{Abbeville District}		
Sheppard, William	____ ____ (illegitimate daughter of Mrs. Caleb Gilbert)	2 McC	36-43	1827
Sheppard, William	Sarah Waters (widow of Philemon Berry Waters)	6 RIEQ	83-87	1813
		{Newberry}		
Sherry, ____	Sarah Schinholster (widow of John Schinholster who died 1781)	2 McC	60-72	1794
		{Beech Island}		
Shuler, ____	Barbara Bowman (daughter of George Bowman)	14 RIEQ	271-279	1826
		{Orangeburg}		
Sifly, ____	Susan Caloff	HARPER	3-5	1824
Simkins, ____	Mary Ardis	2 McC	60-72	1827
		{Beech Island}		
Simmons, ____	Jane Stanyarne (daughter of J. Stanyarne)	1 DESA	127-135	1772
Simmons, Dr. ____	Maria Vanderhorst (daughter of Arnoldus Vanderhorst)	DUDLEY	145-154	1810
		{Charleston}		
Simmons, James	Ann Tyler (daughter of William Tyler)	1 McC	18-22	1825
Simmons, William K.	Susannah A. Pickett	13 RIEQ	366-372	1866
		{Chester}		
Simons, ____	Eliza Lucila Ball	SPEERS	48-87	1843

S.C. Marriages 1749-1867 Implied in S.C. Equity Reports

MAN	WOMAN	VOLUME	PAGES	LIVED
Simons, B. P.	_____ Lloyd (daughter of John Lloyd)	DUDLEY	141-145	1836
Simons, Charles Dewar (marriage settlement 25 September 1807) (daughter of Thomas Barksdale) (Simons died 21 January 1812) {Charleston}	Sarah Barksdale	3 RIEQ	271-281	1807
Simons, Dr. Thomas Y. (daughter of Charles E. Rowand, Sr.) [See also 4 RIEQ pages 416-420 in footnotes of 1917 Edition] {Charleston}	Mary E. Rowand	4 STRO	37-58	1849
Simons, Keating (widow of John Wilson who died 1790; Wilson's marriage settlement 1 January 1789, recorded 16 August 1790)	Eleanor Wilson	1 DESA	401-409	1790
Simons, William	Catharine Hume	5 RIEQ	270-274	1852
{Charleston}				
Simpson, Dr. Edward G. (daughter of Dr. Robert Campbell of Laurens District) {Abbeville District}	_____ Campbell	5 RIEQ	405-421	1848
Sims, _____ (widow of Andrew Snoddy who died November 1841) {Spartanburg}	Elizabeth Snoddy	1 STRO	84-89	1846
Sims, John J. (daughter of Thomas Mackey) {Lancaster}	Agnes Mackey	6 RIEQ	75-78	1841
Sims, Thaddeus C.	_____ Robbs	8 RIEQ	286-290	1855
{Spartanburg}				
Sineath, Jesse S. (married 1832/33) (widow of Henry Broxson of Colleton District) {Walterborough}	Rebecca Broxson	2 STRO	31-34	1832
Singletary, Daniel M. (granddaughter of Elisha Mellard of St. James Goose Creek) (she died 1835) {Charleston}	Celia Ann _____	11 RIEQ	393-404	1830
Singleton, Thomas (marriage settlement 25 August 1790) (daughter of John Roberts) {Beaufort District}	Elizabeth Roberts	2 McC	410-419	1790
Sinkler, James (daughter of Charles Cantey who died 10 October 1780)	Margaret Cantey	2 DESA	127-140	1791
Sinkler, James (daughter of Charles Cantey who died 10 October 1780)	Sarah Cantey	2 DESA	127-140	1780
Sinkler, William H. (daughter of John Linton Thompson) {St. Matthew's Parish}	Anna Thompson	5 RIEQ	370-403	1848
Skellon, T. (daughter of James Oswald) {Beaufort}	Susan Oswald	RICHEQ	326-352	1817

83

S.C. Marriages 1749-1867 Implied in S.C. Equity Reports

MAN	WOMAN	VOLUME PAGES	LIVED
Skinner, James W.	Mary A. S. Green (daughter of Richard G. Green)	10 RIEQ 27-37 {Georgetown District}	1857
Slappy, _____	Margarett Geiger (widow of Harmon Gieger)	2 STRO 359-370 {Newberry}	1827
[In footnotes of 1917 Edition]			
Slaughton, _____	Ann Rugely	RICHEQ 235-246 {St. Phillip's Parish}	1776
Slawson, _____	Mary Ann Albergottie	2 RIEQ 136-143 {Beaufort}	1815
Slowman, _____	Sarah Oswald	RICHEQ 326-352 {Beaufort}	1831
Slowman, _____	Sarah Oswald	RILEY 38-41 {Beaufort District}	1836
Slowman, James	Sarah Oswald	2 HILL 504-511 {Beaufort District}	1835
Smelie, William (married 1783)	Mary Lowrey (widow) (he died December 1800) (she died 1788)	2 DESA 66-79	1783
Smith, _____	Karen Davidson (widow)	4 RIEQ 307-314 {York}	1818
Smith, _____	Elizabeth Dill	1 DESA 237-244	1791
Smith, _____	Lucy Liles	HARPER 298-301 {Newberry District}	1824
Smith, _____	Lucy Nettles (daughter of Zachariah Nettles)	10 RIEQ 394-407 {Darlington}	1803
Smith, Archer	_____ Smith (daughter of George Smith who died 17 June 1784) [In footnotes of 1917 Edition]	2 DESA 124	1802
Smith, David	Ann Musgrove (widow of Edward Musgrove who died 1790)	HARPER 175	1824
Smith, George (lived in Charleston) (George Smith died September 1818)	_____ Smith (daughter of Josiah Smith)	3 RIEQ 465-542 {Georgetown}	1807
Smith, George P. (marriage settlement 6 April 1813)	Rebecca J. Clayton (his first marriage)	1 HILL 101-106 {Barnwell District}	1813
Smith, John	Mary Dinkins (daughter of John Dinkins who died 1811) (she died 1813)	HARPER 160-164	1810
Smith, John Holmes	Ann Lockwood	3 DESA 12-18	1800
Smith, O. B.	_____ Skirving (daughter of James Skirving)	1 DESA 158-159	1780
Smith, Philip (Smith died January 1796)	_____ Skirving (daughter of Col. James Skirving)	BAILEY 244-267 {Charleston}	1791

S.C. Marriages 1749-1867 Implied in S.C. Equity Reports

MAN	WOMAN	VOLUME PAGES	LIVED
Smith, Roger Moor (married March 1796)	Ann Downs	3 DESA 417-465 {Charleston}	1796
Smith, Savage (he died April 1817) (daughter of Wm. Cuttino)	____ Cuttino	3 RIEQ 465-542 {Georgetown}	1807
Smith, W. L.	Charlotte Izard (daughter of Ralph Izard who died 30 May 1804)	2 DESA 308-313	1805
Smith, W. L.	____ Wragg	3 DESA 31-38 {Charleston District}	1809
Smith, William E.	Caroline Trescot (daughter of Doctor John Sen Trescot)	1 RIEQ 123-130 {Charleston}	1845
Smoot, Josiah H.	____ Cummings (widow)	9 RIEQ 440-458 {Sumter District}	1857
Smoot, Josiah H.	____ Michau (daughter of Manassah Michau who died 1805) [See also 2 RIEQ pages 285-287] {Sumter}	SPEERS 312-321	1843
Snell, ____	Catharina Horger (daughter of Jacob Horger) {Orangeburg}	4 DESA 268-273	1792
Snowden, Aaron (married 1788)	____ Hughson (she was a widow)	4 DESA 87-92 {Cheraw District}	1788
Snowden, James David (married February 1816) (daughter of Capt. William Pope, Sen. of St. Luke's Parish, who died 1823) (Snowden of Charleston, died August 1818/19)	Sarah Pope	RICE 174-198 {Beaufort District}	1816
Sollee, ____	Harriet Neyle	CHEVES 21-26	1839
Sollee, Frederick W. (he died September 1851) (she died 1840) (Sollee died October 1837) (to Marengo County, Alabama)	Florida (Florilla) P. Croft (daughter of Edward Croft who	7 RIEQ 34-53 {Greenville}	1829
Sollee, Frederick W. (he was born 19 May 1827) (daughter of Richard Ward)	____ Ward	7 RIEQ 34-53 {Greenville}	1848
Sommers, James D. (he died 1817)	Susan B. Farr	4 STRO 37-58 {Charleston and Colleton Districts}	1817
Sommers, John	Martha Perry (daughter of Edward Perry, Sr.)	4 STRO 37-58 {Charleston}	1809
Southard, Hancock	Jemima Etheredge	10 RIEQ 207-216 {Edgefield}	1855
Spann, James L. (married 1824) (Spann died 1827)	Elizabeth O'Quin (daughter of Daniel O'Quin, Jr.)	1 HILL 324-325 {Sumter}	1833

S.C. Marriages 1749-1867 Implied in S.C. Equity Reports

MAN	WOMAN	VOLUME PAGES	LIVED
Spann, John R.	Margaret C. Richardson (daughter of James Burchell Richardson who died 28 April 1836)	DUDLEY 184-201	1826
Spear, James E.	Laura Ann Wood (marriage settlement 11 November 1840, Savannah, Georgia) (she died 16 September 1851) {Charleston}	9 RIEQ 184-202	1840
Spearman, Edmund (he died 1827)	Susan Abney (widow of John Abney) {Newberry}	RICHEQ 54-61	1827
Spearman, James S.	Lucy Crosswhite (widow of William Crosswhite who died 1833) {Newberry}	6 RIEQ 88-95	1852
Spears, _____	Mary Rogers	RICHEQ 287-293 {Walterboro}	1810
Speights, J. (married 1794) [In footnotes of 1917 Edition]	Catharine Meggs (widow of J. Meggs) (she died 1802)	3 DESA 139	1794
Spencer, _____	Elizabeth Swan	1 McC 227-233 {Virginia}	1801
Spencer, Samuel	Mary Ellerbe (daughter of Capt. William Ellerbe who died May 1830) {Cheraw}	SPEERS 328-342	1841
Spierin, Thomas P.	Elizabeth Lahiffe (marriage settlement 6 January 1797) (widow) (she died 1804)	2 DESA 459-471	1797
Spiva, David	Rebecca Lee (marriage agreement 26 September 1844) (widower) (widow) (he died about 1855 out West) {Union District}	9 RIEQ 434-439	1844
Stackhouse, H. M.	Martha J. Manning (widow of William L. Manning who died August 1862) {Marlborough District}	12 RIEQ 410-429	1866
Staggers, James M.	Eliza Ann Matthews (widow of Samuel P. Matthews) {Williamsburg}	13 RIEQ 142-164	1866
Stairley, George (he died June 1835)	P. Lester	McMULL 22-26 {Greenville District}	1833
Stallings, _____	_____ Foreman (daughter of Isaac Foreman) {Barnwell}	2 HILL 401-410	1835
Stanyarne, Archibald	Sarah Elliott	1 DESA 183-190	1790
Stapleton, John	Catherine Beale (daughter of John Beale) {Charleston District}	3 DESA 22-25	1809
Starke, Philemon (married about 1800)	Margaret (Peggy) Perry (daughter of James Perry)	1 HILL 35-48	1800
Starke, Reuben	_____ Knox	4 DESA 92-94	1810

S.C. Marriages 1749-1867 Implied in S.C. Equity Reports

MAN	WOMAN	VOLUME PAGES	LIVED
Statham, Barnet	Caroline Lamkin Seibels	2 HILL 605-611 {Edgefield}	1837
Stevens, Henry	Elizabeth Davis	4 DESA 532-536 {Pinckney District}	1814
Stevenson, ____	Elizabeth Brice	4 RIEQ 322-329	1837

(married about 1837) (daughter of William Brice, Sen. who died Mary 1849) {Fairfield}

Stevenson, ____	____ Dunlap	4 DESA 305-329	1812

(sister of Rev. David Ellison Dunlap)

Stewart, ____ (Stuart)	Ann Reeves	1 DESA 500-515	1777
Stewart, James	Ann Sabb (she died 1813)	5 RIEQ 370-403 {St. Matthew's Parish}	1808
Stiles, B.	Sarah M. Waight (widow of Abraham Waight)	2 DESA 66-79	1802
Stillman, ____	Rebecca Teulon	7 RIEQ 89-94 {Abbeville District}	1852
Stitt, Thomas (Stith)	Sarah Watson (daughter of Hardaway D. Watson)	3 STRO 1-15 {Fairfield District}	1837
Stitt, Thomas	Sarah S. Watson	7 RIEQ 100-105 {Fairfield}	1854
Stokes, Joseph H.	Anna R. Hodges	11 RIEQ 135-155	1850

(he died 7 August 1853) (daughter of Gen. George W. Hodges) (she died 1858) {Abbeville District}

Stoney, John	Elizabeth Gaillard	1 RIEQ 222-264	1826

(he died November 1838) (daughter of Capt. Peter Gaillard) [See also pages 275-277; 352-361] {Charleston}

Storms, ____	Sophie J. Jewell	RICHEQ 112-115	1818

(married 1818) (separated from Benjamin Jewell who died 1828) (to Barnwell then Charleston) [In footnotes]

Storne, Joseph (of Charleston) (married about 1820)	Sophia Prevost Jewell	11 RIEQ 296-322 {Charleston District}	1820
Stovall, Lewis	Jane Griffin (daughter of Richard Griffin) (in Lincoln County, Georgia)	2 RIEQ 99-114 {Abbeville}	1845
Stovall, Stephen	Jane Stovall (widow of Lewis Stovall) (in Lincoln County, Georgia)	2 RIEQ 99-114 {Abbeville}	1845
Street, ____	Terza Lee (widow of Eleazar Lee) (she died 1843)	SPEERS 373-374 {Chester}	1841
Strobhart, David	Margaret Winckler	2 DESA 640-646 {Beaufort District}	1808
Stroman, John	Catharina Snell	4 DESA 268-273 {Orangeburg}	1812

S.C. Marriages 1749-1867 Implied in S.C. Equity Reports

MAN	WOMAN	VOLUME PAGES	LIVED
Stuckey, Darius L.	Margaret Herron (daughter of William H. Herron) {Darlington}	5 RIEQ 441-450	1853
Sturkie, Gabriel (married 1844)	Martha (Patsey) Martin (widow of William O. Martin) {Lexington District}	10 RIEQ 118-129	1844
Sturkie, Richard	Jerusha Hoover {Lexington District}	10 RIEQ 118-129	1832
Sturman, _____ (in Indiana)	Martha Durham {Newberry District}	2 STRO 258-262	1843
Suggs, J. H.	_____ Youngblood {York}	1 STRO 122-128	1845
Sumner, Albert	Catharine S. Barclay (widow) [See also pages 518-532] [See also 1 RIEQ pages 361-389; 419-426]	SPEERS 48-87	1843
Sumner, Samuel [In footnotes of 1917 Edition]	Charlotte Palmer {Union}	6 RIEQ 150-154	1851
Swan, Thomas (marriage contract 24 October 1801 in Virginia) (Thomas Swan was married before) (widow of Thomas Thompson Swan)	Judith Swan	1 McC 227-233	1826
Swinton, _____	Susannah Platt	2 McC 440-445	1827
Szemere, Barthelemy	Leopoldine de Turkovics {Paris, France}	11 RIEQ 344-392	1852

(T)

Taggart. See Tygart			
Talbird, John	Elizabeth Bell (daughter of Thomas Bell who died 7 September 1795) (Talbird's first marriage) {Beaufort}	RICHEQ 361-369	1795
Talbird, John	Elizabeth Bell (married 10 May 1799) (daughter of Thomas Bell who died 7 September 1795)	1 DESA 592-595	1799
Talbird, John (married 1801) (she died 1819)	Elizabeth Bell (daughter of Thomas Bell who died 1795) {Beaufort District}	BAILEY 535-566	1801
Talbird, John (married 1822)	Mary Palmer (widow of William Palmer) (she died 1825) {Coosawhatchie}	1 HILL 142-145	1822
Talbird, John Elizabeth Bell)	Mary Palmer (widow) (sister of his first wife (Mary Talbird died November 1825) {Beaufort}	RICHEQ 361-369	1825

S.C. Marriages 1749-1867 Implied in S.C. Equity Reports

MAN	WOMAN	VOLUME	PAGES	LIVED
Talbird, William H.	_____ Givens	RICE	132-158	1839
		{Beaufort District}		
Tally, _____	Frances Barns	4 STRO	179-186	1849
		{Edgefield}		
Tattnell, Josiah	Harriet Fenwick	1 DESA	143	1787
Taveau, Augustus	Martha Caroline	1 McC	7-17	1825
	Ball (widow of John Ball, Sen. who died 29 June 1822)			
Taveau, Augustus	Martha Caroline	SPEERS	48-87	1843
	Ball (widow) [See also pages 518-532]			
[See also 1 RIEQ pages 361-386; 419-426]				
Taylor, _____	Providence Dawson	RICE	243-274	1820
(daughter of Richard Dawson, Sr. of St. Luke's Parish, who died 25 August 1836) {Beaufort District}				
Taylor, _____	Providence Dawson	2 STRO	34-39	1820
	(daughter of Richard Dawson, Sr.)			
		{Gillisonville}		
Taylor, John	_____ Sibley	2 HILL	430-442	1833
	[In footnotes of 1917 Edition] {Newberry}			
Taylor, Simon	Eliza Maria	4 DESA	505-517	1814
	Henderson (daughter of General Wm. Henderson)	{Richland District}		
Teasdale. See Tisdale				
Templeton, Alexander	Polly Phillips	3 RIEQ	543-555	1847
	(daughter of Stephen Phillips) (she died 1847)	{Barnwell}		
Terry, _____	_____ Coiel	2 HILL	108-111	1834
	(widow of Alston Coiel) {Lancaster}			
Terry, _____	Ann McDowell	RILEY	152-155	1834
		{Charleston}		
Terry, John (he died 1817)	Anna Maria Minter (daughter of Joseph Minter)	1 RIEQ	78-91	1807
		{Ninety-Six District}		
Terry, Thomas	Martha Hopkins	1 HILL	1-10	1819
(married February 1819) (widow of George W. Hopkins)				
Terry, Wm.	Sarah Minter	1 RIEQ	78-91	1807
	(daughter of Joseph Minter)			
		{Ninety-Six District}		
Thackum, Francis	_____ Milliken	2 HILL	267-277	1835
Thayer, Thomas Heyward	Catharine Barnwell Livingston	7 RIEQ	136-169	1843
(marriage settlement 6 February 1843) (he was married before)		{Charleston}		
Theus, _____	Magdalina Myers	2 McC	214-269	1804
		{Lexington District}		

S.C. Marriages 1749-1867 Implied in S.C. Equity Reports

MAN	WOMAN	VOLUME PAGES	LIVED
Thomas, _____	Sarah J. McJunkin (daughter of Joseph McJunkin) (her first marriage) {Union}	11 RIEQ 527-535	1856
Thomas, Capt. _____	_____ Threewits	4 DESA 560-578	1815
Thomas, Daniel	_____ Johnson (daughter of Col. Wm. Johnson)	HARPER 197-202	1819
Thomas, E. G. [Referred to in another case]	Emily Wakefield	RILEY 279	1831
Thomas, Edward (marriage agreement 3 April 1832) (widow of Legrand Guerry Walker who died 26 March 1829) (Thomas died December 1851) (she died 1836) {Georgetown District}	Mary E. Walker	7 RIEQ 230-247	1832
Thomas, Edward G.	Emily Cannon	BAILEY 222 {Georgetown}	1830
Thomas, Eli	_____ Hamer	4 STRO 124-133 {Marlborough District}	1847
Thomas, John	_____ Gilbert (daughter of Caleb Gilbert)	2 McC 36-43	1827
Thomas, John S.	_____ Neyle	CHEVES 21-26	1839
Thomas, W. R.	_____ Priester (daughter of Nicholas Priester, Senr.)	RICHEQ 26-35 {Barnwell}	1831
Thomasson, _____	Emily C. Youngblood	1 STRO 122-128 {York}	1845
Thompson, _____	Maria H. Chick (daughter of Burwill Chick of Greenville, who died 1847)	10 RIEQ 178-190 {Greenville, Newberry and Union Districts}	1846
Thompson, _____ [See also 2 HILL pages 146-152]	_____ Maybin (daughter of Andrew Maybin)	1 HILL 122-128 {Chester}	1827
Thompson, James (separated 1852)	Jane _____	10 RIEQ 416-427 {Charleston}	1852
Thompson, James (common-law marriage)	Mary Ellis	10 RIEQ 416-427 {Charleston}	1852
Thompson, James	Jane Murray (widow of John M. Murray) {Charleston}	2 HILL 204-215	1832
Thompson, John P.	_____ Powel (widow of James Powel)	4 DESA 162-165 {Pinckney District}	1811
Thompson, O. R. (of Winnsboro) District}	Eliza Ann Barkley (she died 17 March 1866) {Charleston	14 RIEQ 12-26	1864
Thompson, William R. (he died 1807) (she died November 1838)	Elizabeth Sabb	5 RIEQ 370-403 {St. Matthew's Parish}	1807

S.C. Marriages 1749-1867 Implied in S.C. Equity Reports

MAN	WOMAN	VOLUME	PAGES	LIVED
Thomson, David L. (of Beaufort)	_____ Porter	4 STRO	58-66	1840 {St. Helena's Parish}
Thomson, Hezekiah	_____ Scott	1 McC	32-42	1825
Threewits, Lewellin	Catharine Daniel (married February 1810)	4 DESA	560-578	1810
Tims, Amos (to Alabama)	Mary Cabeen (daughter of Thomas Cabeen)	1 HILL	51-59	1833 {Chester}
Tindall, _____	Lydia A. Wells	5 RIEQ	20-31	1842 {Sumter}
Tindall, _____	Martha P. Wells	5 RIEQ	20-31	1842 {Sumter}
Tisdale, Christopher	Susannah Mitchell (daughter of Stephen Mitchell)	12 RIEQ	263-276	1820 {Sumter District}
Tobin, Cornelius (common-law marriage)	Elizabeth Neilson (wife of John Neilson)	DUDLEY	161-174	1829 {Barnwell}
Tobin, Cornelius (common-law marriage)	Elizabeth Nelson (he died October 1830)	RILEY	64-76	1830 {Barnwell}
Tobin, John E.	Sarah E. Owens (daughter of John A. Owens of Beaufort District, who died 12 December 1830)	2 STRO	289-296	1848 {Barnwell}
Tompkins, Samuel	Elizabeth Adams	1 STRO	114-128	1827 {Edgefield}
Tonge, Edward, Sr.	Susannah Perry (daughter of Edward Perry, Sr.) (she died August 1828)	4 STRO	37-58	1822 {Charleston and St. Bartholomew's Parish}
Toomer, _____	_____ Baker (sister of Robert L. Baker)	1 STRO	129-169	1846 {Colleton and Beaufort Districts}
Toomer, _____	Elizabeth Price (daughter of William Price, Jr.) (she was born 1818-1820)	2 RIEQ	412-472	1846 {Charleston}
Towles, Daniel	Scythia Burton (he died December 1829) (daughter of William Burton who died April 1826) (she died about 1825)	RICHEQ	146-164	1812 {Newberry}
Townsend, Stephen	_____ Arthur (marriage settlement 28 December 1785) (widow)	3 DESA	223-241	1785
Townsend, W. S. (he went to Georgia, remarried and went to Tennessee)	Maria Hutson (she died June 1840)	6 RIEQ	249-254	1840 {Beaufort}
Trapp, Benjamin	_____ Billings	2 McC	403-405	1827
Trott, Captain John	Mary Finden (she was born about 1768)	7 RIEQ	358-374	1789 {Charleston}
Turner, _____	Jemima Bowers	10 RIEQ	551-556	1857 {Lancaster}

S.C. Marriages 1749-1867 Implied in S.C. Equity Reports

MAN	WOMAN	VOLUME	PAGES	LIVED
Turner, _____	Hannah Snelgrove (daughter of Henry Snelgrove)	4 DESA	274-304	1812
Turpin, Wm., Jr.	_____ Brazilman	3 STRO {Newberry}	149-158	1828
Tuttle, William (to Georgia)	Harriet Moore	2 STRO {Charleston}	27-30	1818
Tygart, William	_____ Smith	9 RIEQ {Union}	46-52	1856
Tyler, William (his first marriage)	Elizabeth Young (she died July 1813)	1 McC	18-22	1792

(U)

Ulmer, James	_____ Priester (daughter of Nicholas Priester, Senr.) {Barnwell}	RICHEQ	26-35	1831

(V)

Vaigneur, _____	Elizabeth Winckler	2 DESA {Beaufort District}	640-646	1808
Valk, Jacob R.	Sarah Wightman	DUDLEY {Charleston}	212-224	1838
Valk, Jacob R.	Sarah Wightman	10 RIEQ {Charleston}	518-533	1838
Vance, _____	Susan Mary Dart (daughter of Thomas L. Dart) {Charleston}	DUDLEY	128-132	1835
Vance, Allen	_____ Gary	RICE {Laurens}	2-3	1838
Vanderhorst, Elias	Sarah C. Withers (her first marriage) (daughter of Richard Withers) {Charleston District}	2 STRO	51-63	1829
Vanderhorst, Richard W.	Mary Shackleford (widow of Richard Shackleford)	BAILEY	48-57	1828
Vanderhorst, Thomas C.	Mary Hannah Beale (daughter of John Beale)	3 DESA	22-25	1809
Vandersmissen, Baron	_____ Graves (daughter of Admiral _____ Graves) {Charleston}	BAILEY	268-274	1829
Vandersmissen, Baron (or Chevalier)	Louisa Catherine Colleton Graves (married 1819) (daughter of Admiral Richard Graves)	RILEY	219-247	1819

S.C. Marriages 1749-1867 Implied in S.C. Equity Reports

MAN	WOMAN	VOLUME	PAGES	LIVED
Vandersmissen, Jacques Louis Dominique (married 20 October 1816, Antwerp, the Netherlands) (daughter of Admiral Richard Graves)	Louisa Catharina Colleton Graves	5 RIEQ	519-530 {Charleston}	1828
Varn, James G.	Laura Snider (stepdaughter of John Snider of St. Bartholomew's Parish)	9 RIEQ {Colleton District}	303-310	1847
Varn, Littleberry	Ann Snider (stepdaughter of John Snider of St. Bartholomew's Parish)	9 RIEQ {Colleton District}	303-310	1847
Vauters, Cornelius H.	Elizabeth McGrew	4 DESA	155-162	1811
Venning, _____	Ann Pearce (widow?) (she died 1854)	14 RIEQ {Charleston}	84-89	1854
Verdier, Henry (married 12 February 1839) (daughter of Rev. Paul T. Gervais) (Verdier died August 1839)	Margaret J. Gervais {St. Bartholomew's Parish}	McMULL	106-114	1839
Vickory, _____ (in Illinois)	Ruth Davis	4 RIEQ {Abbeville}	16-22	1851
Vidal, _____	_____ Bennett (sister of Peter Bennett of Wadmalaw Island)	SPEERS {Charleston}	402-412	1844
Viers, Maurice	Sarah Dubon	3 DESA	273-296	1795
Villard, B.	_____ McKenzie (widow of Daniel W. McKenzie)	2 STRO {Gillisonville}	40-44	1848
Villard, Wm. B. (married 2 November 1843) (daughter of Daniel W. McKenzie)	Harriet McKenzie	1 STRO {Gillisonville}	393-420	1843

(W)

Wactor, _____	Eliza Patterson (daughter of Anthony Patterson who died 31 May 1850)	4 RIEQ {Orangeburg}	340-348	1852
Wade, James T.	Agnes Rives (she died November 1850)	7 RIEQ {Charleston}	353-357	1833
Wade, James T.	Martha Rives	7 RIEQ {Charleston}	353-357	1854
Wade, Nathaniel (married 1811)	Laura Simpson	2 McC	130-136	1811
Wade, Thomas H. (marriage settlement 12 September 1826) (she died 8 July 1846)	Rebecca Moore	9 RIEQ {Richland}	362-364	1826

S.C. Marriages 1749-1867 Implied in S.C. Equity Reports

MAN	WOMAN	VOLUME	PAGES	LIVED

Wadkins. See Watkins
Wadlington, _____ Dorothy Cates   HARPER   224-242   1816
                   (daughter of Aaron Cates)
Wadlington, _____ Dorothy Cates   1 McC   252-267   1824
                                          {Newberry District}
Wagner, Charles   Mary Ann Gourlay   2 STRO   1-13   1836
   George (marriage settlement 20 December 1836)
                                          {Charleston}
Wagner, Effingham Franciade Maria   2 STRO   1-13   1845
                   Godard (daughter of Rene Godard of
   Charleston, who died 3 May 1845)   {Charleston}
Waight, Abraham   Sarah Maxwell   2 DESA   66-79   1787
                   Lowrey (her first marriage)
Waight, Isaac   Elizabeth Tucker   BAILEY   351-359   1814
   (common-law marriage)   {John's Island}
Waldo, Horace   _____ Hazard   4 RIEQ   266-275   1839
   (in New York City)   {Beaufort District}
Walker, _____   Mary Ann Elizabeth   3 RIEQ   23-33   1850
                   Allen (daughter of Matthew Allen who
   died 1834, Georgetown District)   {Marlborough District}
Walker, _____   _____ Templeton   3 RIEQ   543-555   1847
                   (daughter of Alexander Templeton)
                                          {Barnwell}
Walker, Edward C. _____ Hall   1 HILL   397-405   1829
   [Must also see 2 HILL pages 22-24]   {Colleton District}
Walker, Hasford   Mary A. Elizabeth   6 RIEQ   255-275   1847
                   Allen (married August 1847)
   (daughter of Mathew Allen of Georgetown District, who
   died 1834) (Walker died September 1851) {Georgetown
   and Marlboro Districts}
Walker, Jeremiah   Lucinda Griffin   2 RIEQ   99-114   1811
                   (daughter of Richard Griffin)
                   (in Lincoln County, Georgia) {Abbeville}
Walker, Thomas P. Mary Frances Hamner   9 RIEQ   459-473   1857
                   (daughter of George B. Hamner, Jr.
                   who went to Tennessee) {Richland}
Walker, William   Mary B. Dean   9 RIEQ   423-428   1856
                   (daughter of John Dean) {Spartanburg}
Wallace, W. L.   _____ Gill   RICHEQ   141-142   1831
                                          {York}
Walter, Alfred   Mary Peters   2 DESA   577-578   1808
Wamer, William   Amanda Pendarvis   DUDLEY   154-160   1836
                   (daughter of Joshua Pendarvis) {Colleton}
Warden, John   _____ Sims   2 McC   73-77   1827
Waring, _____   Lydia Jane Ball   2 STRO   24-27   1839
                   (she died 1840)   {Charleston}

S.C. Marriages 1749-1867 Implied in S.C. Equity Reports

MAN	WOMAN	VOLUME PAGES	LIVED
Waring, Joseph Ioor	Mary E. Perry	5 RIEQ 202-220	1824
	{Colleton and St. George's Parish}		
Waring, Joseph Joor (his first marriage) (daughter of Isaac Perry of St. Paul's Parish, who died 1818) (Waring died December 1852)	Perry	8 RIEQ 136-144 {Colleton}	1820
Waring, Richard	Jane L. Farr	4 STRO 37-58 {Charleston}	1849
Waring, Thomas	Lydia Catharine Ball	SPEERS 48-87	1843
Warren, George	Harriet Ann Risher	CHEVES 44-47 {Walterborough}	1839
Warren, John	Sarah Robinson (daughter of William Robinson who died 1805)	RICHEQ 390-397 {Union}	1828
Washington, Col. William [See also pages 183-190; 360-365]	Jane Riley Elliott (daughter of Charles Elliott)	1 DESA 263-271	1792
Washington, Major Thomas (alias Thomas Walsh) (married 1783) (daughter of David Murray who died 29 April 1771) (he died 1791) (she died 1804)	Charles Murray	McMULL 157-200 {Beaufort District}	1783
Washington, Thomas (he died 1791) (daughter of David Murray who died 1770/71 Savannah, Georgia)	Charles Murray	RILEY 102-112	1783
Washington, William	Theodosia Narcissa McPherson (daughter of James E. McPherson of Prince William's Parish) {Gillisonville}	3 STRO 171-182	1848
Waters, Philemon Berry (he died 1807) (daughter of Robert Gillam who died 1814)	Sarah Gillam	6 RIEQ 83-87 {Newberry}	1807
Waties, _____	Ann Elizabeth Rives	7 RIEQ 353-357 {Charleston}	1850
Watkins, Culpepper R. (Wadkins) (in Stanley County, North Carolina)	_____ Tomlinson (daughter of Thomas Tomlinson, Sr.) {Chesterfield District}	11 RIEQ 52-72	1856
Watson, _____	Catharine Ann McLennan (daughter of John McLennan who died 1853)	9 RIEQ 129-136 {Abbeville}	1856
Watson, _____	Harriet Moore (daughter of Henry Moore) (she died June 1852)	7 RIEQ 100-105 {Fairfield}	1839
Watson, Elijah	_____ Wright	2 McC 185-206 {Laurens}	1825
Weatherford, _____	Charlotte Moore	2 STRO 27-30 {Charleston}	1818

S.C. Marriages 1749-1867 Implied in S.C. Equity Reports

MAN	WOMAN	VOLUME	PAGES	LIVED
Weathers, _____	_____ Collier	3 RIEQ	555-558	1849
	(daughter of John Collier) {Orangeburg}			
Webb, John, Sr.	Jane Kerr	9 RIEQ	369-375	1827
(he died about 1827, Edgefield)		{Kershaw}		
Webb, William	_____ Wilbourne	1 HILL	10-14	1831
	(daughter of William Wilbourne)			
Wedeman, _____	Catharine Welch	SPEERS	256-263	1843
		{Newberry}		
Wells, _____	Jane Dawson	RICE	243-274	1820
(daughter of Richard Dawson, Sr. of St. Luke's Parish, who died 25 August 1836)				
		{Beaufort District}		
Wells, _____	Jane Dawson	2 STRO	34-39	1820
	(daughter of Richard Dawson, Sr.)			
		{Gillisonville}		
Wells, _____	Hester Perdriau	5 RIEQ	20-31	1842
		{Sumter}		
Wells, John D.	Nancy Haigood	1 HILL	59-61	1823
(married 1823) (widow of William Haigood) {Winnsboro}				
Wessenger, Jesse	Elizabeth Hamner	9 RIEQ	459-473	1857
	(daughter of George B. Hamner, Jr. who went to Tennessee) {Richland}			
West, John	Lucy B. Williams	5 RIEQ	531-579	1790
(married April 1790) (her first marriage) (daughter of Thomas Williams of Brunswick County, Virginia, who died January 1787)				
		{Edgefield District}		
Westmoreland, John L.	_____ West	9 RIEQ	418-419	1857
		{Greenville}		
Whaley, _____	Aley Davis	2 STRO	334-341	1832
		{Marion}		
Whaley, _____	Eliza Edings	4 RIEQ	276-301	1834
	(daughter of William Edings) {Charleston}			
Whaley, Benjamin	Eliza Edings	1 RIEQ	301-319	1819
(married 30 March 1819) (daughter of William Edings who died April 1836) (she died 26 June 1823) (Whaley's first marriage)				
Whaley, Benjamin	Maria Ferdinand	1 RIEQ	301-319	1832
(his second marriage) (he died 11 March 1832)				
Whaley, Wm. J.	Martha Mary Murray Clarke (daughter of William M. Clarke)	3 RIEQ	318-341	1841
		{Charleston}		
Whatley, Col. Abner	_____ Lamkin	2 HILL	605-611	1826
		{Edgefield}		
Wheeler, Edward B.	Josephine Livingston	3 RIEQ	452-465	1851
		{Marion}		

S.C. Marriages 1749-1867 Implied in S.C. Equity Reports

MAN	WOMAN	VOLUME PAGES	LIVED
Wheeler, William	Sarah A. Evans	2 HILL 222-228	1827
(did not marry; had child only) (he died July 1829)			
(daughter of John Evans)		{Charleston District}	
Wheeler, William	Susan A. Evans	BAILEY 507-509	1830
(common-law marriage)		{Charleston}	
Whitaker, _____	Mary Hutchinson	10 RIEQ 1-3	1848
(daughter of Mathias Hutchinson)			
(she died 1848)		{Charleston}	
White, _____	Eliza Alston	4 DESA 94-102	1803
		{Georgetown}	
White, _____	Jane Carnes	4 DESA 405-421	1812
		{Camden}	
White, _____	_____ Taylor	5 RIEQ 426-434	1821
(daughter of William Taylor)			
		{Williamsburg}	
White, James, Sr.	Martha Leger	McMULL 115-125	1813
(married June 1813) (his first marriage) {Georgetown}			
White, James, Sr.	Eliza Palmer	McMULL 115-125	1821
(married 1821) (daughter of Jesse Palmer)			
(White's second marriage)		{Georgetown}	
White, William	_____ Brown	2 RIEQ 99-114	1845
(daughter of Frederick Brown)			
(in Lincoln County, Georgia)		{Abbeville}	
Whitridge, Dr. J. B.	Sarah M'Leod	1 RIEQ 155-186	1842
(daughter of Rev. Doctor Donald M'Leod)		{Charleston District}	
Wicker, Uriah	Catharine Sligh	1 HILL 376-382	1808
(he died 1808)		{Newberry}	
Wideman, _____	Catharine Welch	2 STRO 348	n.d.
[Referred to in another case]			
Wideman. See Wedeman			
Wier, Dr. Thomas	_____ Long	2 RIEQ 283-285	1842
(daughter of Robert Long) {Laurens}			
Wightman, William	Sarah Brown	1 DESA 166	1787
Wightman, William J.	Ann Moore	SPEERS 357-372	1837
		{Edgefield}	
Wilder, William	Elizabeth Youngblood	1 STRO 122-128 {York}	1844
Wilie, William	Amanda Johnson	5 RIEQ 91-94	1852
(she of Camden)		{Lancaster}	
Wilkins, G. A.	_____ Taylor	8 RIEQ 291-297	1846
(widow of Henry Taylor)			
		{Beaufort District}	
Wilkins, John H.	Mary Jane Pickett	13 RIEQ 366-372	1866
(widow of Phillip H. Pickett who died July 1862)		{Chester}	

S.C. Marriages 1749-1867 Implied in S.C. Equity Reports

MAN	WOMAN	VOLUME PAGES	LIVED
Willard, Captain Prentiss (married 1812) (daughter of John Berners Barnwell) (Willard died 1812)	Jane H. Barnwell	RICE 198-242 {Beaufort District}	1812
Williams, _____	Jane Beasley (daughter of Thomas Beasley)	1 HILL 112-113	1833
Williams, _____	Elizabeth G. Caston (daughter of Samuel Caston who died May 1831)	2 RIEQ 1-3 {Lancaster}	1845
Williams, _____	_____ Hicks (daughter of Claudius P. Hicks)	RICHEQ 5-23 {Darlington}	1830
Williams, Isham [Referred to in another case]	_____ Shrewsbury (daughter of Edward Shrewsbury)	10 RIEQ 137	1793
Williams, Isham (he died August 1846) (daughter of Edward Shrewsbury who died 1793) (she died 20 October 1844) {Charleston}	Eliza Shrewsbury	3 STRO 211-224	1793
Williams, Jones M.	Rebecca T. Priester (daughter of William Priester) {Barnwell}	12 RIEQ 361-378	1863
Williams, Thomas	_____ Crawford	2 McC 171-181	1827
Williams, Thomas	Mary Shrewsbury	3 STRO 211-224 {Charleston}	1848
Williams, William	_____ Youngblood (daughter of William Youngblood) {York}	1 STRO 122-128	1846
Williams, William W. (he died 1845) (daughter of William Jeter who died 7 September 1820) {Edgefield}	Martha Jeter	1 STRO 103-113	1820
Williamson, Dr. Leander Z.	Prudence Harriet Stewart (daughter of John Stewart who died 1857)	10 RIEQ 323-328 {Lancaster}	1841
Williamson, Robert	_____ King (daughter of John King who died July 1818)	BAILEY 154-156 {Cheraw}	1818
Willis, James T.	_____ Head	5 RIEQ 128-143 {Barnwell District}	1833
Willis, Smith	Sarah Long (daughter of William Long) {Union}	1 STRO 43-53	1846
Wilson, _____	Rebecca Simons (widow of Samuel B. Simons)	2 McC 385-395	1827
Wilson, George (married 1789) (he died 1791)	Ann Withers	1 DESA 543-557	1789
Wilson, John (marriage bonds 8 May 1781, 2 June 1781) (widow of Archibald Baird who died 1777)	Winifred Baird	1 DESA 219-237	1781
Wilson, John died 5 May 1783) (she died 1804)	Elizabeth Stanyarne (daughter of William Stanyarne who {Charleston}	2 HILL 550-553	1804

S.C. Marriages 1749-1867 Implied in S.C. Equity Reports

MAN	WOMAN	VOLUME	PAGES	LIVED
Wilson, John H.	_____ Freer (daughter of Charles Freer who died 1808)	HARPER	56-65	1824
Wilson, Thomas (married 1840) (she died 1845)	Mary McJunkin (daughter of Joseph McJunkin) (Wilson of Columbia or Lexington) {Union}	11 RIEQ	527-535	1840
Wilson, William	Emeline McJunkin (daughter of Joseph McJunkin) {Union}	11 RIEQ	527-535	1856
Wimbish, James (to Virginia)	Rachael O. Patterson (daughter of Anthony Patterson who died 31 May 1850) {Orangeburg}	4 RIEQ	340-348	1852
Winckler, Nicholas, Sen. (common-law marriage) [See also BAILEY page 196]	Anna Barbara (or Mary Barbara) Wonderly (widow of David Wonderly) {Beaufort District}	2 DESA	640-646	1768
Winningham, _____	Mary Carson (widow of James Carson) {Orangeburgh}	3 STRO	86-93	1840
Winslow, Edward D. (marriage settlement May 1809) (widow) {Charleston}	_____ Berry	1 RIEQ	114-122	1809
Winter, John (married about 1749) (widow of Patrick Lindsay who died 1744) (Winter died 1785) (she died 1781/82)	_____ Lindsay	1 DESA	150-154	1749
Wirtemburgh, _____	_____ Boyer (daughter of Jacob H. Boyer who died 1817) {Charleston}	BAILEY	334-342	1817
Wise, Finklea G.	Ansy Bird (daughter of Peter Bird) (she was born about 1832) {Marion District}	11 RIEQ	536-540	1860
Wise, Major Samuel	_____ Boak	4 DESA	330-350 {Richland District}	1812
Wiseman, _____ (in Tennessee)	Sarah Finley	14 RIEQ	167-175 {Abbeville}	1867
Wolfe, _____	Catharine Holman (daughter of John C. Holman who died 1839) {Orangeburg}	4 RIEQ	329-334	1852
Wood, _____	_____ Coburn (daughter of John Coburn)	RILEY	187-193	1830
Wood, _____	Eliza Cook (daughter of Daniel Cook) {Charleston}	5 RIEQ	351-355	1852
Wood, J. J. (he died 1855/56)	Laura Patrick (she died 1856) {Barnwell}	10 RIEQ	130-138	1847
Wood, W. S.	Jane Youngblood	1 STRO	122-128 {York}	1845
Woodberry, _____	Mary Collins (daughter of Jonah Collins)	BAILEY	48-57	1828

S.C. Marriages 1749-1867 Implied in S.C. Equity Reports

MAN	WOMAN	VOLUME PAGES	LIVED
Woodward, _____	_____ McMullen (daughter of Hugh McMullen of Chester District, who died December 1841) {Chester}	4 RIEQ 117-135	1846
Woodward, William T.	Eliza Henry (marriage settlement 14 October 1839) (widow of George Henry who died August 1837) (Woodward died August 1842) {Charleston}	4 STRO 84-102	1839
Woodward, William T.	Eliza Henry (widow of George Henry who died 1837) {Charleston}	5 RIEQ 187-202	1840
Wotton, John A.	Ann Dunlap (daughter of James Dunlap) {Charleston}	11 RIEQ 405-415	1860
Wrenn, _____	Jane White (widow) {Camden}	4 DESA 405-421	1812
Wright, Jonathan	Eliza Herron (daughter of William H. Herron) {Darlington}	5 RIEQ 441-450	1853
Wright, Dr. Thomas W.	Sarah E. Screven (he died about 1825) {Sumter}	1 HILL 326-334	1824
Wurtz, Thomas (married 1819)	_____ _____ {Charleston}	2 HILL 171-180	1819

(Y)

MAN	WOMAN	VOLUME PAGES	LIVED
Yancey, William L. (to Alabama)	Sarah Earle {Greenville}	9 RIEQ 429-433	1852
Yancey, William L. (to Alabama)	Sarah Earle {Greenville}	7 RIEQ 16-19	1854
Yeates, Thomas	Mary Minter (daughter of Joseph Minter) (her first marriage) {Ninety-Six District}	1 RIEQ 78-91	1777
Young, James M., Jun.	Catharine Davenport (daughter of Jonathan Davenport) {Newberry}	3 RIEQ 559-578	1849
Young, William	Ann M. Cummings {Sumter District}	9 RIEQ 440-458	1857
Youngblood, David (he died 7 July 1791)	Lucretia Sharpless	2 DESA 295-299	1790

S.C. Marriages 1749-1867 Implied in S.C. Equity Reports

MAN   WOMAN   VOLUME PAGES   LIVED

(Z)

Zimmerman, Daniel   Elizabeth Holman   4 RIEQ   329-334   1821
                    (daughter of Conrad Holman of St.
    Matthew's Parish, who died 16 August 1816) {Orangeburg}
Zimmerman, Jacob   Mary Moore   BAILEY 195-204   1803
    (he died about 1803) (widow) (she died about 1803)
                                               {Coosawhatchie}
Zimmerman, Russel   Elizabeth Holman   4 RIEQ   329-334   1852
                    (daughter of John C. Holman who
                    died 1839)   {Orangeburg}

S.C. Marriages 1749-1867 Implied in S.C. Equity Reports

WOMAN	MAN	VOLUME PAGES	LIVED

(A)

Abney, Susan   Edmund Spearman   RICHEQ 54-61   1827
(widow of John Abney) (Spearman died 1827) {Newberry}
Adams, _____   _____ Gunter   4 RIEQ 152-164   1851
(daughter of Shockley Adams who died 10 October
1824)   {Marlborough}
Adams, Caroline   A. J. McQueen   4 RIEQ 152-164   1841
(married 1838/41) (daughter of Shockley Adams who
died 10 October 1824) (she was born October 1824)
(to Richmond County, North Carolina) {Marlborough}
Adams, Elizabeth   Samuel Tompkins   1 STRO 114-128   1827
    {Edgefield}
Adams, Gracey W.   B. F. Davis   3 STRO 55-59   1846
(daughter of James Adams)   {Columbia}
Adams, Mary   J. Jaffray   1 DESA 567-570   1797
(daughter of N. Adams)
Adams, Rebecca   George Holloway   1 STRO 114-128   1846
    {Edgefield}
Adams, Sarah   Daniel O'Quin, Jr.   1 HILL 324-325   1817
(daughter of Ephraim Adams) (she died 1818) {Sumter}
Adamson, Amelia   Francis A.   2 HILL 200-204   1832
    Delesseline
(daughter of John Adamson of Camden, who died May 1816)
(she died July 1832) [See also pages 235-243]
Adamson, Charlotte   John Boykin   2 HILL 200-204   1814
Adamson, Sarah   Lewis Ciples   2 HILL 200-204   1814
(daughter of John Adamson of Camden, who died May 1816)
[See also pages 235-243]
Addison, _____   _____ Sergeant   3 DESA 535-539   1813
(daughter of James Addison)   {Charleston}
Addison, Emeline S.   Dr. Edward J. Mims   9 RIEQ 58-70   1849
(daughter of Allen B. Addison who died November 1854)
    {Edgefield}
Adger, Isabella   George W. Boggs   4 RIEQ 408-413   1851
(widow of William Adger, Jun.)   {Fairfield}
Albergottie, _____   Benjamin Chaplin   2 RIEQ 136-143   1846
(daughter of William J. Albergottie) {Beaufort}
Albergottie, Mary   _____ Carney   2 RIEQ 136-143   1815
(daughter of Anthony Albergottie)   {Beaufort}
Albergottie, Mary   _____ Slawson   2 RIEQ 136-143   1815
Ann   {Beaufort}
Albergottie,   Benjamin Chaplin   10 RIEQ 428-434   1856
Rebecca (daughter of William J. Albergottie)
    {Beaufort District}

102

S.C. Marriages 1749-1867 Implied in S.C. Equity Reports

WOMAN	MAN	VOLUME	PAGES	LIVED
Alexander, _____	Thomas O. Hood	9 RIEQ	311-330	1845
		{Lancaster}		
Allen, _____	David Crosland	3 RIEQ	23-33	1839
(widow of Matthew Allen who died 1834, Georgetown				
District)		{Marlborough District}		
Allen, Ann A.	Seth Daniel	2 RIEQ	99-114	1838
(married 30 November 1838) (daughter of Josiah G.				
Allen)		{Beaufort and Barnwell Districts}		
Allen, Eliza Ann	_____ Cook	2 RIEQ	68-74	1839
(widow of Matthew Allen who died 1834)				
		{Georgetown District}		
Allen, Eliza Ann	David Crossland	6 RIEQ	255-275	1839
(widow of Mathew Allen of Georgetown District,				
who died 1834) (to Florida)		{Georgetown}		
Allen, Janet	George Rumph	2 HILL	1-6	1805
(married 1805) (separated 1816/17) (widow of				
Josiah Allen who died about 1796) (she died 1828)				
		{Walterborough}		
Allen, Mary A.	Hasford Walker	6 RIEQ	255-275	1847
Elizabeth (married August 1847) (daughter of Mathew				
Allen of Georgetown District, who died 1834) (Walker				
died September 1851) {Georgetown and Marlboro Districts}				
Allen, Mary Ann	_____ Walker	3 RIEQ	23-33	1850
Elizabeth (daughter of Matthew Allen who died 1834,				
Georgetown District)		{Marlborough District}		
Allston, Rachel	H. C. Flagg	1 DESA	164	1789
(widow)				
Alston, Eliza	_____ White	4 DESA	94-102	1803
		{Georgetown)		
Alston, Sarah	John Izard	4 STRO	37-58	1849
(Sally)	Middleton	{Charleston}		
Anderson, _____	_____ Quarles	9 RIEQ	137-148	1842
(daughter of Allen Anderson, Sr. who died 1842)				
		{Edgefield}		
Anderson, Margaret	_____ Brooks	1 STRO	344-346	1844
S. (daughter of Silas Anderson who died March 1845)				
		{Marion}		
Anderson, Mary E.	_____ Brown	1 STRO	344-346	1844
(daughter of Silas Anderson who died March 1845)				
(she died about April 1845)		{Marion}		
Andrews, Mary	Andrew Hunter	2 HILL	483-492	1819
(marriage settlement 10 February 1819) {Darlington}				
Antheaume,	Jacques Magnus	1 RIEQ	187-221	1836
Madelaine Julie	Guillemot	{Paris, France}		
Ardis, _____	Miledge Galphin	2 McC	60-72	1827
		{Beech Island}		

S.C. Marriages 1749-1867 Implied in S.C. Equity Reports

WOMAN	MAN	VOLUME	PAGES	LIVED
Ardis, _____	Adam Hiles (he died 1785/86)	2 McC {Beech Island}	60-72	1786
Ardis, _____	Casper Naily, Jun.	2 McC {Beech Island}	60-72	1827
Ardis, Mary	_____ Simkins	2 McC {Beech Island}	60-72	1827
Arnett, Elizabeth (married 1817) (widow of John Arnett) {Williamsburg District}	William Camlin	4 STRO	189-203	1817
Arnett, Eliza Elmira (daughter of John Arnett) (she was born 23 March 1813) (he was born 1816) {Williamsburg District}	Samuel Brockington	4 STRO	189-203	1834
Arnett, Sarah M. (daughter of John Arnett) (she was born 13 October 1810) {Williamsburg District}	David Nesmitte	4 STRO	189-203	1834
Arthur, _____ (widow) (marriage settlement 28 December 1785)	Stephen Townsend	3 DESA	223-241	1785
Ash, _____	George Barksdale	1 DESA	603-605	1795
Ash, Ann (widow) (she died 1794)	_____ Berwick	1 DESA	603-605	1786
Ashby, _____ (married 1835) [Must see footnotes in 1917 Edition]	William McGrath	7 RIEQ {Union District}	430-449	1835
Ashby, Mary	_____ I'On	2 DESA	210-214	1802
Ashe, Eliza (daughter of John Ashe)	_____ Livingston	RICHEQ {Charleston}	380-384	1832
Ashe, Eliza Ann (daughter of Richard C. Ashe, Sr. who died 1837) [Must also see 5 RIEQ pages 5, 6] {Barnwell}	Lawrence P. Hext	2 STRO	250-258	1848
Ashe, Maria Louisa (daughter of Richard C. Ashe, Sr. who died 1837) {Barnwell}	Medicus Powell	2 STRO	250-258	1841
Ashe, Mary	Dr. James Fraser (he died 1803)	RILEY {Charleston}	271-282	1787
Ashe, Mary D. (daughter of Richard C. Ashe, Sr. who died 1837) {Barnwell}	Edward K. Garvin	2 STRO	250-258	1848
Ashe, Sarah (widow) (she died November 1801)	_____ Odingsell	RILEY {Charleston}	271-282	1798
Askew, Charlotte (daughter of Dr. _____ Askew who died 18 January 1841) {Union}	Henry Anderson	5 RIEQ	162-170	1852
Askew, Eunice (daughter of Dr. _____ Askew who died 18 January 1841) {Union}	Newton Anderson	5 RIEQ	162-170	1852

S.C. Marriages 1749-1867 Implied in S.C. Equity Reports

WOMAN	MAN	VOLUME PAGES	LIVED
Askew, Jemima	W. P. Anderson	5 RIEQ 162-170	1849
(daughter of Dr. _____ Askew who died 18 January 1841) {Union}			
Askew, Mary	W. B. Matheney	10 RIEQ 163-177	1858
(widow of Seth Askew)		{Barnwell}	
Askew, Rebecca E.	Irvine R. Hair	10 RIEQ 163-177	1853
(married 13 October 1853) (daughter of Seth Askew) {Barnwell}			
Askew, Sarah	W. T. Crenshaw	5 RIEQ 162-170	1852
(daughter of Dr. _____ Askew who died 18 January 1841) {Union}			
Atchison, Sarah	George W. Brown	2 HILL 542-548	1836
(widow of John Atchison who died April 1833) {Charleston}			

(B)

WOMAN	MAN	VOLUME PAGES	LIVED
Bache, Helena	Samuel Patterson	CHEVES 29-32	1836
(married 2 August 1836) (he died 1839)			
Badger, Delia Ann	Robert Harden	6 RIEQ 147-149	1842
(daughter of Nathaniel Badger who died 1842) {Barnwell}			
Bailey, _____	Andrew McDaniel	11 RIEQ 114-134	1846
		{Chester}	
Bailey, _____	Green B. Montgomery Jr.	11 RIEQ 114-134 {Chester}	1849
Bailey, Mary	_____ Eddings	1 DESA 355-359	1794
(widow of Henry Bailey)		{Beaufort District}	
Bailey, Sarah	William Reynolds	1 DESA 355-359	1784
(daughter of Henry Bailey) (she died 1789) {Beaufort District}			
Baird, Winifred	John Wilson	1 DESA 219-237	1781
(marriage bonds 8 May 1781, 2 June 1781) (widow of Archibald Baird who died 1777)			
Baker, _____	_____ Toomer	1 STRO 129-169	1846
(sister of Robert L. Baker)		{Colleton and Beaufort Districts}	
Baker, Rhoda	Henry Gardner	1 RIEQ 392-395	1839
(married 1839) (widow of William Baker who died 1837) {Lancaster}			
Ball, Ann	E. H. Deas	2 STRO 24-27 {Charleston}	1845
Ball, Ann	John Hunt	1 DESA 137-142	1769
Ball, Beulah	_____ Sealy	1 DESA 137-142	1775
(widow of Samuel Ball)			
Ball, Caroline	_____ Laurens	SPEERS 48-87	1843
Ball, Eliza Lucila	_____ Simons	SPEERS 48-87	1843

S.C. Marriages 1749-1867 Implied in S.C. Equity Reports

WOMAN	MAN	VOLUME	PAGES	LIVED
Ball, Lydia Catharine	Thomas Waring	SPEERS	48-87	1843
Ball, Lydia Jane (she died 1840)	____ Waring	2 STRO {Charleston}	24-27	1839
Ball, Martha Caroline (widow of John Ball, Sen. who died 29 June 1822)	Augustus Taveau	1 McC	7-17	1825
Ball, Martha Caroline (widow) [See also pages 518-532] [See also 1 RIEQ pages 361-386; 419-426]	Augustus Taveau	SPEERS	48-87	1843
Ball, Susan E. (or S.)	William E. Haskell	SPEERS	48-87	1843
Ballard, ____ (daughter of Thomas Ballard, Senr.)	Samuel Caston	RICE {Kershaw District}	13-17	1821
Ballentine, Jane (daughter of Dougal Ballentine)	Patrick Harbeson	2 McC {Chester District}	112-118	1827
Barber, Martha (daughter of John M. Barber)	William Jackson	5 RIEQ {Chester}	38-55	1849
Barclay, Catharine S. (widow) [See also pages 518-532] [See also 1 RIEQ pages 361-389; 419-426]	Albert Sumner	SPEERS	48-87	1843
Barkley, Catharine (daughter of Robert Barkley)	____ Beard	SPEERS {Lancaster}	264-268	1842
Barkley, Eliza Ann (she died 17 March 1866) (he of Winnsboro) {Charleston District}	O. R. Thompson	14 RIEQ	12-26	1864
Barksdale, Adelaide (daughter of Thomas Barksdale, Jr.)	C. C. Huguenin	7 RIEQ {Charleston}	125-135	1854
Barksdale, Eliza	____ Edwards	2 HILL {Coosawhatchie}	184-200	1798
Barksdale, Elizabeth (daughter of Thomas Barksdale) {Charleston}	____ Edwards	3 RIEQ	271-281	1850
Barksdale, Elizabeth (daughter of Thomas Barksdale, Sr.)	____ Edwards	7 RIEQ {Charleston}	125-135	1854
Barksdale, Emma Julia (daughter of Thomas Barksdale, Jr.) {Charleston}	George Edwards	7 RIEQ	125-135	1854
Barksdale, Martha (married October 1812) (daughter of Joseph Barksdale)	B. T. Saxon	4 DESA {Abbeville}	522-529	1812
Barksdale, Mary (daughter of Thomas Barksdale, Jr.)	James Macbeth	7 RIEQ {Charleston}	125-135	1854
Barksdale, Mary (daughter of George Barksdale) (she died 30 November 1843) (Mathews died 22 July 1848)	William Mathews	4 STRO {Charleston}	1-25	1793
Barksdale, Sabina (daughter of Thomas Barksdale)	____ Payne	3 RIEQ {Charleston}	271-281	1850

S.C. Marriages 1749-1867 Implied in S.C. Equity Reports

WOMAN	MAN	VOLUME PAGES	LIVED
Barksdale, Sarah	Charles Dewar Simons (he died 21 January 1812) (marriage settlement 25 September 1807) (daughter of Thomas Barksdale)	3 RIEQ 271-281 {Charleston}	1807
Barksdale, Sarina	_____ Bonneau (daughter of Thomas Barksdale, Sr.)	7 RIEQ 125-135 {Charleston}	1800
Barnett, _____	Allen Lancaster (daughter of Jorial Barnett)	6 RIEQ 111-114 {Spartanburg}	1853
Barnett, _____	William Seay (daughter of Jorial Barnett)	6 RIEQ 111-114 {Spartanburg}	1853
Barns, Elizabeth (widow)	William Robertson	4 STRO 179-186 {Edgefield}	1831
Barns, Frances	_____ Tally	4 STRO 179-186 {Edgefield}	1849
Barnwell, E. C.	_____ Deveaux (daughter of J. J. Barnwell)	1 DESA 497-500	1795
Barnwell, Jane H.	Captain Prentiss Willard (he died 1812) (married 1812) (daughter of John Berners Barnwell)	RICE 198-242 {Beaufort District}	1812
Barsh, Catherine M.	Abner Lewis Hammond (marriage settlement 19 November 1834) (she of Columbia)	10 RIEQ 149-156 {Orangeburg}	1834
Baynard, Elizabeth (widow of William Baynard)	Mungo Mackie	2 DESA 342-361	1805
Beale, _____	_____ Bull (daughter of Othniel Beale)	3 DESA 22-25 {Charleston District}	1809
Beale, Catherine	John Stapleton (daughter of John Beale)	3 DESA 22-25 {Charleston District}	1809
Beale, Mary Hannah	Thomas C. Vanderhorst (daughter of John Beale)	3 DESA 22-25	1809
Beard, _____	George R. Allen	SPEERS 264-268 {Lancaster}	1842
Beasley, Jane	_____ Williams (daughter of Thomas Beasley)	1 HILL 112-113	1833
Beaty, Margaret (Peggy) (daughter of James Beaty)	Thomas Ketchin	5 RIEQ 83-90 {Fairfield}	1852
Beaty, Nancy	_____ Cathcart (daughter of James Beaty)	5 RIEQ 83-90 {Fairfield}	1852
Beazley, _____	Peter H. Larey (daughter of W. B. Beazley) (she was born 1838)	9 RIEQ 119-128 {Barnwell}	1856
Bee, Mary R. (widow)	_____ McCord	5 RIEQ 370-403 {St. Matthew's Parish}	1820
Bee, Rachel Susan	John R. Cheves	5 RIEQ 370-403 {St. Matthew's Parish}	1843

S.C. Marriages 1749-1867 Implied in S.C. Equity Reports

WOMAN	MAN	VOLUME PAGES	LIVED

Bell, _____ William Bell   9 RIEQ 42-45   1856
  (daughter of Thomas Bell)   {Fairfield}
Bell, _____ William M. Martin 9 RIEQ 42-45   1854
  (daughter of Thomas Bell)   {Fairfield}
Bell, Elizabeth   John Talbird   RICHEQ 361-369   1795
  (daughter of Thomas Bell who died 7 September 1795)
  (Talbird's first marriage)   {Beaufort}
Bell, Elizabeth   John Talbird   1 DESA 592-595   1799
  (married 10 May 1799) (daughter of Thomas Bell
  who died 7 September 1795)
Bell, Elizabeth   John Talbird   BAILEY 535-566   1801
  (married 1801) (daughter of Thomas Bell who died 1795)
  (she died 1819)   {Beaufort District}
Bell, Mary   _____ Palmer RICHEQ 361-369   1795
  (daughter of Thomas Bell who died 7 September 1795)
  (her first marriage)   {Beaufort}
Bell, Mary   William Palmer 1 HILL 142-145   1817
  (her first marriage) (he died November 1817)
                                 {Coosawhatchie}
Bennett, _____ _____ Vidal SPEERS 402-412   1844
  (sister of Peter Bennett of Wadmalaw Island) {Charleston}
Benson, Esther   Seth Dyches   2 STRO 343-379   1829
  (daughter of Moses Duke of Barnwell District)
  [See also pages 353-358, in footnotes in 1917 Edition]
Benson, Mary   John Bruce   4 DESA 463-465   1814
  (widow of Joshua Benson)
Berry, _____ Edward D. Winslow 1 RIEQ 114-122   1809
  (widow) (marriage settlement May 1809) {Charleston}
Berwick, Ann Eliza Thomas Legare 1 DESA 603-605   1794
Billings, _____ Benjamin Trapp 2 McC 403-405   1827
Birch, Dorcas   _____ Bergamy McMULL 279-289   1839
  (widow of Michael Birch) (to Alabama) {Sumter}
Bird, _____ Edmund Herrin   11 RIEQ 536-540   1860
  (daughter of Arthur Bird who died 1835) {Marion District}
Bird, _____ Phillip Owens   11 RIEQ 536-540   1860
  (daughter of Peter Bird)   {Marion District}
Bird, Ann   John Blackman, Jr. 11 RIEQ 536-540   1849
  (daughter of Arthur Bird who died 1835) {Marion District}
Bird, Ansy   Finklea G. Wise 11 RIEQ 536-540   1860
  (daughter of Peter Bird) (she was born about 1832)
                                 {Marion District}
Bird, Maria   Wilson Herrin 11 RIEQ 536-540   1849
  (daughter of Arthur Bird who died 1835) {Marion District}
Bird, Mary   _____ Owens 11 RIEQ 536-540   1849
  (daughter of Arthur Bird who died 1835) {Marion District}
Bird. See Byrd

108

S.C. Marriages 1749-1867 Implied in S.C. Equity Reports

WOMAN	MAN	VOLUME PAGES	LIVED

Black, Rachel   Richard Fryer   RICHEQ 85-109   1831
   (married 1794/95 or common-law marriage) (common-law
   wife of William Black) (she died 29 April 1831)
   (Fryer died 1821)   {Spartanburg}
Blackburne, _____   B. W. Capehart   1 HILL 405-412   1832
   (daughter of William Blackburne)   {Abbeville}
Blackburne, Lydia   John Huey   1 HILL 405-412   1830
   (widow of William Blackburne) (Huey died 1830)
                                            {Abbeville}
Blake, Sarah B.   _____ Purcell   RILEY   282-284   1795
   (daughter of Edward Blake) (she died 1834)
Blakely, Ellen   George A. Huggins   9 RIEQ 408-410   1857
                                            {Sumter}
Blankton, Lovey   _____ Salisbury   6 RIEQ 388-398   1850
            {Goose Creek Parish and Charleston District}
   [Referred to in another case in footnotes of 1917 Edition]
Blewer, _____   James B. Coleman   2 STRO 285-289   1843
   (widow of John G. Blewer)   {Lexington}
Blewer, _____   Robert Hankinson   2 STRO 285-289   1842
   (daughter of John G. Blewer)   {Lexington}
Blewer, _____   Robert Haukison   10 RIEQ 191-201   1842
   (daughter of John G. Blewer) (Hankison) {Lexington}
Blewer, _____   Peter Redheimer   10 RIEQ 191-201   1842
   (daughter of John G. Blewer)   {Lexington}
Blewer, _____   Peter Redheimer   2 STRO 285-289   1842
   (daughter of John G. Blewer)   {Lexington}
Blewer, Elizabeth   James B. Coleman   10 RIEQ 191-201   1838
   M. (marriage settlement 29 August 1838) (widow of
   John G. Blewer) (Coleman widower)   {Lexington}
Blount, Elizabeth   Thomas E. Searson   8 RIEQ 130-135   1844
   M. (daughter of Stephen W. Blount of Georgia) {Beaufort}
Boak, _____   Major Samuel Wise   4 DESA 330-350   1812
                                            {Richland District}
Bobo, _____   Robert Martin   McMULL 304-310   1840
   (daughter of Barron Bobo)
Bobo, _____   John J. Murril   McMULL 304-310   1840
   (daughter of Barron Bobo)
Bocket, Floride   _____ Peyre   2 DESA 221-226   1793
   (Boquet) [Must also see pages 210-214; 419-422]
Bocket, Magdalene   John Ashby   2 DESA 221-226   1793
   (Boquet) (she died 1801/02) (he died 1793)
   [See also pages 210-214; 419-422]
Bona, _____   George Barksdale   2 HILL 184-200   1798
                                            {Coosawhatchie}
Bond, Epsiby   John Bates   1 STRO 1-26   1836
   (daughter of John P. Bond, Sr. of Lexington District,
   who died 1823) (in Lexington County) {Edgefield}

S.C. Marriages 1749-1867 Implied in S.C. Equity Reports

WOMAN	MAN	VOLUME PAGES	LIVED

Bond, Hepsebah   John Bates   DUDLEY 71-84   1837
   (daughter of John P. Bond of Lexington District,
   who died September 1823)   {Edgefield}
Bond, Lucinda   Jonathan Hill   3 STRO 94-105   1844
   (she died 7 October 1847) (he went to Texas) {Edgefield}
Bond, Lucinda   Jonathan M. Hill   1 STRO 1-26   1834
   (daughter of John P. Bond, Sr. of Lexington District,
   who died 1823) (in Alabama 1834)   {Edgefield}
Bond, Lucinda   Jonathan M. Hill   DUDLEY 71-84   1837
   (daughter of John P. Bond of Lexington District,
   who died September 1823)   {Edgefield}
Bond, Martha   Henry H. Hill   1 STRO 1-26   1836
   (daughter of John P. Bond, Sr. of Lexington District,
   who died 1823)   {Edgefield}
Bond, Martha   Henry H. Hill   DUDLEY 71-84   1837
   (daughter of John P. Bond of Lexington District,
   who died September 1823)   {Edgefield}
Bond, Matilda   ____ Daniel   1 STRO 1-26   1836
   (daughter of John P. Bond, Sr. of Lexington District,
   who died 1823)   {Edgefield}
Bonds, Ann   Joseph H. Hoell   4 DESA 21-26   1809
   (widow of William Bonds who died 1804) {Camden}
Bonneau, Sabina   John W. Payne   RILEY   174-179   1815
   (widow) (separated) (he died 6 October 1826) [Must also
   see DUDLEY pages 124-128]   {Charleston}
Bonneau, Sarina   John W. Payne   7 RIEQ 125-135   1854
   (widow)   {Charleston}
Booker, Martha   George W. Hopkins   1 HILL 1-10   1799
   (daughter of Bird Booker) (Hopkins died 1805)
Bookter, Judith   Judah Barret   4 DESA 447-458   1806
   (marriage settlement 19 November 1806) (widow of
   Jacob Bookter)
Boone, Maria   George Fraser   3 DESA 88-89   1810
   (daughter of John Boone)   {Charleston District}
Bostick, Eliza A. Daniel W. McKenzie 1 STRO 393-420   1821
   (married February 1821) (he died 1826) {Gillisonville}
Boulware, Catharine William G. Raines 4 RIEQ 399-408   1828
                                      {Fairfield}
Boulware, Sarah   Dr. H. H. Paulling 4 RIEQ 317-322   1845
   (married 1845) (daughter of Thomas Boulware who
   died 1842) (Paulling died April 1849) {Fairfield}
Boulware. See Bowler
Bowers, Elizabeth ____ Graham   10 RIEQ 551-556   1835
   Jemima   {Lancaster}
Bowers, Elizabeth ____ Robertson   10 RIEQ 551-556   1835
   Jemima (widow of Edward Bowers)   {Lancaster}

S.C. Marriages 1749-1867 Implied in S.C. Equity Reports

WOMAN	MAN	VOLUME PAGES	LIVED
Bowers, Jemima	_____ Turner	10 RIEQ 551-556 {Lancaster}	1857
Bowler, Sarah	John Hunter	HARPER 69-71	1824

(daughter of J. H. Bowler who died 1804)

Bowman, Barbara	_____ Shuler	14 RIEQ 271-279	1826
(daughter of George Bowman)		{Orangeburg}	
Bowman, Catharine	_____ Crum	14 RIEQ 271-279	1826
(daughter of George Bowman)		{Orangeburg}	
Bowman, Clarissa	_____ Scott	14 RIEQ 271-279	1826
(daughter of George Bowman)		{Orangeburg}	
Bowman, Margaret	_____ Felder	14 RIEQ 271-279	1826
(daughter of George Bowman)		{Orangeburg}	
Bowman, Sarah	John Dinkins	RICHEQ 185-191	1820

(married June/July 1820) (he died 1825) {Sumter}

Box, _____	Edward Bingley	1 McC 333-352 {Charleston District}	1815
Boyd, Malinda	John Keith	7 RIEQ 509-520	1838

(married 10/12 October 1838) (widow of Samuel Boyd)
(Keith died 7 November 1842) {Fairfield}

Boyd, Nancy	Joseph Cummings	7 RIEQ 509-520	1851
(daughter of Samuel Boyd)		{Fairfield}	
Boyer, _____	John Schroder	BAILEY 334-342	1817

(daughter of Jacob H. Boyer who died 1817) {Charleston}

Boyer, _____	_____ Wirtemburgh	BAILEY 334-342	1817

(daughter of Jacob H. Boyer who died 1817) {Charleston}

Boyle, Rosa Sarah D.	Wade Hampton Schultz	SPEERS 533-544 {Colleton District}	1834

(daughter of John Boyle, Sr. of St. Paul's Parish, who died 1827) [See also 1 RIEQ pages 280-282]

Bradley, Cecilia A.	Isaac McKnight	10 RIEQ 157-162	1853

(marriage settlement 18 December 1853)
(daughter of Dr. _____ Bradley) {Williamsburg}

Bradley, Jane J.	A. Isaac McKnight	10 RIEQ 557-572	1854

(daughter of Dr. James Bradley) {Williamsburg District}

Brailsford, _____	_____ M'Leod	2 HILL 277-298	1835

(daughter of Robert Brailsford)

Brailsford, Julia M.	Wm. L. Felder	McMULL 55-62 {Sumter District}	1840
Branford, Ann	Thomas Horry	2 DESA 115-127	1771

(married 1771) (daughter of William Branford)

Branford, Elizabeth	Elias Horry	2 DESA 115-127	1770

(married 1770) (daughter of William Branford)
(she died 1785) (Horry died 11 February 1785)

Bratton, _____	_____ Gracey	9 RIEQ 376-391	1857

(daughter of Dr. William Bratton of Winnsboro, who
died 1 December 1850) (Gracey of Columbia) {Fairfield}

S.C. Marriages 1749-1867 Implied in S.C. Equity Reports

WOMAN	MAN	VOLUME	PAGES	LIVED

Bratton, Christina　Clement C. Faust　9 RIEQ　294-302　1837
　W. (married 12 April 1837) (divorced October 1852,
　Georgia) (daughter of Dr. William Bratton of
　Winnsboro, who died 1 December 1850) {Fairfield}
　[See also pages 376-391]
Brazilman, _____　Wm. Turpin, Jr.　3 STRO　149-158　1828
　　　　　　　　　　　　　　　　　　　　　{Newberry}
Brazilman, Mary　Rev. Benjamin S.　3 STRO　149-158　1828
　Louisa Graff　Ogletree
　(she died 1834) (his first marriage) {Newberry}
Breeland, _____　Richard Dawson　RICE　243-274　1820
　　　　　　　　(his second marriage)
　　　　　　　　　　　　　　　　　{Beaufort District}
Brewton. See Bruton
Brice, Elizabeth　_____ Stevenson　4 RIEQ　322-329　1837
　(married about 1837) (daughter of William Brice, Sen.
　who died May 1849)　　　　　　　　{Fairfield}
Brice, Jane　John Douglass　4 RIEQ　322-329　1818
　(married about 1818) (daughter of William Brice, Sen.
　who died May 1849)　　　　　　　　{Fairfield}
Bride, Elizabeth　_____ King　1 McC　399-406　1826
　(widow)
Brisbane, Sarah　Alexander Gillon　1 McC　148-155　1821
Britton, Sarah Jane　Wesley W. Brunson　8 RIEQ　271-285　1856
　(daughter of Henry Britton who died 20 July 1842)
　(she was born 1830)　　　　　　　　{Sumter}
Brooks, Nancy　Barkley M. Blocker　2 STRO　113-134　1828
　(daughter of Col. Z. S. Brooks)　　{Edgefield}
Brown, _____　_____ Dunn　1 DESA　196-201　1789
　(sister of Cornelius Brown)　　　　{England}
Brown, _____　William White　2 RIEQ　99-114　1845
　(daughter of Frederick Brown) (in Lincoln County,
　Georgia)　　　　　　　　　　　　　{Abbeville}
Brown, Almedia　_____ Harley　3 RIEQ　379-384　1845
　(daughter of Colonel Tarlton Brown who died
　September 1845)　　　　　　　　　　{Barnwell}
Brown, Cynthia W.　James Y. Calhoun　6 RIEQ　155-182　1821
　(daughter of Bartlett Brown who died November 1822)
　　　　　　　　　　　　　　　　　　　{Barnwell}
Brown, Mary　Aaron Loocock　1 DESA　471-480　1791
Brown, Mary A. R.　_____ Lowry　4 RIEQ　262-266　1851
　(widow of William Brown who died 1815) {Colleton}
Brown, Sarah　William Wightman　1 DESA　166　1787
Brown, Susan　_____ Hay　4 RIEQ　378-389　1852
　Cynthia (daughter of Charles J. Brown)

S.C. Marriages 1749-1867 Implied in S.C. Equity Reports

WOMAN	MAN	VOLUME	PAGES	LIVED

Brown, Susan   Col. Frederick J.   3 RIEQ   384-397   1849
  Cynthia   Hay (he died 10 August 1849)
  (daughter of Charles J. Brown)   {Barnwell District}
Broxson, Henrietta Wm. Booth   2 STRO   31-34   1846
  (married 8 October 1846) (daughter of Henry Broxson
  of Colleton District)   {Walterborough}
Broxson, Rebecca   Jesse S. Sineath   2 STRO   31-34   1832
  (married 1832/33) (widow of Henry Broxson of
  Colleton District)   {Walterborough}
Brummet, Comfort   Zadock Perry   2 HILL   638-644   1792
  (daughter of William Brummet)   {Lancaster}
Brummet, Elizabeth John Lewis   1 RIEQ   1-25   1816
  C. (daughter of Daniel Brummet who died 1816)
  (Lewis died 1822)   {Union}
Bruton, _____   Charles DeWitt   2 HILL   367-371   1835
  (widow of George Bruton)   {Barnwell}
Bruton, Elizabeth   Jacob R. Harley   2 HILL   367-371   1835
  (daughter of George Bruton)   {Barnwell}
Bryan, Eliza L.   Nicholas H.   DUDLEY   201-212   1831
  (widow)   Rutledge (he died 1835)
  (marriage settlement 1831)   {Charleston}
Bryson, _____   George Nichols   2 HILL   113-121   1835
                                       {Laurens}
Buist, Mary S.   James Lamb   4 STRO   37-58   1845
  (daughter of Rev. George Buist)   {Charleston}
Buist, Mary S.   Jas. Lamb   4 RIEQ   416-420   1852
  [In footnotes of 1917 Edition]
Bullein, Susannah   _____ Keith   1 DESA   353-355   1794
Burgess, Eliza Ann James L. Mouzon   13 RIEQ 142-164   1850
  (married 10 December 1850) (widow of James A.
  Burgess) (Mouzon died 9 December 1855) {Williamsburg}
Burke, Catharine R. John Kerr   McMULL   475-484   1831
  (daughter of Dr. Michael Burke) (in Georgia) {Fairfield}
Burke, Elizabeth   Thomas T. Holt   McMULL   475-484   1831
  Ellen (daughter of Dr. Michael Burke) (in Georgia)
                                       {Fairfield}
Burton, Phebe   William Ragan   RICHEQ   146-164   1812
  (daughter of William Burton who died April 1826)
                                       {Newberry}
Burton, Scythia   Daniel Towles   RICHEQ   146-164   1812
  (daughter of William Burton who died April 1826) (she
  died about 1825) (Towles died December 1829) {Newberry}
Butler, Elizabeth   Duncan Hill   2 DESA   279-285   1785
  (marriage settlement 3 December 1785)
Butler, Mary   _____ Savage   2 McC   435-440   1778
  Elliott

S.C. Marriages 1749-1867 Implied in S.C. Equity Reports

WOMAN	MAN	VOLUME PAGES	LIVED
Buzzard, Nancy	Tarlton Murphy	3 RIEQ 20-23 {Newberry}	1828
Byers, Elizabeth (married 8 May 1801) (daughter of William Byers) (she was born 1783/84) (she died 8 June 1802)	Charles M. Picton	2 DESA 592-602 {Charleston}	1801
Byrd, Elizabeth (daughter of Joseph Byrd) (to Tennessee) {Lancaster}	Abner Buckalew	6 RIEQ 129-137	1844
Byrd, Sarah (daughter of Joseph Byrd)	John B. Fry	6 RIEQ 129-137 {Lancaster}	1845
Byrd. See Bird			

(C)

Cabeen, Mary (daughter of Thomas Cabeen) (to Alabama) {Chester}	Amos Tims	1 HILL 51-59	1833
Cabeen, Nancy (daughter of Thomas Cabeen)	_____ Hill	1 HILL 51-59 {Chester}	1833
Cain, Catharine (widow) (married 12 January 1797)	George Caborne	3 DESA 514-528	1797
Calder, _____	Ephraim Mikell	2 DESA 342-361	1805
Caldwell, _____	Dr. Joseph Chapman	11 RIEQ 73-82 {Newberry}	1848
Caldwell, _____ (daughter of John M. Caldwell of Orangeburgh, who died June 1824)	_____ Footman	BAILEY 397-411 {Charleston}	1824
Caldwell, Harriet	_____ Reid	11 RIEQ 73-82 {Newberry}	1848
Caldwell, Mary Ann	_____ Glenn	11 RIEQ 73-82 {Newberry}	1848
Calhoun, Cynthia W. (widow)	_____ Nobles	6 RIEQ 155-182 {Barnwell}	1853
Calhoun, Mary L. (married 1835) (daughter of Downes Calhoun) (she died October 1838)	W. B. Beazley	9 RIEQ 119-128 {Barnwell}	1835
Caloff, Susan	_____ Sifly	HARPER 3-5	1824
Campbell, _____ (daughter of Dr. Robert Campbell of Laurens District)	Dr. Edward G. Simpson	5 RIEQ 405-421 {Abbeville District}	1848
Campbell, E. B.	Wm. Harrison	9 RIEQ 376-391 {Fairfield}	1857
Campbell, Elizabeth E. (she was born 1804)	William M'Cants, Jun.	1 McC 383-394	1826

114

S.C. Marriages 1749-1867 Implied in S.C. Equity Reports

WOMAN	MAN	VOLUME	PAGES	LIVED
Campbell, Sarah	_____ Cunningham	5 RIEQ	405-421	1851
(she was born about 1779) (she died 28 April 1851)				
		{Abbeville District}		
Campbell, Sarah	George Jones	2 DESA	380-388	1796
		{Pendleton District}		
Canady, _____	William Buckhalter	6 RIEQ	103-110	1851
		{Barnwell}		
Canady, Vashti	_____ Cook	6 RIEQ	103-110	1853
(daughter of John Canady)		{Barnwell}		
Cannon, _____	William Doughty	2 STRO	101-104	1784
(daughter of Daniel Cannon)		{Charleston}		
Cannon, _____	John Lloyd	2 DESA	232-233	1804
(orphan raised by Daniel Cannon)				
Cannon, Emily	Edward G. Thomas	BAILEY	222	1830
		{Georgetown}		
Cannon, Harriet	Abraham (Abram) Duke	10 RIEQ	380-388	1834
(daughter of Russell Cannon who died 1824)				
		{Pendleton and Pickens Districts}		
Canter, Charlotte	Abram Sasportas	10 RIEQ	38-52	1826
(married about 16 September 1778, Charleston)				
(she died 1851, Bordeaux, France) (he died 1823, France)		{Charleston District}		
Cantey, Margaret	James Sinkler	2 DESA	127-140	1791
(daughter of Charles Cantey who died 10 October 1780)				
Cantey, Sarah	James Sinkler	2 DESA	127-140	1780
(daughter of Charles Cantey who died 10 October 1780)				
Carn, Elizabeth	Christian Rhode	2 HILL	41-45	1831
(daughter of Frederick Carn)		{Orangeburgh}		
Carne, Catharine	Barnaby Coffie	RICHEQ	294-301	1793
(widow) (marriage settlement 15 June 1793) (she died 1805) (he died 1830)		{Charleston}		
Carnes, Jane	_____ White	4 DESA	405-421	1812
		{Camden}		
Carr, Eliz.	_____ Dawson	2 STRO	105-111	1825
(widow of John Carr)		{Walterborough}		
Carr, Emeline M. E.	Thomas Pye	2 STRO	105-111	1844
(married November 1844) (daughter of Dr. William Carr of St. George Dorchester) (she was born 1825)				
		{Walterborough}		
Carr, Susan	Charles J. Brown	1 STRO	363-370	1847
		{Barnwell}		
Carroll, Jane	John Gallagher	5 RIEQ	170-185	1819
(daughter of Thomas Carroll) (she died March 1832)				
(Gallagher died 6 March 1825)		{York}		

S.C. Marriages 1749-1867 Implied in S.C. Equity Reports

WOMAN	MAN	VOLUME PAGES	LIVED
Carson, Julia A. (married 2 December 1838) (she was born 24 January 1823) (he was born 10 May 1819)	William R. Bull	3 STRO 86-93 {Orangeburgh}	1838
Carson, Juliana (daughter of James Carson who died 1826) {Orangeburg}	Wm R. Bull	8 RIEQ 259-270	1856
Carson, Mary (widow of James Carson)	____ Winningham	3 STRO 86-93 {Orangeburgh}	1840
Cash, Elizabeth E. (married 1835) (widow)	James Ellerbe	SPEERS 328-342 {Cheraw}	1835
Cason, Cynthia (married 28 December 1849) (daughter of William Cason) (she was born 6 March 1829)	James Long	4 RIEQ 60-70 {Anderson}	1849
Caston, ____	James F. Secrest	2 RIEQ 54-56 {Lancaster}	1843
Caston, Elizabeth G. (daughter of Samuel Caston who died May 1831)	____ Williams	2 RIEQ 1-3 {Lancaster}	1845
Cates, Dorothy (daughter of Aaron Cates)	____ Wadlington	HARPER 224-242	1816
Cates, Dorothy	____ Wadlington	1 McC 252-267 {Newberry District}	1824
Cates, Dorothy Ann	Jefferson L. Edmonds	1 McC 252-267 {Newberry District}	1824
Cattell, ____ (widow of William Cattell)	____ Brown	1 DESA 112-113	1784
Cave, Dorcas (daughter of David Cave who died October 1834) {Barnwell}	____ Kirkland	6 RIEQ 43-57	1834
Cave, Elizabeth (daughter of David Cave who died October 1834) {Barnwell}	____ Nix	6 RIEQ 43-57	1834
Cave, Martha (married 6 December 1838) (daughter of David Cave who died October 1834) (she was born about 1802) (she died 29 June 1851)	Robert Bradley	6 RIEQ 43-57 {Barnwell}	1838
Champion, Mary (daughter of Jacob Champion)	James Bailey	3 RIEQ 156-159 {Kershaw}	1826
Chandler, Mary	____ Marshall	RICE 373-388 {Charleston District}	1825
Channing, Ann Elizabeth (married 8 March 1827, Boston) (daughter of Walter Channing of Boston) (Ball was born 18 October 1808) (Ball and wife died 14 June 1838) [See also pages 518-532] [See also 1 RIEQ pages 361-389; 419-426]	Hugh Swinton Ball	SPEERS 48-87	1827
Channing, Catharine S. (daughter of Walter Channing of Boston)	____ Barclay	SPEERS 48-87	1843
Channing, Mary Ann (daughter of Walter Channing of Boston) [See also pages 518-531] [See also 1 RIEQ pages 361-389; 419-426]	Ferris Pell	SPEERS 48-87	1843

S.C. Marriages 1749-1867 Implied in S.C. Equity Reports

WOMAN	MAN	VOLUME PAGES	LIVED
Chaplin, Ann	___ Adams	1 HILL 265-284	1776

(daughter of Benjamin Chaplin of St. Helena's Parish)

Chaplin, Isabella (widow)	Robert L. Baker	3 RIEQ 208-218 {Beaufort District}	1844
Chaplin, Isabella C. (widow)	___ Fields	1 STRO 129-169 {Colleton and Beaufort Districts}	1843
Cheves, Anna	T. Pinckney Huger	10 RIEQ 534-550	1854

(daughter of Hon. Langdon Cheves who died 27 June 1857)

Cheves, Louisa	David J. McCord	10 RIEQ 534-550	1854

(daughter of Hon. Langdon Cheves who died 27 June 1857)

Cheves, Sophia	Charles T. Haskell	10 RIEQ 534-550	1854

(daughter of Hon. Langdon Cheves who died 27 June 1857)

Chick, Caroline T.	___ Hodges	10 RIEQ 178-190	1846

(daughter of Burwill Chick of Greenville, who died 1847)
{Greenville, Newberry and Union Districts}

Chick, Louisa V.	___ Farr	10 RIEQ 178-190	1846

(daughter of Burwill Chick of Greenville, who died 1847)
{Greenville, Newberry and Union Districts}

Chick, Maria H.	___ Thompson	10 RIEQ 178-190	1846

(daughter of Burwill Chick of Greenville, who died 1847)
{Greenville, Newberry and Union Districts}

Chick, Wilhelmina	___ Chaplin	10 RIEQ 178-190	1846

(daughter of Burwill Chick of Greenville, who died 1847)
{Greenville, Newberry and Union Districts}

China, Harriet A.	David M. Mason	5 RIEQ 426-434 {Williamsburg}	1852

(daughter of Thomas China)

China, Magdaline	Peter R. Keals	5 RIEQ 426-434 {Williamsburg}	1852

(daughter of Thomas China)

Chitty, Ann Eugenia	Henry W. Schroeder	McMULL 422-430	1841

(daughter of Charles C. Chitty) {Charleston}

Clark, Elizabeth Mary	John Hanahan	CHEVES 129-142 {Charleston}	1839

(widow of William M. Clark) [See also pages 80-93]

Clarke, Elizabeth	John Hannahan	3 RIEQ 318-341 {Charleston}	1839

(widow of William M. Clarke)

Clarke, Elizabeth Grimball	___ Jenkins	3 RIEQ 318-341 {Charleston}	1830
Clarke, Elizabeth Jenkins	___ Hanckel	3 RIEQ 318-341	1841

(daughter of William M. Clarke) {Charleston}

Clarke, Lydia Calon Millivan Murray		3 RIEQ 318-341 {Charleston}	1830
Clarke, Martha Mary Murray	Wm. J. Whaley	3 RIEQ 318-341	1841

(daughter of William M. Clarke) {Charleston}

Clarkson, ___	___ Johnson	3 RIEQ 305-318	1850

(sister of John Clarkson)

Clausen, Elizabeth	___ Brandis	RILEY 117-120	1819

(she died 10 February 1819, Hildeshein, Germany)

S.C. Marriages 1749-1867 Implied in S.C. Equity Reports

WOMAN	MAN	VOLUME	PAGES	LIVED

Clausen, Margaret ____ Frautz RILEY 117-120 1822
   Theresa (she died 17 December 1826, Halberstadt, Germany)
Clausen, Maria ____ Retmeyer RILEY 117-120 1822
   Agnes (she died 18 August 1826, Paderborn, Prussia)
Clayton, Rebecca J. George P. Smith 1 HILL 101-106 1813
   (marriage settlement 6 April 1813) (his first marriage)
                                                           {Barnwell District}
Clegg, Lydia Paul Micheau 3 RIEQ 465-542 1795
                                                           {Georgetown}
Clegg, Lydia Paul Micheau RILEY 88-96 1795
                                                           {Georgetown}
Cleland, Ann Captain M. S. Howe 4 RIEQ 254-260 1849
   Timothy   {Charleston}
Clements, Mary Olley Mattison 1 STRO 377-385 1840
   (married 1840)   {Anderson}
Clendinen, Mary ____ Hemingway 2 RIEQ 321-354 1835
   (widow)   {Richland and Union}
Clifton, Mary James McClure BAILEY 107-112 1827
   (widow of James Clifton)   {Chester}
Clifton, Susannah William Miller BAILEY 107-112 1827
   (daughter of James Clifton)   {Chester}
Cloud, Margaret W. William L. Calhoun 10 RIEQ 358-376 1853
   (married 5 January 1853) (daughter of William Cloud
   of Chester) (she died 9 April 1855) (Calhoun of
   Abbeville) (his first marriage) {Abbeville}
Coachman, Ann Patrick Donnelly 1 STRO 81-84 1818
   Waties (daughter of James Coachman of Prince
   George Winyah) (she died August 1844)
Coachman, Hannah ____ Postell 1 STRO 81-83 1789
   (daughter of James Coachman of Prince George Winyah)
Coate, ____ John N. Lindsey 2 McC 16-22 1827
   (daughter of Henry Coate)
Coburn, ____ ____ Wood RILEY 187-193 1830
   (daughter of John Coburn)
Cochran, ____ Archibald Douglas 4 DESA 143-145 1810
                                                           {Ninety-Six District}
Cochran, Phebe ____ Hearst 4 DESA 143-145 1810
   (widow)   {Ninety-Six District}
Cogdell, ____ ____ Barnup 3 DESA 346-393 1807
   (sister of John Cogdell)
Cogdell, ____ ____ Egerton 3 DESA 346-393 1807
   (sister of John Cogdell) (Eagerton)
Cogdell, Elizabeth ____ Potts 1 DESA 454-458 1795
   (Eliza) (daughter of George Cogdell)
Cogdell, Mary R. Johnston 1 DESA 454-458 1795
   (daughter of George Cogdell) (Johnson)

S.C. Marriages 1749-1867 Implied in S.C. Equity Reports

WOMAN	MAN	VOLUME PAGES	LIVED
Cohen, Dinah	____ Minis	4 DESA 215-226 {Georgetown}	1812
Coiel, ____ (widow of Alston Coiel)	____ Terry	2 HILL 108-111 {Lancaster}	1834
Colburn, Susan C. (daughter of James B. Colburn)	Parker J. Holland	14 RIEQ 176-244 {Boston and Charleston}	1856
Cole, Lucy (daughter of John Cole)	Jordan Baily	RICE 17-19 {Union District}	1837
Coleman, Malinda (daughter of Charles Coleman)	Samuel Boyd	7 RIEQ 509-520 {Fairfield}	1837
Collier, ____ (daughter of John Collier)	____ Moorer	3 RIEQ 555-558 {Orangeburg)	1849
Collier, ____ (daughter of John Collier)	____ Weathers	3 RIEQ 555-558 {Orangeburg}	1849
Collier, Lucinda	A. B. Elliot	3 RIEQ 125-132 {Charleston}	1850
Collier, Mariah	J. B. Hart	3 RIEQ 125-132 {Charleston}	1850
Collins, Lucy (widow of George W. Collins)	Barnet M. Enicks	SPEERS 142-158 {Barnwell}	1841
Collins, Lucy J. (widow of George W. Collins)	____ Enecks	3 RIEQ 398-403 {Barnwell}	1851
Collins, Lucy J. (widow of George W. Collins)	____ Enicks	4 RIEQ 314-317 {Barnwell}	1852
Collins, Mary (granddaughter of J. Collins)	____ Shackleford	1 DESA 570-573	1797
Collins, Mary (daughter of Jonah Collins)	____ Woodberry	BAILEY 48-57	1828
Compty, ____ (widow of Maj. John Compty who died February 1799)	Henry M'Gowan	4 DESA 486-504 {Richland District}	1814
Compty, Rebecca (daughter of Maj. John Compty who died February 1799)	Peter M'Guire	4 DESA 486-504 {Richland District}	1814
Conlietle, ____	Abram Felder	2 McC 323-343	1827
Conner, Mary Eliza	____ Picket	3 RIEQ 452-465 {Marion}	1843
Connoly, Elizabeth (marriage settlement 31 December 1829) (daughter of Richard Connoly)	James Murray	2 HILL 204-215 {Charleston}	1829
Connoly, Jane (married May 1821) (daughter of Richard Connoly) (Murray died 1829)	John M. Murray	2 HILL 204-215 {Charleston}	1823
Connors, ____	Robert Henry	2 McC 323-343	1827
Connors, Unity (widow of Charles P. Connors who died 5 March 1843) (Ballard was married before)	John Ballard	10 RIEQ 389-393 {Sumter}	1858

S.C. Marriages 1749-1867 Implied in S.C. Equity Reports

WOMAN	MAN	VOLUME PAGES	LIVED

Conyers, Elizabeth   John Arnett   4 STRO 189-203   1804
   (married 3 January 1804) (daughter of Straud
   Conyers of North Carolina) (Arnett died 1816)
                                        {Williamsburg District}
Cook, Dorothy   _____ Nopie   5 RIEQ 351-355   1852
   Frances (daughter of Daniel Cook)   {Charleston}
Cook, Eliza   _____ Wood   5 RIEQ 351-355   1852
   (daughter of Daniel Cook)   {Charleston}
Cook, Eliza Ann   David Crosland   2 RIEQ 68-74   1839
   (widow)   {Georgetown District}
Cook, Elizabeth A.   _____ Avery   5 RIEQ 351-355   1852
   (daughter of Daniel Cook)   {Charleston}
Cook, Nubilia   _____ Blewer   5 RIEQ 351-355   1852
   (daughter of Daniel Cook)   {Charleston}
Cooper, Rebecca   _____ Graham   3 STRO 261-262   n.d.
   (widow of George Cooper) [Referred to in another case]
Corbett, Margaret   _____ Laurens   5 RIEQ 301-326   1837
   Harleston (daughter of Thomas Corbett)
   (she was born 7 June 1805)   {Charleston}
Cornwell, Hannah   _____ Douglass   12 RIEQ 379-392   1848
   (daughter of Eli Cornwell)   {Chester District}
Cotchet, Sarah   _____ Robson   2 McC   269-317   1823
Coulietle, Ann   Richard Felder   2 McC   168-171   1827
Covington, _____   George Anderson   9 RIEQ 137-148   1849
                                        {Edgefield}
Cox, Bethana   _____ Pace   12 RIEQ 349-360   1857
                                        {Abbeville District}
Cox, Jane   _____ McKinney   12 RIEQ 349-360   1828
                                        {Abbeville District}
Cox, Jane   _____ McKinney   1 STRO 27-43   1828
                                        {Abbeville}
Cox, Pheraby   _____ Price   12 RIEQ 349-360   1857
                                        {Abbeville District}
Craddock, Anne   James Saxon   1 HILL 69-76   1818
   (Nancy) (widow of Edmund Craddock)   {Laurens}
Craddock, Judith   William Clarke   1 HILL 69-76   1815
   (daughter of Edmund Craddock)   {Laurens}
Crawford, _____   Thomas Williams   2 McC   171-181   1827
Crawford, Charity   _____ Porter   McMULL 81-86   1815
   (she was born 8 June 1776)   {Marion District}
Crocker, Patsey   _____ McBee   SPEERS 20-28   1833
   (daughter of Solomon Crocker)   {Spartanburgh District}
Croft, Florida   Frederick W. Sollee 7 RIEQ 34-53   1829
   (Florilla) P. (daughter of Edward Croft who died
   September 1851) (she died 1840) (he died October
   1837) (to Marengo County, Alabama)   {Greenville}

S.C. Marriages 1749-1867 Implied in S.C. Equity Reports

WOMAN	MAN	VOLUME PAGES	LIVED
Croft, Isabella	Col. Bird M. Pearson	7 RIEQ 34-53	1838
(daughter of Edward Croft who died September 1851)			
(to Alabama)		{Greenville}	
Cromwell, Elizabeth	Thomas Rivers	3 DESA 190-199	1811
(widow)	(widower)	{Charleston}	
Crosswhite, Betsey	_____ Roebuck	6 RIEQ 88-95	1825
(daughter of Jacob Crosswhite)		{Newberry}	
Crosswhite, Lucy	James S. Spearman	6 RIEQ 88-95	1852
(widow of William Crosswhite who died 1833) {Newberry}			
Crosswhite, Sarah	_____ Davidson	6 RIEQ 88-95	1825
(daughter of Jacob Crosswhite)		{Newberry}	
Cummings, _____	Josiah H. Smoot	9 RIEQ 440-458	1857
(widow)		{Sumter District}	
Cummings, Ann M.	William Young	9 RIEQ 440-458	1857
		{Sumter District}	
Cummings, Elizabeth	Robert R. Cannon	9 RIEQ 440-458	1857
		{Sumter District}	
Cummings, Joanna	Peter A. Brunson	9 RIEQ 440-458	1857
		{Sumter District}	
Cummings, Susan	John McSween	9 RIEQ 440-458	1857
		{Sumter District}	
Cunningham, Isabella L.	Thomas F. McDow	9 RIEQ 475-482	1856
(daughter of John S. Cunningham) {Lancaster}			
Cunningham, Mary	Dixon Barnes	9 RIEQ 475-482	1855
(married May 1855) (widow of John S. Cunningham)			
(she died 12 September 1855)		{Lancaster}	
Cunningham, Mary M.	_____ Cureton	4 RIEQ 135-151	1850
(daughter of Joseph Cunningham)		{Kershaw}	
Cureton, Ann	_____ Potts	13 RIEQ 104-110	1858
		{Lancaster District}	
Cureton, Elizabeth	_____ Massey	13 RIEQ 104-110	1858
		{Lancaster District}	
Cureton, Mary	_____ Haile	13 RIEQ 104-110	1858
		{Lancaster District}	
Cureton, Sarah	_____ Kimbrell	13 RIEQ 104-110	1858
		{Lancaster District}	
Curtis, Catharine	John Bailer, Sr.	3 STRO 258-262	1807
(daughter of Thomas Curtis) (she died about 1841)			
Cuttino, _____	Savage Smith	3 RIEQ 465-542	1807
(daughter of Wm. Cuttino) (Smith died April 1817)			
		{Georgetown}	

S.C. Marriages 1749-1867 Implied in S.C. Equity Reports

WOMAN	MAN	VOLUME PAGES	LIVED

(D)

WOMAN	MAN	VOLUME PAGES	LIVED
Daniel, Catharine (married February 1810)	Lewellin Threewits	4 DESA 560-578	1810
Dantzler, _____ (daughter of David Dantzler)	John Poole	12 RIEQ 224-228 {Spartanburg}	1860
Dart, Martha Motte	James E. Robinson	DUDLEY 128-132 {Charleston}	1835
Dart, Susan Mary (daughter of Thomas L. Dart)	_____ Vance	DUDLEY 128-132 {Charleston}	1835
Davenport, Aimy (daughter of Jonathan Davenport)	_____ Hill	3 RIEQ 559-578 {Newberry}	1842
Davenport, Catharine (daughter of Jonathan Davenport)	James M. Young, Jun.	3 RIEQ 559-578 {Newberry}	1849
Davenport, Elizabeth G. (daughter of Jonathan Davenport)	_____ Rudd	3 RIEQ 559-578 {Newberry}	1842
Davenport, Maria Louisa (daughter of Jonathan Davenport)	Carey McLure	3 RIEQ 559-578 {Newberry}	1842
David, Sarah (widow of Benjamin David)	Philip Pledger	4 DESA 264-266 {Cheraw District}	1812
Davidson, Karen (widow)	_____ Smith	4 RIEQ 307-314 {York}	1818
Davis, _____ (daughter of Col. Jonathan Davis)	Rev. J. C. Furman	4 STRO 133-149 {Fairfield, Newberry and Richland Districts}	1846
Davis, Aley	_____ Whaley	2 STRO 334-341 {Marion}	1832
Davis, Ann	W. Bay	4 DESA 505-517 {Richland District}	1814
Davis, Christiana (she died 30 December 1849)	Joseph A. Hamilton	5 RIEQ 434-441 {Abbeville District}	1849
Davis, Elizabeth	William Clarke	1 McC 191-197	1825
Davis, Elizabeth	Henry Stevens	4 DESA 532-536 {Pinckney District}	1814
Davis, Frances (in Illinois)	_____ Ross	4 RIEQ 16-22 {Abbeville}	1851
Davis, Martha	Lewis Presley	7 RIEQ 105-111 {Union}	1835
Davis, Mary [Referred to in another case]	Philip Carolan	2 HILL 1-6	1831
Davis, Ruth (in Illinois)	_____ Vickory	4 RIEQ 16-22 {Abbeville}	1851
Davis, Sarah Clarissa (daughter of Elnathan Davis)	J. P. Prince	SPEERS 29-35 {York District}	1842

S.C. Marriages 1749-1867 Implied in S.C. Equity Reports

WOMAN	MAN	VOLUME PAGES	LIVED
Dawson, _____ (daughter of Richard Dawson)	Samuel Marvin	CHEVES 148-157	1821
Dawson, Harriet (daughter of Lawrence Monk Dawson)	William W. Ancrum	DUDLEY 145-154 {Charleston}	1835
Dawson, Harriet	Wm. M. Ancrum	McMULL 405-409	1842
Dawson, Jane (daughter of Richard Dawson, Sr. of St. Luke's Parish, who died 25 August 1836)	_____ Wells	RICE 243-274 {Beaufort District}	1820
Dawson, Jane (daughter of Richard Dawson, Sr.)	_____ Wells	2 STRO 34-39 {Gillisonville}	1820
Dawson, Mary (daughter of Richard Dawson, Sr. of St. Luke's Parish, who died 25 August 1836)	Samuel Marvin	RICE 243-274 {Beaufort District}	1820
Dawson, Providence (daughter of Richard Dawson, Sr. of St. Luke's Parish, who died 25 August 1836)	_____ Taylor	RICE 243-274 {Beaufort District}	1820
Dawson, Providence (daughter of Richard Dawson, Sr.)	_____ Taylor	2 STRO 34-39 {Gillisonville}	1820
Dawson, Rebecca Ann (daughter of Richard Dawson, Sr.)	Samuel R. McKensie	2 STRO 34-39 {Gillisonville}	1836
Dawson, Rebecca Ann (daughter of Richard Dawson)	_____ M'Kenzie	CHEVES 148-157	1836
Dawson, Rebecca Ann (daughter of Richard Dawson, Sr. of St. Luke's Parish, who died 25 August 1836) (she was born September 1805)	_____ McKenzie	RICE 243-274 {Beaufort District}	1836
Day, Eliza Maria (married 28 December 1823) (daughter of George Day) (she was born 9 September 1797)	John Bonner	RILEY 162-165 {Charleston}	1823
Dean, Amelia B. (daughter of John Dean)	Lowry Lanford	9 RIEQ 423-428 {Spartanburg}	1856
Dean, Emily G. (daughter of John Dean)	David Patton	9 RIEQ 423-428 {Spartanburg}	1856
Dean, Mary Ann	William Miller	9 RIEQ 423-428 {Spartanburg}	1857
Dean, Mary B. (daughter of John Dean)	William Walker	9 RIEQ 423-428 {Spartanburg}	1856
Dean, Rosannah (daughter of John Dean)	Miles Brewton	9 RIEQ 423-428 {Spartanburg}	1856
Deas, Maria (widow of John Deas, Jun. who died 20 October 1790)	Dr. John Ramsay	2 DESA 233-239	1804
Deas, Mary	C. R. Holmes	7 RIEQ 328-343 {Charleston}	1843
Deas, Mary	Alexander Inglis	1 DESA 333-340	1785
Deas, Mary [Referred to in another case]	Alexander Inglis	10 RIEQ 137	1793

S.C. Marriages 1749-1867 Implied in S.C. Equity Reports

WOMAN	MAN	VOLUME PAGES	LIVED
De Graffenreid, ___	Thomas G. Blewit	2 McC 90-105	1815
(daughter of Allen De Graffenreid who died 7 January 1821)		{Chester}	
De Graffenreid, ___	S. Chisholme	2 McC 90-105	1827
		{Chester}	
De Graffenreid, ___	William Foote	2 McC 90-105	1827
		{Chester}	
De Graffenreid, ___	John M'Caw	2 McC 90-105	1821
(daughter of Allen De Graffenreid who died 7 January 1815)		{Chester}	
De Graffenreid, ___	John McCaw	BAILEY 98-102	1823
(daughter of Allen De Graffenreid)		{Chester}	
De Graffenried, ___	James B. Pickett	10 RIEQ 346-355	1837
		{Chester}	
Delk, Nancy	William H. Herron	5 RIEQ 441-450	1836
(daughter of Newit Delk) (she died 1848) {Darlington}			
Delk, Nancy H.	William H. Herron	6 RIEQ 339-342	1830
(daughter of Newitt Delk) (she died 1848) {Darlington}			
Dennis, _____	_____ Curry	4 RIEQ 307-314	1818
(daughter of John Dennis who died 10 October 1850) {York}			
Dennis, Karen	_____ Davidson	4 RIEQ 307-314	1818
(daughter of John Dennis who died 10 October 1850) {York}			
Dennis, Sarah	Robert H. De Hay	14 RIEQ 27-30	1860
(widow of William J. Dennis)		{Charleston}	
de Rochefort, Gabrielle Emelie	Charles Gregorie Arnauld Lacoste	1 RIEQ 187-221	1836
de Turkovics, Leopoldine	Barthelemy Szemere	11 RIEQ 344-392 {Paris, France}	1852
De Veaux, _____	_____ Moore	9 RIEQ 535-571	1856
(daughter of Robert Marion De Veaux) {Sumter District}			
De Veaux, Esther (widow) (she died November 1821)	Hon. Robert Marion	1 STRO 283-294 {Charleston}	1810
De Veaux, Esther Gabriella (daughter of Stephen Gabriel De Veaux)	John Huger	1 STRO 283-294 {Charleston}	1843
De Veaux, Videau M. (widow?)	Robert Marion De Veaux (he was born November 1812) (he died May 1843)	1 STRO 283-294 {Charleston}	1834
De Veaux, Videau Marion	Rev. Augustus L. Converse	9 RIEQ 535-571	1849
(marriage settlement 27 March 1849) Robert Marion De Veaux)		(widow of {Sumter District}	
Dill, Elizabeth	_____ Smith	1 DESA 237-244	1791
Dinkins, Emily E.	Benjamin D. Hodge	SPEERS 268-280	1838
(daughter of Gilbert Dinkins)		{Sumter District}	
Dinkins, Harriet B.	Benjamin B. Hodge	SPEERS 268-280	1838
(daughter of Gilbert Dinkins)		{Sumter District}	

S.C. Marriages 1749-1867 Implied in S.C. Equity Reports

WOMAN	MAN	VOLUME	PAGES	LIVED
Dinkins, Mary (daughter of Gilbert Dinkins)	John M. Hodge	SPEERS {Sumter District}	268-280	1838
Dinkins, Mary (daughter of John Dinkins who died 1811) (she died 1813)	John Smith	HARPER	160-164	1810
Dinkins, Sarah (widow of John Dinkins)	D. D. Richbourg	RICHEQ {Sumter}	185-191	1829
Dixon, Mary (daughter of John Dixon)	James Perry	4 DESA	504-510	1814
Donald, Nancy (daughter of Alexander Donald who died about 1806) (Gray died about 1811)	Robert Gray	RICE {Abbeville}	330-342	1803
Donnelly, Mary C. (married 1840) (daughter of Patrick Donnelly) (she was born about 1818) (living in Savannah) {Marion}	Francis B. Durant	1 STRO	81-83	1840
Dougherty, Judith	_____ Frost	4 DESA	447-458	1806
Douglass, Hannah (married 1848) (widow) (she died December 1855) {Chester District}	John T. McAfee	12 RIEQ	379-392	1848
Downs, Ann (married March 1796)	Roger Moor Smith	3 DESA {Charleston}	417-465	1796
Downs, Mildred (daughter of Jonathan Downs)	Lydall Allen	6 RIEQ {Laurens}	364-369	1818
Dozier, _____	Miles Gayle	McMULL {Greenville}	236-253	1832
Dozier, Nancy	John Ramsey (he died 9 June 1825) (he of Edgefield District) {Greenville}	McMULL	236-253	1825
Dragaud, _____ (widow of Pierre Dragaud)	_____ Abrahams	3 DESA {Charleston District}	25-28	1809
Drayton, _____ (daughter of Thomas Drayton)	_____ Grimke	RICHEQ {Charleston}	321-325	1831
Drayton, _____ (married December 1806) (daughter of Glen Drayton) (to Pendleton 1808)	John L. North	HARPER	34-46	1806
Drayton, Maria	Thomas Parker	RICE {Charleston District}	373-388	1793
Drayton, Rose	Frederick A. Ford	7 RIEQ {Charleston}	328-343	1843
Drayton, Susannah (married 10 March 1795) (daughter of John Drayton)	Tobias Bowles	1 DESA	489-497	1795
Dubon, Sarah	Maurice Viers	3 DESA	273-296	1795
Dugan, _____ (daughter of John Dugan)	Francis A. Shell	DUDLEY {Newberry}	1-14	1837
Dugan, _____ (daughter of John Dugan)	Harmon Shell	DUDLEY {Newberry}	1-14	1837
Dugan, Lucy (daughter of Park Dugan)	William Davis	DUDLEY {Newberry}	1-14	1837

S.C. Marriages 1749-1867 Implied in S.C. Equity Reports

WOMAN	MAN	VOLUME PAGES	LIVED
Dugan, Margaret (daughter of Col. Thomas Dugan)	James Murray	DUDLEY 1-14 {Newberry}	1822
Duke, Louisa (common-law marriage or married 1835) (she died October 1848)	William Fulmer	5 RIEQ 121-128 {Lexington}	1835
Duke, Louisa (common-law marriage, eloped March 1822, Jones County, Georgia)	Samuel Godby	5 RIEQ 121-128 {Lexington}	1822
Dumont, Ursule (marriage settlement 12 January 1810) [daughter of Guillaume (William) Dumont] (Schmidt was married before) (Schmidt died 1853)	Dr. John W. Schmidt	7 RIEQ 201-218 {Charleston}	1810
Dunbar, Lucy E.	_____ Patrick	10 RIEQ 130-138 {Barnwell}	1847
Dunlap, _____ (sister of Rev. David Ellison Dunlap)	_____ Stevenson	4 DESA 305-329	1812
Dunlap, Ann (daughter of James Dunlap)	John A. Wotton	11 RIEQ 405-415 {Charleston}	1860
Dunlap, Elizabeth (daughter of James Dunlap)	William T. O'Neale	11 RIEQ 405-415 {Charleston}	1860
Dunlap, Margaret (daughter of James Dunlap)	Thomas Divine	11 RIEQ 405-415 {Charleston}	1860
Dupont, Agnes (widow)	Dr. Henry Field	McMULL 369-404 {Gillisonville}	1828
Dupont, Elvira	William M. Pelot	McMULL 369-404 {Gillisonville}	1841
Dupree, Sarah (widow of James Dupree)	_____ McDonald	4 DESA 209-215 {Georgetown}	1812
Durham, Martha	_____ Sturman (in Indiana)	2 STRO 258-262 {Newberry District}	1843
Durham, Sarah	_____ Pitts (in Indiana)	2 STRO 258-262 {Newberry District}	1843
Durr, _____ (widow of Jacob Durr)	Henry Rhodes	2 McC 368-376	1827
Dwight, Elizabeth (unrecorded marriage settlement 8 January 1814, Georgetown District)	Henry Hanion	HARPER 170-174	1824

(E)

| Earle, Sarah | William L. Yancey (to Alabama) | 9 RIEQ 429-433 {Greenville} | 1852 |
| Earle, Sarah | William L. Yancey (to Alabama) | 7 RIEQ 16-19 {Greenville} | 1854 |

S.C. Marriages 1749-1867 Implied in S.C. Equity Reports

WOMAN	MAN	VOLUME	PAGES	LIVED
Eddings, Mary (widow)	_____ Hughes	5 RIEQ	274-289	1852

Eddings. See Edings

Edgerton, Elizabeth George W. Muse DUDLEY 179-183 1831
(married 5 May 1831) {Barnwell}
Edgerton, Elizabeth George W. Muse 2 HILL 51-53 1834
(widow of Otis Edgerton) {Barnwell}
Edings, Eliza _____ Whaley 4 RIEQ 276-301 1834
(daughter of William Edings) {Charleston}
Edings, Eliza Benjamin Whaley 1 RIEQ 301-319 1819
(married 30 March 1819) (daughter of William Edings
who died April 1836) (she died 26 June 1823)
(Whaley's first marriage)
Edings, Elizabeth William Seabrook McMULL 201-230 1836
Emma (daughter of Joseph Edings) (Seabrook was
married before) {Edisto Island}
Edings, Mary _____ Chisholm 4 RIEQ 276-301 1834
{Charleston}
Edings, Mary John A. Fripp 1 RIEQ 301-319 1822
(married 12 February 1822) (daughter of William
Edings who died April 1836)
Edings, Mary John A. Fripp 4 RIEQ 276-301 1834
(daughter of William Edings) {Charleston}
Edings, Sarah George Chisholm 1 RIEQ 301-319 1823
(married 14 January 1823) (daughter of William
Edings who died April 1836) (she died 19 October 1834)
Edings, Sarah George Chisolm, Jr. 4 RIEQ 276-301 1834
(daughter of William Edings) {Charleston}

Edings. See Eddings

Edmondston, Beatrix _____ Sandford RICHEQ 357-361 1817
{Charleston}
Edwards, Mary _____ Hammond 3 RIEQ 271-281 1850
[See also 7 RIEQ pages 125-135] {Charleston}
Edwards, Mary Daniel Holbrook 2 HILL 184-200 1835
{Coosawhatchie}
Elbert, Catharine John Burke McMULL 475-484 1799
{Fairfield}
Elbert, Elizabeth Dr. Michael Burke McMULL 475-484 1799
(married 1799) (she was born 1779) (she died 1804/05)
{Fairfield}
Ellerbe, Elizabeth _____ Cash SPEERS 328-342 1822
E. (daughter of Capt. William Ellerbe who died May 1830)
{Cheraw}
Ellerbe, Harriet William Cole SPEERS 328-342 1841
(daughter of Capt. William Ellerbe who died May 1830)
{Cheraw}

S.C. Marriages 1749-1867 Implied in S.C. Equity Reports

WOMAN	MAN	VOLUME	PAGES	LIVED

Ellerbe, Mary   Samuel Spencer   SPEERS 328-342 1841
   (daughter of Capt. William Ellerbe who died May 1830)
                                          {Cheraw}
Ellerbe, Obedience Zachariah Ellerbe   SPEERS 328-342 1841
   (daughter of Capt. William Ellerbe who died May 1830)
                                          {Cheraw}
Elliott, _____   Glen Drayton   HARPER 34-46   1783
   (daughter of Samuel Elliott) (Drayton died June 1796)
Elliott, Ann   Hon. Richard   1 DESA 263-271 1792
                Beresford
   (widow of Charles Elliott)
   [See also pages 174-183, 360-366]
Elliott, Eliza   Glen Drayton   3 DESA 29-31   1809
   (daughter of Samuel Elliott who died 1777)
                                    {Charleston District}
Elliott, Elizabeth _____ Butler   2 McC   435-440 1775
   (she died about 1775)
Elliott, Jane Riley Col. William   1 DESA 263-271 1792
                    Washington
   (daughter of Charles Elliott)
   [See also pages 183-190; 360-365]
Elliott, Mary   Robert Rowand   1 DESA 183-190 1790
   [See also pages 262-269]
Elliott, Mary   Colonel Bernard 1 DESA 183-190 1766
  Bellinger   Elliott
   (married April 1766) (his first marriage)
   (daughter of Thomas Law Elliott who died
   7 December 1756) (she died 11 December 1774)
   (he died October 1778/88) [See also pages 263-271]
Elliott, Sarah   Archibald Stanyarne 1 DESA 183-190 1790
Elliott, Susannah _____ Carnes   2 DESA 299-304 1805
   (widow of Col. Barnard Elliott)
Ellis, Jane   Stephen Shell   4 DESA 611-613 1815
   (daughter of John Ellis who died 1772)
                                  {Washington District}
Ellis, Mary   James Thompson 10 RIEQ 416-427 1852
   (common-law marriage)   {Charleston}
Ellis, Mary Ann L. E. Madison Scurry 9 RIEQ 19-33   1852
   (married 1852)   {Williamsburg District}
Ellis, Sarah M.   _____ De Treville BAILEY 35-42   1827
                                        {Coosawhatchie}
Ellison, Susannah Rev. David Ellison 4 DESA 305-329 1804
  Potts   Dunlap
   (daughter of Robert Ellison) (he and she died 10
   September 1804)
Elms, Hannah   Arthur Hughes   3 DESA 155-164 1810
   (widow of William Elms)   {Charleston}

S.C. Marriages 1749-1867 Implied in S.C. Equity Reports

WOMAN	MAN	VOLUME PAGES	LIVED
Ernest, Rachel	William Lindsay	RICHEQ 439-448	1836
(or Margaret) (daughter of Henry Ernest who died 1834)			
		{Spartanburg}	
Etheredge, Jemima	Hancock Southard	10 RIEQ 207-216	1855
		{Edgefield}	
Etheredge, Sarah	Nathaniel Corley	10 RIEQ 207-216	1855
		{Edgefield}	
Evans, _____	G. W. Holcombe	HARPER 202-204	1824
(daughter of John Evans)			
Evans, Mary G.	William H. Adams	1 STRO 72-78	1830
(marriage settlement 17 October 1830)			
(widow of Cadwell Evans)		{Edgefield}	
Evans, Sarah A.	Edward Meray	2 HILL 222-228	1835
(daughter of John Evans)		{Charleston District}	
Evans, Sarah A.	William Wheeler	2 HILL 222-228	1827
(did not marry; had child only) (daughter of			
John Evans) (Wheeler died July 1829)			
		{Charleston District}	
Evans, Susan A.	Edward Meray	BAILEY 507-509	1830
		{Charleston}	
Evans, Susan A.	William Wheeler	BAILEY 507-509	1830
(common-law marriage)		{Charleston}	
Ewing, Agnes	Archibald Simpson	1 HILL 228-242	1807
Johnston (he died 15 September 1819)			
(marriage contract 8 April 1807) (she died 27 March			
1828)		{Charleston}	
Ewing, Ann	_____ Johnston	2 DESA 451-456	1806
(daughter of Adam Ewing who died October 1796)			
Exum, Sarah	Hugh Humphrey	McMULL 81-86	1836
Porter (he was born January/February			
1815) (daughter of William Exum who died about 1821)			
		{Marion District}	

(F)

Fable, Catharine	_____ Franks	2 HILL 378-401	1835
		{Philadelphia, Pennsylvania}	
Fair, Jane Caroline	George Anderson	5 RIEQ 55-76	1830
(daughter of Isaac Fair)		{Edgefield District}	
Fair, Lucilla	John B. Covington	5 RIEQ 55-76	1830
(widow of Isaac Fair)		{Edgefield District}	
Falconer, _____	James House	4 DESA 86-87	1810
Lavinia (widow of William Falconer who died June 1805)			
		{Cheraws}	

S.C. Marriages 1749-1867 Implied in S.C. Equity Reports

WOMAN	MAN	VOLUME PAGES	LIVED
Farr, Jane L.	Richard Waring	4 STRO 37-58 {Charleston}	1849
Farr, Susan B.	James D. Sommers (he died 1817)	4 STRO 37-58 {Charleston and Colleton Districts}	1817
Faucheraud, Mary (daughter of Gideon Faucheraud)	John Paul Grimke	1 DESA 366-382	1751

Faust, Christina W. William W. Eaton 9 RIEQ 294-302 1853
(married 1 November 1853, Georgia) (she had been
divorced) [See also pages 376-391] {Fairfield}
Felder, Ann James J. Andrews 4 RIEQ 349-358 1829
Catherine (married April 1829) (widow of Henry Felder)
{Orangeburg}
Felder, Eliza M. Joseph Pou 5 RIEQ 509-518 1852
[See also 6 RIEQ pages 58-71] {Orangeburg}
Felder, Eugenia M. John Buchanan 5 RIEQ 509-518 1852
(daughter of Samuel J. Felder) {Orangeburg}
Felder, Henrietta Wesley Keitt 4 RIEQ 349-358 1852
(daughter of Henry Felder) {Orangeburg}
Felder, Louisa ____ Federick 5 RIEQ 509-518 1852
(daughter of Samuel J. Felder) {Orangeburg}
Felder, Olivia George D. Keitt 4 RIEQ 349-358 1843
(daughter of Henry Felder) {Orangeburg}
Felder, Sarah A. Henry M. Moorer 4 RIEQ 349-358 1841
(daughter of Henry Felder) {Orangeburg}
Fennel, Susannah Col. Aromanos 1 HILL 76-94 1817
Lyles (he died September 1817)
(married February 1817) (widow of Cullen Fennel)
Fennell, Susannah Philip James HARPER 288-295 1817
(Fannell) (she of Lexington District)
Fennell, Susannah Aromanus Lyles, Sr. HARPER 288-295 1817
(Fannell) (she of Lexington District) (marriage
settlement 6 February 1817) (he was married before)
Fenwick, Harriet Josiah Tattnell 1 DESA 143 1787
Ferdinand, Maria Benjamin Whaley 1 RIEQ 301-319 1832
(his second marriage) (he died 11
March 1832)
Ferguson, ____ ____ Sanders 3 DESA 555-556 1813
(widow of Charles Ferguson)
Ferguson, Ann Charles Elliott 1 DESA 174-183 1790
(daughter of Charles Ferguson) (her first marriage)
Field, Isabel C. Robert L. Baker 7 RIEQ 386-394 1847
{Colleton}
Field, Isabella C. Robert L. Baker 1 STRO 129-169 1843
(marriage settlement 8 June 1843) (married Charleston)
(separated) (widow) (she was born 1789-1793)
{Colleton and Beaufort Districts}

S.C. Marriages 1749-1867 Implied in S.C. Equity Reports

WOMAN	MAN	VOLUME PAGES	LIVED
Finch, _____ (daughter of Edward Finch)	_____ Crenshaw	4 DESA 185-199 {Newberry District}	1811
Fincher, Ann	John Rogers	1 STRO 370-377	1836
(marriage settlement 2 June 1836) (widow) (widower) (she died February 1838) (he died July 1838) {Union}			
Finden, Mary (she was born about 1768)	Captain John Trott	7 RIEQ 358-374 {Charleston}	1789
Finklea, Elizabeth Ann (widow of Hugh Finklea)	A. B. Jordan	14 RIEQ 160-166 {Marion}	1867
Finley, Ann	_____ Green	14 RIEQ 167-175 {Abbeville}	1859
Finley, Sarah	_____ Wiseman (in Tennessee)	14 RIEQ 167-175 {Abbeville}	1867
Fitzpatrick, Mary	_____ Gallagher	1 DESA 340-346	1793
Flanagan, _____	Henry Gray	2 HILL 644-653	1829
(daughter of Dr. Reuben Flanagan of Newberry) (Gray died 5 April 1831) {Newberry and Abbeville}			
Footman, Mary Elizabeth (daughter of William C. Footman of Bryan County, Georgia)	Robert A. McKelvy	2 STRO 317-324 {Williamsburg District}	1845
Ford, _____	William Fox	5 RIEQ 349-351 {Colleton}	1852
Ford, Elizabeth (daughter of John Ford)	James McElray	1 RIEQ 474-476 {Greenville}	1843
Ford, Mary W.	Josiah Beck	SPEERS 579-592	1837
(marriage settlement February 1837) {Colleton District}			
Foreman, _____ (daughter of Isaac Foreman)	_____ Stallings	2 HILL 401-410 {Barnwell}	1835
Foreman, Caroline A. (marriage settlement 12 August 1835) (daughter of Benjamin Foreman)	Samuel B. Bush	1 STRO 377-385 {Barnwell}	1835
Foreman, Caroline A. (daughter of Benjamin Foreman of Barnwell District)	Samuel B. Bush	3 STRO 131-136	1835
Foster, Cynthia	_____ Burrows	SPEERS 569-577 {Spartanburg}	1841
Foster, Dorcas	_____ McDowell	SPEERS 569-577 {Spartanburg}	1841
Fowke, Jane	Hugh Johnson	SPEERS 233-249	1837
(marriage settlement 4 October 1837) {Barnwell}			
Foxworth, Jane Maria	Benjamin Dehay	1 RIEQ 266-270	1845
Fraser, Jane	Thomas Boone (daughter of J. B. Fraser)	2 McC 105-112	1825
Fraser, Jane Baxter	Thomas Boone (daughter of John B. Fraser) {Sumter}	1 HILL 360-369	1833

S.C. Marriages 1749-1867 Implied in S.C. Equity Reports

WOMAN	MAN	VOLUME	PAGES	LIVED
Fraser, Mary (daughter of J. B. Fraser)	G. S. C. Deschamps	2 McC	105-112	1823
Fraser, Mary	Dr. Henry Richardson	RILEY	271-282	1801

(marriage settlement 27 October 1801) (daughter of Dr. James Fraser) (she died 1812) {Charleston}

Frazier, _____	John Gomillian	2 HILL	304-318	1824
		{Edgefield}		
Frazier, _____	James Jeter	2 HILL	304-318	1824
		{Edgefield}		
Frazier, _____	John Livingston	2 HILL	304-318	1824
		{Edgefield}		
Frazier, Martha	Charles J. Glover	1 STRO	79-81	1833

(married June 1833) (daughter of Benjamin Frazier) (she was born about 1816) {Edgefield}

Freer, _____	William Robertson	HARPER	56-65	1824

(daughter of John Freer who died November 1787)

Freer, _____	John H. Wilson	HARPER	56-65	1824

(daughter of Charles Freer who died 1808)

Fretwell, Amanda	John Burrow	11 RIEQ	559-573	1856

(daughter of William Fretwell of Greene County, Georgia) {Anderson}

Fretwell, Elizabeth	_____ Mims	11 RIEQ	559-573	1856

(Betsey) (daughter of William Fretwell of Greene County, Georgia) {Anderson}

Fretwell, Julia	Edward Cobb	11 RIEQ	559-573	1856

(daughter of William Fretwell of Greene County, Georgia) {Anderson}

Fretwell, Nancy	William H. Kelly	11 RIEQ	559-573	1856

(daughter of William Fretwell of Greene County, Georgia) {Anderson}

Fretwell, Sally	Benjamin Scott	11 RIEQ	559-573	1856

(daughter of William Fretwell of Greene County, Georgia) {Anderson}

Fripp, Harriet	Hamilton Fripp	RICE	84-109	1832

(married 4 July 1832) (widow of William P. Fripp) {Beaufort District}

Fripp, Harriet	William P. Fripp	RICE	84-109	1828

(daughter of Isaac Perry Frip who died 5/6 January 1832) (William P. Fripp died October 1828) {Beaufort} District}

Frost, Judith (widow)	Jacob Bookter	4 DESA	447-458	1806
Fulmer, Elizabeth	Joseph Counts	5 RIEQ	121-128	1848
		{Lexington}		

S.C. Marriages 1749-1867 Implied in S.C. Equity Reports

WOMAN   MAN   VOLUME   PAGES   LIVED

(G)

Gadsden, _____   Andrew Lord   1 DESA   208-219   1780
    (widow of Thomas Gadsden) (Lord died 1780)
Gaillard, Elizabeth John Stoney   1 RIEQ   222-264   1826
    (daughter of Capt. Peter Gaillard) (Stoney died November
    1838) [See also pages 275-277; 352-361] {Charleston}
Gallagher, Esther   Jackson Poag   5 RIEQ   170-185   1832
    (daughter of John Gallagher) (she died 1839) {York}
Gallagher, Martha   Alfred Abshier   5 RIEQ   170-185   1832
    (daughter of John Gallagher)   {York}
Gallagher, Matilda   Leander Poag   5 RIEQ   170-185   1832
    (daughter of John Gallagher)   {York}
Gallman, Susan A.   Stanmore B. Ryan   McMULL   451-457   1838
    (daughter of Benjamin Gallman)   {Edgefield}
Galphin, _____   Joseph Grant   1 McC   280-300   1826
                                             {Edgefield District}
Galphin, Ann   B. M'Kinney   1 McC   280-300   1816
                                             {Edgefield District}
Galphin, B.   C. Scriven   1 McC   280-300   1826
                                             {Edgefield District}
Garden, _____   John Miles   2 HILL   277-298   1835
    (widow of Alexander Garden, Garden's second marriage)
Garden, Harriott   _____ Benson   1 DESA   521-537   1796
Gardner, Rebecca   _____ Old   2 McC   32-36   1827
    (daughter of Robert Gardner)
Gardner, Sarah   William Harden   2 McC   32-36   1827
    (widow of Robert Gardner)
Garrett, Amy   John A. Houston   1 STRO   96-103   1843
                                             {Edgefield}
Garrett, Amy   John A. Houston   2 STRO   272-284   1843
                                             {Edgefield}
Garrett, Elizabeth   Richard M. Johnson   2 STRO   272-284   1843
                                             {Edgefield}
Garrett, Elizabeth   Richard W. Johnson   1 STRO   96-103   1843
                                             {Edgefield}
Garrett, Mary   Henry Key   1 STRO   96-103   1843
                                             {Edgefield}
Garrett, Mary   Henry Key   2 STRO   272-284   1843
                                             {Edgefield}
Garrett, Mary Ann   Britton Mims   1 STRO   66-72   1825
    (married 15 December 1825) (daughter of Stephen
    Garrett)   {Edgefield}
Garth, _____   Rollin H. Kirk   11 RIEQ   259-263   1855
    (she went to Kentucky)   {Beaufort}

S.C. Marriages 1749-1867 Implied in S.C. Equity Reports

WOMAN	MAN	VOLUME	PAGES	LIVED

Garvin, _____ John N. Copeland RICE 69-72 1839
 (widow of James M. Garvin who died 1836)
 (to Calhoun County, Florida Territory)
                                    {Barnwell District}
Garvin, Laura L. A. M. Baker 4 RIEQ 392-399 1852
                                    {Barnwell}
Gary, _____ Allen Vance RICE 2-3 1838
                                    {Laurens}
Geiger, _____ George Bell CHEVES 162 1840
Geiger, Margarett _____ Slappy 2 STRO 359-370 1827
 (widow of Harmon Geiger)   {Newberry}
 [In footnotes of 1917 Edition]
George, Rachael John Canady 6 RIEQ 103-110 1851
 (common-law marriage) (he died 9 April 1851) {Barnwell}
Gervais, _____ _____ Miller McMULL 106-114 1841
 (daughter of Rev. Paul T. Gervais)
Gervais, _____ _____ Robinson McMULL 106-114 1841
 (daughter of Rev. Paul T. Gervais)
Gervais, Margaret Henry Verdier McMULL 106-114 1839
 J. (married 12 February 1839) (daughter of Rev.
 Paul T. Gervais) (Verdier died August 1839)
                                    {St. Bartholomew's Parish}
Gervais, Martha P. Dr. _____ North McMULL 106-114 1841
 (daughter of Rev. Paul T. Gervais)
Gibbes, Caroline L. George W. Brown 5 RIEQ 291-300 1844
                                    {Charleston}
Gilbert, _____ John Johnson 13 RIEQ 42-49 1860
 (daughter of Jesse Gilbert, Sr. of Darlington
 District, who died 20 July 1852) {Darlington District}
Gilbert, _____ William K. Johnson 13 RIEQ 42-49 1860
 (daughter of Jesse Gilbert, Sr. of Darlington
 District, who died 20 July 1852) {Darlington District}
Gilbert, _____ John Thomas 2 McC 36-43 1827
 (daughter of Caleb Gilbert)
Gill, _____ W. L. Wallace RICHEQ 141-142 1831
                                    {York}
Gillam, Sarah Philemon Berry 6 RIEQ 83-87 1807
             Waters (he died 1807)
 (daughter of Robert Gillam who died 1814) {Newberry}
Gillett, Julia J. Higgenbottom 3 RIEQ 398-403 1832
                                    {Barnwell}
Gillett, Julia James Higginbottom SPEERS 142-158 1829
 (daughter of Dr. Elijah Gillett who died 1818) {Barnwell}
 [See also 4 RIEQ pages 314-316]
Gillett, Lavinia J. S. Powell 3 RIEQ 398-403 1832
                                    {Barnwell}

134

S.C. Marriages 1749-1867 Implied in S.C. Equity Reports

WOMAN	MAN	VOLUME PAGES	LIVED
Gillett, Lavinia	Jacob S. P. Powell	2 STRO 196-207 {Barnwell}	1832
Gillett, Lavinia	Rev. J. S. Powell	SPEERS 142-158	1829

(daughter of Dr. Elijah Gillett who died 1818)
(she died 12 November 1832) {Barnwell}

Gillett, Lucy	George W. Collins	SPEERS 142-158	1841

(daughter of Dr. Elijah Gillett who died 1818) {Barnwell}

Gillett, Lucy J.	George W. Collins	3 RIEQ 398-403	1826

(married 1826) (daughter of Elijah Gillett) {Barnwell}
(Collins died 1836) [Must also see 5 RIEQ page 114]

Gillett, Lucy J.	George W. Collins	4 RIEQ 314-317	1852

(daughter of Elijah Gillett) {Barnwell}

Gillison, Adela	Isadore Lartigue	4 RIEQ 213-222	1847

(daughter of Samuel R. Gillison who died 1847) {Beaufort}

Gilmore, Jane	_____ Monks	DUDLEY 14-23 {York District}	1837
Givens, _____	William H. Talbird	RICE 132-158 {Beaufort District}	1839
Givens, Elizabeth	Randal Chaplin	RICE 132-158	1831

(daughter of John Givens who died 1822) (she was born May 1810) (Chaplin died about 1831) {Beaufort District}

Givens, Mary	_____ Firth	RICE 132-158 {Beaufort District}	1810
Glenn, Hannah	_____ Carlisle	1 HILL 357-360	1833

(daughter of James Glenn of Chester)

Glover, _____	John Huger	2 HILL 515-528 {Colleton District}	1832

(daughter of Col. Wilson Glover)

Glover, Elizabeth	_____ Harris	4 RIEQ 25-38 {Abbeville}	1851

(daughter of Wiley Glover, Sen.)

Glover, Elizabeth	_____ Jones	1 RIEQ 141-154 {Colleton}	1845
Glover, Jane M.	Alfred J. Lemacks (Lamacks)	1 RIEQ 141-154 {Colleton}	1845
Glover, Jemima	Nathan Lipscomb	4 RIEQ 25-38	1808

(married 9 March 1808) (widow of Wiley Glover, Sen.)
(she died 29 January 1850) (Lipscomb died 1820)
{Abbeville}

Glover, Sarah	John Nail	RICHEQ 115-121	1822

(daughter of Andrew Glover who died 3 August 1822)
(Nail died 1 November 1825) {Edgefield}

Glover, Sarah	John Nail	1 RIEQ 24	1823

(he died 1825)
[Referred to in another case]

Godard, Franciade Maria	Effingham Wagner	2 STRO 1-13	1845

(daughter of Rene Godard of Charleston, who died 3 May 1845) {Charleston}

S.C. Marriages 1749-1867 Implied in S.C. Equity Reports

WOMAN	MAN	VOLUME PAGES	LIVED
Godard, Jane Eliza (daughter of Rene Godard of Charleston, who died 3 May 1845)	Henry Bailey	2 STRO 1-13 {Charleston}	1845
Godbold, Elizabeth (her first marriage) (daughter of General _____ Goldbold of Marion District, who died 1825)	John Haseldon	4 RIEQ 334-340	1844
Godbold, Elizabeth (her first marriage) (daughter of General Thomas Godbold)	John Haseldon	6 RIEQ 26-42 {Marion}	1853
Godbold, Mary (daughter of General Thomas Godbold)	James Haseldon	6 RIEQ 26-42 {Marion}	1853
Godbold, Sarah Ann (daughter of General _____ Godbold of Marion District, who died 1825)	William Evans	4 RIEQ 334-340	1852
Godbold, Sarah Ann (daughter of General Thomas Godbold)	William Evans	6 RIEQ 26-42 {Marion}	1853
Goodman, Huldah (married 1823)	Finsley Chewning	2 McC 11-15	1823
Goodwyn, Eliza (daughter of Major James Goodwyn)	John H. Blake	BAILEY 141-148 {Fairfield}	1824
Goodwyn, Eliza H. (daughter of Major James Goodwyn)	J. H. Blake	2 HILL 629-638 {Fairfield}	1824
Goodwyn, Sarah C.	Ainsley Hall (he died August 1823)	2 McC 269-317 {Columbia}	1823
Gourdin, Eliza	Peter Gaillard	RILEY 167-173 {Charleston}	1834
Gourdin, Esther	Silas E. Holbrook	RILEY 167-173 {Charleston}	1834
Gourlay, Mary Ann (marriage settlement 20 December 1836) {Charleston}	Charles George Wagner	2 STRO 1-13	1836
Gourley, Ann Jane (daughter of Joseph Gourley) (she died September 1835)	Robert Harlee	DUDLEY 42-54 {Marion}	1835
Graham, Elizabeth Jemima (married in Camden) (widow) (he had been married before) (he died December 1835)	Edward Bowers	10 RIEQ 551-556 {Lancaster}	1835
Graham, Janet M.	Washington Cockfield	7 RIEQ 95-99 {Williamsburg}	1850
Graham, Mary T.	_____ Frierson	7 RIEQ 95-99 {Williamsburg}	1850
Graves, _____ (widow of Samuel Colleton Graves) [See also pages 219-231]	_____ Cleary	RILEY 232-247	1828
Graves, _____ (widow of Samuel Colleton Graves)	Nathaniel G. Cleary	BAILEY 268-274 {Charleston}	1829

S.C. Marriages 1749-1867 Implied in S.C. Equity Reports

WOMAN	MAN	VOLUME	PAGES	LIVED
Graves, _____ (daughter of Admiral _____ Graves)	Baron Vandersmissen	BAILEY	268-274 {Charleston}	1829
Graves, Caroline M. (daughter of Samuel Colleton Graves)	Loftus C. Clifford	3 RIEQ	218-225 {Charleston}	1850
Graves, Louisa Catherine Colleton (daughter of Admiral Richard Graves)	Baron Vandersmissen (or Chevalier) (married 1819)	RILEY	219-247	1819
Graves, Louisa Catharina Colleton (married 20 October 1816, Antwerp, the Netherlands) (daughter of Admiral Richard Graves)	Jacques Louis Dominique Vandersmissen	5 RIEQ	519-530 {Charleston}	1828
Graves, Septima Sexta Colleton (married 12 December 1819 at the Hague and February 1820 in London) (daughter of Admiral Richard Graves)	Sir James Roupel Colleton (or Baronet)	RILEY	219-247	1819
Graves, Sophia Louisa (daughter of Admiral Richard Graves) [See also pages 233-247]	_____ Radcliffe	RILEY	219-232	1821
Graves, Susan (widow of Samuel C. Graves)	N. G. Cleary	1 HILL	135-138	1833
Graves, Susan (widow of Samuel Colleton Graves) (she died 19 July 1848)	Nathaniel G. Cleary	3 RIEQ	218-225 {Charleston}	1848
Graves, Susan M. (widow of Samuel C. Graves)	Nathaniel G. Cleary	1 RIEQ	319-324 {Colleton District}	1829
Gray, _____ (daughter of John Gray)	_____ Scott	4 RIEQ	1-9 {Edgefield}	1846
Gray, Elizabeth (daughter of Robert Gray)	James Donald	RICE	330-342 {Abbeville}	1838
Gray, Mary Ann (daughter of Robert Gray)	West Donald	RICE	330-342 {Abbeville}	1838
Gray, Nancy (married 1825) (widow of Robert Gray)	_____ Paul	RICE	330-342 {Abbeville}	1825
Green, _____ (widow of Col. _____ Green)	Major James Goodwyn	BAILEY	141-148 {Fairfield}	1824
Green, Mary A. S. (daughter of Richard G. Green)	James W. Skinner	10 RIEQ	27-37 {Georgetown District}	1857
Green, Rebecca	John M. Barber	DUDLEY	238-241 {Chester}	1829
Green, Rebecca	John M. Barber	5 RIEQ	38-55 {Chester}	1831
Green, Rebecca	John M. Barber	1 HILL	95-101 {Chester}	1833
Greenland, Elizabeth (married March 1787/88)	Cornelius Brown	1 DESA	196-201	1788

S.C. Marriages 1749-1867 Implied in S.C. Equity Reports

WOMAN	MAN	VOLUME PAGES	LIVED
Griffin, Agnes (daughter of Richard Griffin) (in Lincoln County, Georgia)	John Calhoun	2 RIEQ 99-114 {Abbeville}	1845
Griffin, Amelia (widow of Richard Griffin) (she died February 1841) (Cowan died 1822) (in Lincoln County, Georgia) (to Missouri)	John Cowan	2 RIEQ 99-114 {Abbeville}	1803
Griffin, Eugenia (daughter of Richard Griffin who died 20 November 1850)	Dr. ____ Leland	9 RIEQ 71-84 {Edgefield}	1856
Griffin, Jane (daughter of Richard Griffin) (in Lincoln County, Georgia)	Lewis Stovall	2 RIEQ 99-114 {Abbeville}	1845
Griffin, Lucinda (daughter of Richard Griffin) (in Lincoln County, Georgia)	Jeremiah Walker	2 RIEQ 99-114 {Abbeville}	1811
Griffin, Margaret (daughter of Richard Griffin who died 20 November 1850)	Z. W. Carwile	9 RIEQ 71-84 {Edgefield}	1856
Griffin, Margaret (daughter of Richard Griffin) (in Lincoln County, Georgia)	James McMillan	2 RIEQ 99-114 {Abbeville}	1845
Grimke, Ann	____ Coslett	1 DESA 366-382	1794
Guerard, Margaret L. (marriage settlement December 1828) (she died September 1848)	William Fuller	7 RIEQ 170-179	1828
Guess, Rachel (daughter of John Guess)	John Matheney	2 HILL 63-70	1834
Guignard, Margaret (marriage settlement 9 February 1793)	Peter Horry	4 DESA 614-616	1793
Gunnels, Eliza (daughter of William C. Gunnels)	William Leak	2 RIEQ 259-270 {Greenville and Laurens Districts}	1845
Gunnels, Maria (daughter of William C. Gunnels)	A. J. Joyce	2 RIEQ 259-270 {Greenville and Laurens Districts}	1845

(H)

Haigood, Nancy (married 1823) (widow of William Haigood) {Winnsboro}	John D. Wells	1 HILL 59-61	1823
Haile, Catherine	C. Matheson	13 RIEQ 104-110 {Lancaster District}	1858
Haile, Elizabeth	____ Knox	13 RIEQ 104-110 {Lancaster District}	1858

S.C. Marriages 1749-1867 Implied in S.C. Equity Reports

WOMAN	MAN	VOLUME	PAGES	LIVED

Haile, Susan _____ Lanier 13 RIEQ 104-110 1858
 {Lancaster District}
Hall, _____ _____ Cotchet 2 McC 269-317 1823
 (sister of Ainsley Hall of Columbia)
Hall, _____ John H. Garrett 2 McC 27-31 1821
Hall, _____ Robert May BAILEY 58-61 1810
 (widow of Andrew Hall) (May died 1823) {Walterborough}
Hall, _____ Edward C. Walker 1 HILL 397-405 1829
 [Must also see 2 HILL pages 22-24] {Colleton District}
Hall, Elizabeth James Day 2 McC 27-31 1820
 (widow of William Hall who died 1812) (she died
 September 1820)
Hall, Eliza May R. P. McCord 2 McC 269-317 1823
Hall, Margaret Robt. May 1 HILL 397-405 1829
 (widow) {Colleton District}
 [Must also see 2 HILL pages 22-24]
Hall, Martha A. Allen S. Barksdale 13 RIEQ 180-189 1861
 (daughter of David Hall who died 15 April 1860)
 {Anderson District}
Hall, Pinckey Josiah Foster 4 RIEQ 390-392 1826
 (daughter of Z. Hall) (she died about 1835)
 (Foster died 1836) {Fairfield}
Hall, Sarah William Cudworth 3 DESA 256-262 1810
 (married February 1810) (widow of Thomas Hall)
Hamer, _____ Eli Thomas 4 STRO 124-133 1847
 {Marlborough District}
Hamer, Mary Charles Gee 4 RIEQ 413-420 1851
 Elizabeth {Marlboro}
Hamilton, _____ _____ M'Leod 2 McC 354-367 1827
 (sister of Paul Hamilton who died about 1797 in England)
 {Charleston}
Hamlin, _____ James Rowland BAILEY 226-227 1829
 (widow of E. Hamlin) {Charleston}
Hamner, Elizabeth Jesse Wessenger 9 RIEQ 459-473 1857
 (daughter of George B. Hamner, Jr. who went to
 Tennessee) {Richland}
Hamner, Margaret Thomas Puryear 9 RIEQ 459-473 1839
 (married 31 May 1839) (daughter of George B. Hamner,
 Sr. of Mecklenburg County, Virginia) (she died 12
 February 1845) {Richland}
Hamner, Maria John C. O'Hanlon 9 RIEQ 459-473 1839
 (married 1839) (daughter of George B. Hamner, Sr.
 of Mecklenburg County, Virginia) (she died July
 1843) (O'Hanlon died 1853) {Richland}
Hamner, Martha William S. Lane 9 RIEQ 459-473 1835
 (daughter of George B. Hamner, Sr. of Mecklenburg
 County, Virginia) {Columbia, Richland}

S.C. Marriages 1749-1867 Implied in S.C. Equity Reports

WOMAN	MAN	VOLUME PAGES	LIVED
Hamner, Mary Frances (daughter of George B. Hamner, Jr. who went to Tennessee)	Thomas P. Walker	9 RIEQ 459-473 {Richland}	1857
Hamner, Nancy (daughter of George B. Hamner, Sr. of Mecklenburg County, Virginia)	Reuben A. Puryear	9 RIEQ 459-473 {Virginia}	1835
Hamner, Sarah (Sally) (daughter of George B. Hamner, Sr. of Mecklenburg County, Virginia)	Howell L. Jeffries	9 RIEQ 459-473 {Richland}	1834
Hancock, Elizabeth (widow of Simon Hancock, Sr.)	David Gurganes	McMULL 298-303 {Edgefield}	1834
Hancock, Elizabeth (widow of Simon Hancock, Sr.)	David Gurganus	1 RIEQ 26-40 {Edgefield}	1829
Hancock, Elizabeth (widow of Simon Hancock, Sr.)	David Gurganus	McMULL 69-74 {Edgefield}	1838
Hancock, Nancy (daughter of Simon Hancock, Sr.)	John M. Cooper	1 RIEQ 26-40 {Edgefield}	1841
Harleston, Eliza (daughter of John Harleston)	Thomas Corbett	DUDLEY 201-212 {Charleston}	1805
Harleston, Elizabeth (married May 1795) (daughter of Col. John Harleston) (she died 17 September 1837) (Corbett died July 1850)	Thomas Corbett	5 RIEQ 301-326 {Charleston}	1795
Harleston, Elizabeth (widow of John Harleston who died April 1781)	Maj. James Hamilton	1 DESA 244-247	1791
Harleston, Jane (marriage settlement 1793) (daughter of John Harleston) (she died 11 November 1835) (Rutledge died 1811)	Edward Rutledge	DUDLEY 201-212 {Charleston}	1793
Harleston, Jane (daughter of Col. John Harleston)	Edward Rutledge	5 RIEQ 301-326 {Charleston}	1795
Harleston, Sarah (daughter of Col. John Harleston)	Dr. William Read	5 RIEQ 301-326 {Charleston}	1793
Harleston, Sarah (daughter of John Harleston)	Dr. Wm. Reed (Read)	DUDLEY 201-212 {Charleston}	1805
Harley, _____ (daughter of William J. Harley)	_____ Langley	10 RIEQ 253-275 {Barnwell}	1857
Harris, _____ (daughter of John Harris)	John R. Carter	4 DESA 60-65 {Camden}	1809
Harris, _____ (daughter of John Harris)	Gilbert Dinkins	4 DESA 60-65 {Camden}	1809
Harris, _____ (widow of John Harris who died 1826) [In footnotes of 1917 Edition]	Nathaniel Saunders	2 STRO 370-377 {Edgefield}	1835
Harris, Ann Jemima	E. S. Irvine	4 RIEQ 25-38 {Abbeville}	1851

S.C. Marriages 1749-1867 Implied in S.C. Equity Reports

WOMAN	MAN	VOLUME	PAGES	LIVED

Harris, Narcissa _____ Hood 9 RIEQ 311-330 1846
 (daughter of John Harris, Sr. who died 1840,
 Mecklenburgh County, North Carolina) {Lancaster}
Harris, Rebecca George A. Addison 4 RIEQ 25-38 1851
   {Abbeville}
Harris, Sarah Joseph Brown 4 DESA 60-65 1798
 (daughter of John Harris) {Camden}
Harris, Sophia S. Moses Moore 9 RIEQ 311-330 1840
 (daughter of John Harris, Sr. who died 1840,
 Mecklenburgh County, North Carolina) {Lancaster}
Harrison, Ann Leroy H. Munday DUDLEY 34-41 1835
 Sophronia (daughter of Edward Harrison who died
 13 April 1829) {Edgefield}
Harrison, Charlotte Wm. M. McDonald 4 STRO 167-170 1812
 (widow) {Chester, Fairfield, Lancaster and Union}
Harrison, Julia B. Caleb Clarke, Sr. 4 STRO 167-170 1831
   {Chester, Fairfield, Lancaster and Union}
Hart, Charlotte Robert H. Goodwyn 5 RIEQ 370-403 1848
 (widow of Derril Hart) {St. Matthew's Parish}
Hart, Rachel Nathan Hart 3 DESA 592-595 1811
 (daughter of Daniel Hart who died 1811)
Harten, Rose Joseph Gibson, Sr. 4 DESA 139-143 1796
 (a married woman, wife of Henry Harten)
 (had child only) (Gibson died about 1805)
   {Fairfield District}
Haseldon, Elizabeth David Monroe 4 RIEQ 334-340 1844
 (widow of John Haseldon) (she died 1844) {Marion}
Haseldon, Elizabeth David Monroe 6 RIEQ 26-42 1853
 (widow of John Haseldon) {Marion}
Haseldon, Sarah C. D. Evans 6 RIEQ 26-42 1853
 Jane (daughter of John Haseldon) {Marion}
Hawie, _____(widow) Thomas Cochran 2 DESA 521-524 1807
Hay, Mary L. Richard A. Gantt 3 RIEQ 384-397 1850
 (daughter of Col. Frederick J. Hay) {Barnwell District}
Hazard, _____ Horace Waldo 4 RIEQ 266-275 1839
 (in New York City) {Beaufort District}
Hazard, Mary E. Edward N. Chisolm 4 RIEQ 266-275 1831
 (marriage contract 1831) (she died November 1838)
 (he died 1 September 1836) {Beaufort District}
Head, _____ James T. Willis 5 RIEQ 128-143 1833
   {Barnwell District}
Heape, Eliza Robert S. Burgess 1 HILL 397-405 1833
 (married 1817/18) {Barnwell}
Hearst, _____ Jacob Clarke 4 DESA 143-145 1810
   {Ninety-Six District}
Heath, _____ William G. Hunt 2 HILL 100-107 1816
 (daughter of Frederick Heath who died 1816) {Orangeburg}

S.C. Marriages 1749-1867 Implied in S.C. Equity Reports

WOMAN	MAN	VOLUME PAGES	LIVED

Heath, _____ John Kaigler 2 HILL 100-107 1831
{Orangeburg}
Henderson, _____ _____ Liles HARPER 298-301 1824
 (daughter of David Henderson) {Newberry District}
Henderson, Eliza Simon Taylor 4 DESA 505-517 1814
 Maria (daughter of General Wm. Henderson)
 {Richland District}
Henry, Anna Boyce _____ Bailey 5 RIEQ 187-202 1852
 (daughter of George Henry) {Charleston}
Henry, Caroline P. James Farrow 7 RIEQ 378-385 1854
 (daughter of James Edward Henry) {Spartanburg}
Henry, Eliza William T. Woodward 4 STRO 84-102 1839
 (marriage settlement 14 October 1839) (widow of
 George Henry who died August 1837) (Woodward died
 August 1842) {Charleston}
Henry, Eliza William T. Woodward 5 RIEQ 187-202 1840
 (widow of George Henry who died 1837) {Charleston}
Henry, Eliza A. H. Nicholas V. Bailey 4 STRO 84-102 1850
 (daughter of George Henry who died August 1837)
 {Charleston}
Herbemont, _____ _____ Bofil 3 RIEQ 1-9 1836
 (daughter of Nicholas Herbemont) {Richland District}
Herron, Eliza Jonathan Wright 5 RIEQ 441-450 1853
 (daughter of William H. Herron) {Darlington}
Herron, Margaret Darius L. Stuckey 5 RIEQ 441-450 1853
 (daughter of William H. Herron) {Darlington}
Hesse, Ann Henry Felder 4 RIEQ 349-358 1826
 Catherine (daughter of Daniel Hesse who died 1826)
 (her first marriage) (Felder died 28 April 1826)
 {Orangeburg}
Heyward, _____ General J. Cuthbert 2 McC 395-403 1814
 (daughter of William Heyward)
Heyward, _____ _____ Glover 2 McC 395-403 1814
 (sister of John Heyward who died 1820)
Heyward, Ann Sarah Nicholas Cruger 2 DESA 94-115 1799
 (married 1799) (widow of Daniel Heyward who died
 February 1796) [Must also see pages 422-431]
Heyward, Eliza _____ Parker 7 RIEQ 289-327 1852
Heyward, Elizabeth _____ Hamilton 7 RIEQ 289-327 1852
 M. (daughter of Daniel Heyward) {Charleston}
Heyward, Margaret Col. Wilson Glover 2 HILL 515-528 1783
 (widow of Daniel Heyward) (she died 1832)
 {Colleton District}
Heyward, Maria William Brailsford 2 DESA 18-37 1800
 (daughter of Daniel Heyward who died 11 October 1777)
 [See also pages 92-114; 291-294]

S.C. Marriages 1749-1867 Implied in S.C. Equity Reports

WOMAN	MAN	VOLUME PAGES	LIVED
Heyward, Susan (widow of James Heyward of Combahee)	Charles Baring	7 RIEQ 289-327 (she died 1845) {Charleston}	1845
Hicklin, Elizabeth	Henry Cole	1 HILL 311-323 {Lancaster}	1823
Hicklin, Sarah	___ Creyon	1 HILL 311-323 {Lancaster}	1823
Hicks, ___ (daughter of Claudius P. Hicks)	___ Williams	RICHEQ 5-23 {Darlington}	1830
Higginbottom, Julia E. D. (marriage settlement November 1838) (widow of James Higginbottom) (Kottman was born August 1818) [See also pages 142-158]	Kottman	SPEERS 29-35 {Barnwell}	1839
Hill, Rhydonia (daughter of Jonathan Hill) (to Arkansas) {Edgefield}	James Goodwin	3 STRO 94-105	1847
Hilton, Jane (she died December 1856) (he died September 1857)	William Rhodus	12 RIEQ 104-113 {Clarendon}	1829
Hodges, ___ (daughter of Richard Hodges)	John Iley	HARPER 295-298 {Laurens}	1824
Hodges, ___	John Iley	1 McC 518-523	1826
Hodges, Anna R. (daughter of Gen. George W. Hodges) (Stokes died 7 August 1853)	Joseph H. Stokes	11 RIEQ 135-155 (she died 1858) {Abbeville District}	1850
Hoff, Jane (marriage settlement 6 April 1805) (widow) (he of Abbeville) (she died 1852/53) {Colleton}	Godfrey Adams	9 RIEQ 247-251	1805
Holland, Martha (daughter of John Holland)	James Miller	BAILEY 479-482 {Charleston}	1830
Holloway, ___	Daniel Prescott	7 RIEQ 9-16 {Edgefield}	1820
Holloway, Lucy	James Reese	7 RIEQ 9-16 {Edgefield}	1847
Holman, Catharine (daughter of John C. Holman who died 1839) {Orangeburg}	___ Wolfe	4 RIEQ 329-334	1852
Holman, Elizabeth (daughter of Conrad Holman of St. Matthew's Parish, who died 16 August 1816)	Daniel Zimmerman	4 RIEQ 329-334 {Orangeburg}	1821
Holman, Elizabeth (daughter of John C. Holman who died 1839) {Orangeburg}	Russel Zimmerman	4 RIEQ 329-334	1852
Holman, Esther	___ Anderson	3 DESA 210-212	1811
Holman, Mary (daughter of Conrad Holman of St. Matthew's Parish, who died 16 August 1816) (she died 1848) (Murph died 1844)	John Murph	4 RIEQ 329-334 {Orangeburg}	1821
Hoof, Sarah (daughter of James D. Hoof)	William W. Holeman	3 STRO 66-75 {Orangeburg District}	1848

S.C. Marriages 1749-1867 Implied in S.C. Equity Reports

WOMAN	MAN	VOLUME PAGES	LIVED

Hoof, Sarah   Thomas Jackson   3 STRO 66-75   1813
   (married about January 1813) (widow of James D. Hoof)
   (widower)   {Orangeburg District}
Hoover, Jerusha   Elijah Jefcoat   10 RIEQ 118-129   1811
   (daughter of John Hoover who died 1832)
   (she died 1818)   {Lexington District}
Hoover, Jerusha   Richard Sturkie   10 RIEQ 118-129   1832
    {Lexington District}
Hopkins, _____   _____ Glenn   1 HILL 1-10   1818
   (daughter of George W. Hopkins)
Hopkins, Martha   Thomas Terry   1 HILL 1-10   1819
   (married February 1819) (widow of George W. Hopkins)
Horger, _____   _____ Snell   4 DESA 268-273   1792
   Catharina (daughter of Jacob Horger) {Orangeburg}
Horry, _____   Judge Edward Frost   10 RIEQ 109   1835
   (daughter of Elias Horry)   {Charleston}
Horry, Emma L.   Charles D.   2 HILL 244-249   1835
    Manigault   {Charleston}
   (daughter of Elias Lynch Horry who died 1831)
Horry, Margaret   Henry Deas   2 DESA 115-127   1802
   (Peggy) (daughter of Elias Horry)
Horry, Margaret   Henry Deas   2 HILL 244-249   1835
   (daughter of Elias Horry who died 1785) {Charleston}
Horry, Margaret   Edward R. Laurens   14 RIEQ 139-145   1866
    {Charleston}
Horry, Margaret H.   Edward R. Laurens   2 HILL 244-249   1835
   (daughter of Elias Lynch Horry who died 1831)
    {Charleston}
Houston, _____   John C. Scott   9 RIEQ 85-99   1856
    {Abbeville}
Houston, Augusta G.   Lewis G. Parks   9 RIEQ 85-99   1856
   (daughter of Alexander Houston) (she was born
   7 May 1835)   {Abbeville}
Howard, _____   Horatio McClenaghan   2 RIEQ 79-84   1829
   (daughter of Richard Howard)   {Marion}
   [See also 1 STRO pages 295-323 and 2 STRO pages 227-230]
Howard, Sarah   Thomas Hall   3 DESA 256-262   1803
   (married 1803) (he died October 1808)
Huff, Susan   Thomas Blankton   6 RIEQ 388-398   1850
   (married April 1850)   {Goose Creek}
   [Referred to in another case in footnotes of 1917
   Edition]
Huger, _____   Allen Smith Izard   9 RIEQ 217-243   1856
   (daughter of Hon. David Elliott Huger of Charleston,
   who died 21 August 1854)   {Charleston}

S.C. Marriages 1749-1867 Implied in S.C. Equity Reports

WOMAN	MAN	VOLUME PAGES	LIVED
Huger, _____	_____ Manigault	9 RIEQ 217-243	1856
(daughter of Hon. Daniel Elliott Huger of Charleston, who died 21 August 1854)		{Charleston}	
Hughes, Elizabeth	David Lawrence	BAILEY 304-311	1824
		{Charleston}	
Hughson, _____	_____ Frazier	4 DESA 87-92	1810
(sister of John Hughson) (she was born 1780)			
		{Cheraw District}	
Hughson, _____	Aaron Snowden	4 DESA 87-92	1788
(married 1788) (she was a widow)		{Cheraw District}	
Hull, Currency	Samuel Sawyer	2 STRO 174-195	1840
		{Connecticut}	
Hull, Zulina	_____ Bryan	2 STRO 174-195	1845
(daughter of Gideon H. Hull) (she was born 1828/29)			
		{Edgefield}	
Hull, Zulina	_____ Bryan	3 RIEQ 65-96	1849
		{Edgefield}	
Hull, Zulina	_____ Langdon	2 STRO 174-195	1845
(daughter of Gideon H. Hull)		{Connecticut}	
Hume, Catharine	William Simons	5 RIEQ 270-274	1852
		{Charleston}	
Hunt, Jane B.	William Mootry	8 RIEQ 166-184	1849
[Must also see 11 RIEQ pages 205-224] {Charleston District and Georgetown}			
Hunt, Jane B.	William Mootry	6 RIEQ 183-199	1853
(daughter of Col. Benjamin F. Hunt) {Charleston}			
Hunter, _____	Ervin Brunson	2 HILL 483-492	1835
(daughter of Andrew Hunter)		{Darlington}	
Hunter, Nancy A.	Ezekiel F. Hyde	13 RIEQ 250-258	1864
		{Laurens}	
Hurst, Jane	Archibald M'Kewn	3 DESA 273-296	1795
(widow of Robert Hurst) (she died October 1807) (M'Kewin)			
Hutchinson, Maria	_____ Dupont	10 RIEQ 1-3	1857
(daughter of Mathias Hutchinson)		{Charleston}	
Hutchinson, Mary	_____ Firth	10 RIEQ 1-3	1848
(daughter of Mathias Hutchinson)		{Charleston}	
Hutchinson, Mary	_____ Whitaker	10 RIEQ 1-3	1848
(daughter of Mathias Hutchinson) (she died 1848)			
		{Charleston}	
Hutson, Maria	W. S. Townsend	6 RIEQ 249-254	1840
(she died June 1840) (he went to Georgia, remarried and went to Tennessee)		{Beaufort}	
Hyams, Sarah	George Prince	1 RIEQ 282-291	1835
(married 2 March 1835, Portsmouth, England, or common-law marriage)			

S.C. Marriages 1749-1867 Implied in S.C. Equity Reports

WOMAN	MAN	VOLUME	PAGES	LIVED

(I)

Inabinit, Eliza M. Daniel V. V.   3 RIEQ   370-378   1849
                    Funchess   {Orangeburgh}
   (daughter of James Inabinit who died 7 March 1849)
Ingram, Mary   Christian   1 RIEQ   465-474   1838
                    Breithaupt (common-law marriage)
                                      {Edgefield}
Ingram, Sarah   ____ Clanton   4 STRO   171-175   1831
                                      {Lancaster}
I'On, ____   Thomas Lowndes   2 DESA   210-214   1802
Ioor, Julia S.   Absalom T. Hodges SPEERS   593-603   1837
   (marriage settlement 9 March 1837)
   (Hodges of Abbeville)   {Edgefield District}
Irby, Mehitabel   Thomas Lide   4 DESA   422-433   1787
   (widow of Charles Irby) (she died February 1804)
   (Lide died 7 November 1787) (Lide was married
   before)   {Cheraw and Marlboro Districts}
Isaacs, Sarah J.   Benjamin Jewell   11 RIEQ 296-322   1813
   (married June 1813, Richmond, Virginia) (he died
   1828, Louisiana)   {Charleston District}
Izard, Ann Stead   Walter Blake   3 RIEQ   225-234   1837
   (married 16 June 1837)   {Charleston}
Izard, Charlotte   W. L. Smith   2 DESA   308-313   1805
   (daughter of Ralph Izard who died 30 May 1804)
Izard, Eliza   Thomas Pinckney   2 RIEQ   218-245   1803
   (marriage contract 27 December 1803) (daughter of
   Ralph Izard) (Pinckney died 7 July 1842, Havre, France)
Izard, Mary   Arthur Middleton 1 DESA   116-123   1785

(J)

Jackson, Ann   James D. Hoof   3 STRO   66-75   1813
   (married April 1813) (daughter of Thomas Jackson)
   (Hoof was born about 1796) (to Edgefield) {Orangeburg
   District}
Jaffray, Mary   Thomas Cape   1 DESA   567-570   1797
   (widow of J. Jaffray)
James, ____   Joseph Gregg   DUDLEY   42-54   1835
   (daughter of George James)   {Marion}
James, Elizabeth   Robert Brailsford McMULL   55-62   1826
                    (he died 1826)   {Sumter District}

S.C. Marriages 1749-1867 Implied in S.C. Equity Reports

WOMAN	MAN	VOLUME	PAGES	LIVED
James, Jane	Daniel Mullins	4 RIEQ	80-87	1829
(married 1829) (widow of John James)				
(Mullins died 1844)		{Spartanburg District}		
James, Judith	Owen Hall	2 McC	143-150	1827
(daughter of George James)		{Wilkes County, North Carolina}		
James, Lucy	Samuel (or William) Hicks	2 McC	143-150	1827
(daughter of George James)		{Wilkes County, North Carolina}		
James, Mary	Thomas N. Johnson	2 HILL	277-298	1818
(she died January 1818)				
James, Nancy	William Gary	4 DESA	185-199	1811
(daughter of John James of Newberry District)				
		{Washington District}		
James, Polly T.	Thomas C. Austin	4 RIEQ	80-87	1851
(daughter of John James)		{Spartanburg District}		
James, Susannah	Joseph Kennerly	1 HILL	76-94	1808
(married 1800/01) (widow of Philip James)				
(Kennerly died about 1808)				
Jefcoat, Martha	William O. Martin	10 RIEQ	118-129	1828
(Patsey) (married about 1828) (he died November 1839)				
		{Lexington District}		
Jeffreys, Jean	Andrew McCullough, Sen.	1 STRO	193-196	1795
		{Walterborough}		
Jeffreys, Mary	Hans McCullough	1 STRO	193-196	1784
		{Walterborough}		
Jeffries, Jeffreys. See Jaffrey				
Jenkins, _____	Rev. Paul T. Gervais	McMULL	106-114	1830
(daughter of Micah Jenkins who died about 1839)				
Jenkins, _____	Benjamin D. Roper	McMULL	106-114	1830
Jenkins, Elizabeth	_____ Gray	2 HILL	511-515	1834
(widow of John H. Jenkins who was born 3 February 1797)				
		{Beaufort}		
Jenkins, Elizabeth	William M. Clarke	3 RIEQ	318-341	1831
Mary (his second marriage) (he died 1831) {Charleston}				
Jenkins, Martha (widow)	Charles Givens	RICHEQ	326-352	1813
		{Beaufort}		
Jenkins, Martha	Charles Givens	2 HILL	511-515	1832
(widow of Joseph John Jenkins who died 1804)				
(she died 1832)		{Beaufort}		
Jennings, Anne	S. K. McClellan	13 RIEQ	172-179	1863
		{Sumter}		
Jeter, _____	Edward Martin	1 STRO	103-113	1820
(daughter of William Jeter who died 7 September 1820)				
		{Edgefield}		

S.C. Marriages 1749-1867 Implied in S.C. Equity Reports

WOMAN	MAN	VOLUME	PAGES	LIVED
Jeter, Charlotte	_____ Phillips	1 STRO	103-113	1820
(daughter of William Jeter who died 7 September 1820) {Edgefield}				
Jeter, Martha	William W. Williams	1 STRO	103-113	1820
(daughter of William Jeter who died 7 September 1820) (Williams died 1845) {Edgefield}				
Jeter, Mary P.	Christopher Mantz	1 STRO	103-113	1826
(daughter of William Jeter who died 7 September 1820) {Edgefield}				
Jewell, _____	A. Bondy	11 RIEQ	296-322	1855
		{Charleston District}		
Jewell, Delia	Jacob Meyers	11 RIEQ	296-322	1834
(daughter of Benjamin Jewell)		{Charleston District}		
Jewell, Hannah	Verg Aigne	11 RIEQ	296-322	1834
(daughter of Benjamin Jewell)		{Charleston District}		
Jewell, Hetty	_____ Mitchell	11 RIEQ	296-322	1855
(daughter of Benjamin Jewell)		{Charleston District}		
Jewell, Juliana	Samuel Rickenbacker	11 RIEQ	296-322	1855
(daughter of Benjamin Jewell) (Charleston or Orangeburg)		{Charleston District}		
Jewell, Sophia	Joseph Storne	11 RIEQ	296-322	1820
Prevost (married about 1820) (he of Charleston) {Charleston District}				
Jewell, Sophie J.	_____ Storms	RICHEQ	112-115	1818
(married 1818) (separated from Benjamin Jewell who died 1828) (to Barnwell then Charleston) [In footnotes]				
Johnson, _____	John Gage, Sr.	HARPER	197-202	1819
(daughter of Col. Wm. Johnson)				
Johnson, _____	Daniel Thomas	HARPER	197-202	1819
(daughter of Col. Wm. Johnson)				
Johnson, Amanda	William Wilie	5 RIEQ	91-94	1852
(she of Camden)		{Lancaster}		
Johnson, Caroline M.	Edward H. Britton	2 HILL	430-442	1835
(daughter of James Johnson who died 1815) {Marion}				
Johnson, Mary	John Canady	6 RIEQ	103-110	1818
(married October 1818)		{Barnwell}		
Johnson, Mary	Wm. King	2 HILL	624-629	1806
(common-law marriage) (he died 1836) {Edgefield}				
Johnson, Sarah	James Dupree	4 DESA	209-215	1785
(marriage agreement 2 February 1785) {Georgetown}				
Johnson, Sarah	Dr. Alexander W. Garden (he died 5 August 1820)	2 HILL	277-298	1818
(daughter of Thomas N. Johnson) (Garden's first marriage)				
Jones, Dorcas	Wm. E. Hall	1 STRO	323-333	1847
		{Fairfield}		
Jones, Jemima	Allen R. Crankfield	1 STRO	323-333	1847
		{Fairfield}		

S.C. Marriages 1749-1867 Implied in S.C. Equity Reports

WOMAN	MAN	VOLUME PAGES	LIVED
Jones, Mercy	Henry Parkman	1 RIEQ 78-91	1807
(widow of Thomas Jones)		{Ninety-Six District}	
Josey, Jane	Thomas Berry	9 RIEQ 369-375	1844
(married 1841-1844) (widow) (she died 1848) {Kershaw}			

(K)

WOMAN	MAN	VOLUME PAGES	LIVED
Kelly, Rebecca	Samuel Adams	2 DESA 214-221	1794
(common-law marriage) (he died October 1794)			
Kennedy, Mary	John J. Aaron	9 RIEQ 411-417	1834
Elizabeth (daughter of Robert Kennedy who died 16 October 1834)		{Barnwell}	
Kennedy, Sarah	Charles Beck	9 RIEQ 411-417	1836
(married 1836) (widow of Robert Kennedy who died 16 October 1834) (Beck died 1855) {Barnwell}			
Kennerly, Susannah	Cullen Fennel	1 HILL 76-94	1810
(widow of Joseph Kennerly)			
Kerr, Jane	John Webb, Sr.	9 RIEQ 369-375	1827
	(he died about 1827, Edgefield) {Kershaw}		
Kerr, Sarah P.	_____ Anderson	9 RIEQ 369-375	1838
		{Kershaw}	
Kershaw, Henrietta	_____ Perkins	1 HILL 344-352	1831
		{Camden}	
Keys, _____	Ezekiel L. Norris	6 RIEQ 388-398	1850
		{Anderson}	
Kimbrough, _____	Lemuel Benton	4 DESA 17-19	1809
(daughter of John Kimbrough)		{Cheraws}	
Kinard, _____	John Enlow	2 RIEQ 247-259	1845
(daughter of John M. Kinard)		{Newberry}	
Kinard, Huldah	John K. Henson	3 STRO 371-379	1842
(married 16 August 1842) (daughter of Martin Kinard) (she died 22 October 1844)		{Newberry and Laurens Districts}	
Kinder, Catharine	Thomas Finley	3 STRO 78-86	1823
(he was born 11 February 1757)		{Abbeville District}	
Kinder, Catherine	Thomas Finley	2 STRO 208-220	1831
(had child only in Virginia) (Finley died 3 December 1831)		{Abbeville}	
King, _____	Robert Williamson	BAILEY 154-156	1818
(daughter of John King who died July 1818) {Cheraw}			
Kingdom, Elizabeth Birch	William Holladay (he died 1819)	McMULL 279-289 {Sumter}	1819
Kittles, _____	_____ Bradley	6 RIEQ 155-182	1822
(daughter of Jacob C. Kittles) (to Florida) {Barnwell}			

S.C. Marriages 1749-1867 Implied in S.C. Equity Reports

WOMAN	MAN	VOLUME PAGES	LIVED
Knox, _____	Reuben Starke	4 DESA 92-94	1810

(L)

La Barthe,   Francis Jelineau   2 DESA 45-52   1800
   Elizabeth F. (widow?) (married February 1800)
Laborde, Zelime   Hollis Dunton   McMULL 448-450   1820
   (daughter of Peter Laborde who died 1821) {Edgefield}
Lacoste, Jeane   Philipe Eugene   1 RIEQ 187-221   1836
   Elvina   Guillemot
   (marriage contract 23 May 1836, Paris, France)
   (daughter of Charles Gregorie Arnauld Lacoste)
Ladson, _____   John Simons Bee   RICHEQ 315-320   1826
   (daughter of Major James Ladson) {Charleston}
Ladson, _____   James Hartley   1 DESA 500-515   1796
   (daughter of Thomas Ladson)
Lahiffe, Elizabeth   Thomas P. Spierin   2 DESA 459-471   1797
   (widow) (marriage settlement 6 January 1797)
   (she died 1804)
Lamb, Mary Jane   John J. Lide   SPEERS 289-302   1843
   (daughter Alexander Lamb who died 1836)
                              {Marlboro District}
Lamkin, _____   Col. Abner Whatley   2 HILL 605-611   1826
                              {Edgefield}
Lane, Martha   Alfred M. Hunt   9 RIEQ 459-473   1838
   (married 15 March 1838) (widow of William S. Lane)
                              {Richland}
Langley, Mary   Henry Cannon   BAILEY 204-207   1812
   (daughter of Christopher Langley who died 1 March
   1812) (she died 16 March 1812) {Coosawhatchie}
Lattimer, Cagy   Robert Elgin   4 DESA 26-33   1809
   (widow of Benjamin Lattimer of Maryland) {Abbeville,
   Ninety-Six District}
Laurens, _____   John Laurens   7 RIEQ 260-280   1846
   (daughter of Edward R. Laurens) {Charleston}
Laurens, Caroline   James W. Read   7 RIEQ 260-280   1853
                              {Charleston}
Laurens, Caroline   James Withers Read   11 RIEQ 285-295   1842
   (married 12 May 1842) (she was born 1823/24)
   (he died 28 June 1851) {Charleston}
Laurens, Eliza R.   John Laurens   14 RIEQ 139-145   1866
   (daughter of Edward R. Laurens) {Charleston}
Laurens, Frances   Francis Henderson   2 DESA 170-171   1803
   (daughter of Col. John Laurens)

S.C. Marriages 1749-1867 Implied in S.C. Equity Reports

WOMAN	MAN	VOLUME PAGES	LIVED
Laurens, Harriet	_____ Ingraham	6 RIEQ 217-226 {Charleston}	1842
Laurens, Harriet (daughter of Henry Laurens, Jr.)	D. N. Ingraham	14 RIEQ 139-145 {Charleston}	1866
Laurens, Martha [See also 6 RIEQ pages 217-266]	Dr. Paul Ramsay	2 DESA 582-592	1806
Lawton, Beulah (daughter of Winborn Lawton)	_____ Hughes	3 DESA 199-203	1811
Leake, Alzira (daughter of George Leake)	Adam Bradock	SPEERS 564-568 {Laurens}	1834
Leake, Jinny (daughter of George Leake)	Wm. Brown	SPEERS 564-568 {Laurens}	1834
Leake, Malinda (married 1833) (daughter of George Leake) (she died 1835)	Middleton W. Cobb	SPEERS 564-568 {Laurens}	1833
Lee, _____ (married 4 March 1819) (daughter of Andrew Lee) (she died 15 November 1820)	Daniel Dubose	BAILEY 166-168 {Darlington}	1819
Lee, _____	Stephen Henderson	4 DESA 459-462 {Abbeville}	1814
Lee, Ann	Simon Lee	11 RIEQ 574-583 {Sumter}	1854
Lee, Rebecca (marriage agreement 26 September 1844) (widow) (widower) (Spiva died about 1855 out West)	David Spiva	9 RIEQ 434-439 {Union District}	1844
Lee, Terza (widow of Eleazar Lee) (she died 1843)	_____ Street	SPEERS 373-374 {Chester}	1841
Lefitt, _____	George Barksdale	2 HILL 184-200 {Coosawhatchie}	1798
Leger, Martha (married June 1813) (his first marriage)	James White, Sr.	McMULL 115-125 {Georgetown}	1813
Lehre, Mary Ann (or Mary R.) [See also pages 271-272]	_____ Greene	1 RIEQ 296-301	1844
Lester, P.	George Stairley (he died June 1835)	McMULL 22-26 {Greenville District}	1833
Lewis, _____ (daughter of John Lewis) (she died 1836)	Peter M. Huson	1 RIEQ 1-25 {Union}	1836
Lewis, _____ (daughter of William Lewis) (Pickett died 1822)	James R. Pickett	2 STRO 157-165 {Fairfield District}	1822
Lewis, _____ (she died 1838) Searson (daughter of Samuel Lewis)	Zachariah Z.	1 STRO 180-184 {Beaufort District}	1836
Lewis, Elizabeth C. (married 1825/26) (widow of John Lewis) (she died February 1835)	Thomas McMeekin	1 RIEQ 1-25 {Union}	1825

151

S.C. Marriages 1749-1867 Implied in S.C. Equity Reports

WOMAN	MAN	VOLUME PAGES	LIVED
Lewis, Ellen	William H. Colcock	5 RIEQ 370-403	1831
(daughter of William L. Lewis)		{St. Matthew's Parish}	
Lewis, Martha	Daniel B. Price	3 RIEQ 172-199	1834
(married 9 January 1834) (widow of Jesse Lewis			
who died 30 October 1832)		{Darlington District}	
Lewis, Martha G.	James R. Pickett	RICE 40-50	1822
(daughter of William Lewis)		{Fairfield}	
Lewis, Sarah	Thomas Gelzer	BAILEY 387-389	1830
		{Charleston}	
Ligon, Nancy T.	John Moon	2 STRO 327-334	1848
[See also pages 407-409]		{Greenville}	
Liles, Lucy	_____ Smith	HARPER 298-301	1824
		{Newberry District}	
Lindsay, _____	John Winter	1 DESA 150-154	1749
(married about 1749) (widow of Patrick Lindsay			
who died 1744) (she died 1781/82) (Winter died 1785)			
Livingston,	Thomas Heyward	7 RIEQ 136-169	1843
Catharine Barnwell Thayer (he was married before)			
(marriage settlement 6 February 1843) {Charleston}			
Livingston,	Edward B. Wheeler	3 RIEQ 452-465	1851
Josephine		{Marion}	
Livingston, Mary	_____ Fraser	2 DESA 573-576	1808
Lloyd, _____	B. P. Simons	DUDLEY 141-145	1836
(daughter of John Lloyd)			
Lockwood, Ann	John Holmes Smith	3 DESA 12-18	1800
Long, _____	Dr. Thomas Wier	2 RIEQ 283-285	1842
(daughter of Robert Long)		{Laurens}	
Long, Caroline	Amasa Ezell	1 STRO 43-53	1846
(daughter of William Long)		{Union}	
Long, Elizabeth	James Farnandes	1 STRO 43-53	1846
(daughter of William Long)		{Union}	
Long, Letitia	_____ Ezell	1 STRO 43-53	1846
(daughter of William Long)		{Union}	
Long, Mary	Daniel Mabray	1 STRO 43-53	1846
(daughter of William Long)		{Union}	
Long, Sarah	Smith Willis	1 STRO 43-53	1846
(daughter of William Long)		{Union}	
Lothrop, _____	_____ McOwen	2 RIEQ 412-472	1846
(daughter of Seth Lothrop)		{Charleston}	
Lothrop, Eliza	William Price, Jr.	2 RIEQ 412-472	1825
(daughter of Seth Lothrop) (Price died May 1831)			
		{Charleston}	
Lott, _____	Benjamin Frazier	1 STRO 79-81	1833
	(he died 1844)	{Edgefield}	
Lowe, _____	Hugh Moore	1 McC 243-247	1826
Lowndes, _____	Frederick Kinloch	1 HILL 190-193	1833
(daughter of Thomas Lowndes)		{Charleston}	

S.C. Marriages 1749-1867 Implied in S.C. Equity Reports

WOMAN	MAN	VOLUME PAGES	LIVED
Lowrey, Mary (married 1783) (widow) (she died 1788) (he died December 1800)	William Smelie	2 DESA 66-79	1783
Lowrey, Sarah Maxwell (her first marriage)	Abraham Waight	2 DESA 66-79	1787
Lowry, Louisa (daughter of James M. Lowry who died May 1837, Perry County, Alabama)	John A. Bradley	SPEERS 1-19 {Chester District}	1836
Lucas, Catharine	____ Hume	5 RIEQ 270-274 {Charleston}	1840
Lushington, Charity (married 14 May 1794) (widow of R. Lushington)	George Forrest	2 DESA 254-263	1794
Luter, Martha E. (married 3/4 December 1841)	Thomas McDowel	1 STRO 347-349 {Fairfield}	1841
Lyles, ____ (daughter of Col. Aromanos Lyles)	William Moody	1 HILL 76-94	1833
Lynch, Elizabeth (her first marriage) (Harleston died April 1781)	John Harleston	1 DESA 244-247	1781

(Mc)

McBee, Martha (widow of Elijah McBee)	David Robertson	McMULL 485-494 {Spartanburg}	1831
McBee, Patsey (widow)	____ Robertson	SPEERS 20-28 {Spartanburgh District}	1833
McClain, Margaret	____ McGrew	4 DESA 155-162	1800
McClenaghan, Mary Ann	C. H. Black	7 RIEQ 407-421 {Darlington}	1854
McClure. See McLure			
McConnell, Mary Jane	W. D. Miller	9 RIEQ 500-520 {York District}	1853
M'Connico, Nancy (daughter of William M'Connico)	____ Connors	2 McC 323-343	1827
McCool, Letitia (she died 1843)	____ Hardin	3 STRO 44-54 {Chester}	1837
McCord, Mary E. (she died 1848)	Christopher F. Hampton	5 RIEQ 403 {St. Matthew's Parish}	1843
McCorkle, Milly	____ Gordon	1 RIEQ 61-66 {Lancaster}	1844
McCreary, Ann	William Fortune	9 RIEQ 34-36 {Barnwell}	1856
M'Culloch, Elizabeth (daughter of Hance M'Culloch)	James T. Buckner	2 HILL 499-504 {Coosawhatchie}	1837

153

S.C. Marriages 1749-1867 Implied in S.C. Equity Reports

WOMAN	MAN	VOLUME	PAGES	LIVED

McCullough, _____ Buchanan 1 STRO 193-196 1822
    Margaret (daughter of Hans McCullough) (she died
    1834-36) (Buchanan died 2 April 1827) {Walterborough}
McCutchen, Margaret Hardy B. Godwin 10 RIEQ 226-231 1833
    (marriage settlement 26 March 1833)
    (Godwin died 1855/56) {Williamsburgh}
McDaniel, _____ James Dugan DUDLEY 1-14 1837
    (widow) {Newberry}
McDaniel, _____ Ary Jeter DUDLEY 1-14 1837
    {Newberry}
McDaniel, _____ William Moore DUDLEY 1-14 1837
    {Newberry}
M'Daniel, _____ Col. James Moorman HARPER 108-116 1824
    (daughter of Charles M'Daniel who died 1801)
M'Daniel, Frances _____ Dugan HARPER 108-116 1824
    (widow of Thomas M'Daniel)
McDaniel, Rosa Wesley Payne 8 RIEQ 9-12 1836
    Manning (daughter of James McDaniel) (she died 1851)
    {Greenville}
McDonald, _____ Paul Jaudon RICHEQ 246-258 1826
    (daughter of Adam McDonald) {Georgetown}
McDonald, Charlotte Hugh McMullan 4 STRO 167-170 1831
    (widow of Wm. M. McDonald) (she died 3 March 1831)
    (McMullan died 1841) {Chester, Fairfield, Lancaster
    and Union}
McDonald, Tirza John Brown 2 HILL 457-467 1817
    (daughter of Middleton McDonald, Sen.) {Chester}
McDow, _____ _____ Gettys 4 STRO 37-58 1839
    (daughter of James McDow of Lancaster District)
McDow, Margaret E. James B. Adams 14 RIEQ 304-310 1867
    (daughter of John J. McDow) {Lancaster}
McDow, Margaret J. Samuel Curry 4 STRO 37-58 1839
    (daughter of James McDow of Lancaster District)
McDow, Martha A. William J. Gamble 4 STRO 37-58 1839
    (daughter of James McDow of Lancaster District)
M'Dowall, _____ Henry Peyton 2 DESA 313-320 1805
    (daughter of Captain Alexander M'Dowall who died 1799)
McDowell, Ann _____ Terry RILEY 152-155 1834
    {Charleston}
M'Dowell, Harriet William Caldwell 2 McC 43-59 1826
    (daughter of Patrick M'Dowell) {Newberry District}
McDowell, Susan _____ Harrison RILEY 152-155 1834
    {Charleston}
M'Gillivray, Mary William Sams 1 DESA 127-135 1785
    (daughter of J. Stanyarne)
McGrath. See Megrath

S.C. Marriages 1749-1867 Implied in S.C. Equity Reports

WOMAN	MAN	VOLUME	PAGES	LIVED
McGrew, Elizabeth	Cornelius H. Vauters	4 DESA	155-162	1811
McGrew, Margaret (common-law marriage)	John Elders	4 DESA	155-162	1800
McJunkin, Amanda (daughter of Joseph McJunkin)	David A. Fant	11 RIEQ {Union}	527-535	1856
McJunkin, Emeline (daughter of Joseph McJunkin)	William Wilson	11 RIEQ {Union}	527-535	1856
McJunkin, Frances (daughter of Joseph McJunkin)	P. A. Davis	11 RIEQ {Union}	527-535	1856
McJunkin, Harriet (daughter of Joseph McJunkin)	William Jeter	11 RIEQ {Union}	527-535	1858
McJunkin, Mary (married 1840) (daughter of Joseph McJunkin) (she died 1845) (Wilson of Columbia or Lexington) {Union}	Thomas Wilson	11 RIEQ	527-535	1840
McJunkin, Sarah J. (daughter of Joseph McJunkin) (her first marriage) {Union}	_____ Thomas	11 RIEQ	527-535	1856
McKenzie, _____ (daughter of Daniel W. McKenzie)	A. E. Chovin	2 STRO {Gillisonville}	40-44	1836
McKenzie, _____ (widow of Daniel W. McKenzie)	B. Villard	2 STRO {Gillisonville}	40-44	1848
McKenzie, Eliza A. (married September 1828) (widow of Daniel W. McKenzie who died 1826) (she died March 1843) {Gillisonville}	Isaac A. E. Chovin	1 STRO	393-420	1828
McKenzie, Harriet (married 2 November 1843) (daughter of Daniel W. McKenzie)	Wm. B. Villard	1 STRO {Gillisonville}	393-420	1843
McKinney, Jane (marriage settlement 21 July 1828, Lincoln County, Georgia) (widow) {Abbeville District}	William R. Reid	12 RIEQ	349-360	1828
McKinney, Jane (marriage contract 31 July 1828) (both of Lincoln County, Georgia) {Abbeville}	William R. Reid	1 STRO	27-43	1828
McLennan, Catharine Ann (daughter of John McLennan who died 1853) {Abbeville}	_____ Watson	9 RIEQ	129-136	1856
M'Leod, Sarah (daughter of Rev. Doctor Donald M'Leod)	Dr. J. B. Whitridge	1 RIEQ {Charleston District}	155-186	1842
McLewrath, _____ (widow)	Daniel Miller (he died 1819)	BAILEY {Barnwell}	187-194	1818
McLewrath, Polly	James Calhoun	2 STRO {Barnwell}	231-237	1831
McLewrath, Polly	James J. Calhoun	RICHEQ {Barnwell}	36-45	1827

S.C. Marriages 1749-1867 Implied in S.C. Equity Reports

WOMAN	MAN	VOLUME PAGES	LIVED
McLure, Araminthia	Joseph Feemster	14 RIEQ 105-120	1866

(daughter of William McLure who died 1859) {York}

| McLure, Caroline | James McKnight | 14 RIEQ 105-120 | 1866 |

(daughter of William McLure who died 1859) {York}

| McLure, Catharine | James Galloway | 14 RIEQ 105-120 | 1866 |

(daughter of William McLure who died 1859) {York}

| McLure, Margaret | William T. Robison | 14 RIEQ 105-120 | 1866 |

(daughter of William McLure who died 1859) {York}

| McMorries, _____ | James P. Caldwell | 11 RIEQ 73-82 | 1848 |

(of Newberry County) (he died October 1848) {Newberry}

| McMorries, Rebecca | _____ Logan | 11 RIEQ 73-82 | 1848 |

{Newberry}

| McMullen, _____ | _____ Clark | 4 RIEQ 117-135 | 1846 |

(daughter of Hugh McMullen of Chester District, who died December 1841) {Chester}

| McMullen, _____ | _____ Woodward | 4 RIEQ 117-135 | 1846 |

(daughter of Hugh McMullen of Chester District, who died December 1841) {Chester}

| McNish, _____ | Alvin N. Miller | 4 STRO 66-83 | 1850 |

(widow of Charles L. McNish) (in Savannah, Georgia) {Beaufort District}

| McNish, Sarah Jane | Alvin N. Miller | 8 RIEQ 112-129 | 1855 |

(widow of Charles Lycurgus McNish who died 1844) [See also 7 RIEQ pages 186-200] {Beaufort District}

| McPherson, _____ | Samuel Colleton Graves | BAILEY 268-274 | 1824 |

{Charleston}

| McPherson, _____ | Samuel Colleton Graves | RILEY 219-247 | 1824 |

| M'Pherson, Elizabeth | James R. Pringle | 2 DESA 524-546 | 1807 |

(daughter of Gen. John M'Pherson of Prince William's Parish, who died 24 August 1806) {Colleton District}

| McPherson, Elizabeth Mary | James Reid Pringle | 3 RIEQ 342-360 | 1807 |

(marriage settlement 18 March 1807) (daughter of General John McPherson) (Pringle died 11 July 1840) (she died 14 August 1843) {Charleston}

| M'Pherson, Susan | Samuel C. Graves | 1 HILL 135-138 | 1833 |
| McPherson, Susan | Samuel Colleton Graves | 3 RIEQ 218-225 | 1818 |

(marriage settlement 15 April 1818) {Charleston}

| M'Pherson, Susan M. | Samuel C. Graves | 1 RIEQ 319-324 | 1829 |

{Colleton District}

| McPherson, Theodosia Narcissa | William Washington | 3 STRO 171-182 | 1848 |

(daughter of James E. McPherson of Prince William's Parish) {Gillisonville}

156

S.C. Marriages 1749-1867 Implied in S.C. Equity Reports

WOMAN	MAN	VOLUME PAGES	LIVED
McRa, Margaret	_____ Houseal	3 RIEQ 96-111 {Kershaw}	1848
McWilliams, _____ (daughter of Samuel McWilliams)	William McGowen	3 RIEQ 10-13 {Laurens}	1849
McWilliams, _____	Thomas Moore	3 RIEQ 10-13 {Laurens}	1849

(M)

Mackey, Agnes   John J. Sims   6 RIEQ 75-78   1841
  (daughter of Thomas Mackey)   {Lancaster}
Manigault, Ann   _____ Middleton   3 DESA 249-256   1811
Manning, Martha J.   H. M. Stackhouse   12 RIEQ 410-429   1866
  (widow of William L. Manning who died August 1862)
                                         {Marlborough District}
Manning, Sarah Jane David W. Bethea   12 RIEQ 410-429   1862
  (daughter of Mealy Manning)   {Marlborough District}
Martin, _____   Joseph D. Aiken   11 RIEQ 205-224   1849
  (daughter of Robert Martin)   {Charleston and Georgetown}
Martin, Martha   Gabriel Sturkie   10 RIEQ 118-129   1844
  (Patsey) (married 1844) (widow of William O.
  Martin)   {Lexington District}
Martin, Temperance   William C. Gunnels   2 RIEQ 259-270   1844
  (daughter of George Martin) (Gunnels died 17/18
  December 1844)   {Greenville and Laurens Districts}
Massey, Charlotte   John B. Cook   2 HILL 492-498   1836
  (daughter of George Massey who died about 1818) {York}
Massey, Harriet C.   James H. Gilmore   2 HILL 492-498   1831
  (daughter of George Massey who died about 1818) {York}
Massey, Mary   John S. Cunningham   9 RIEQ 475-482   1850
  (daughter of James R. Massey) (widower) {Lancaster}
Massey, Mary C.   _____ Haigood   2 HILL 492-498   1836
  (or E.) (daughter of George Massey who died about 1818)
                                         {York}
Mathewes, Ann Ashby B. P. Colburn   4 RIEQ 233-254   1845
                                         {Charleston}
Mathewes, Mary   _____ Boyd   4 RIEQ 233-254   1850
                                         {Charleston}
Mathewes, Susan B.   _____ Hunt   4 RIEQ 233-254   1852
  (daughter of Wm. Mathewes)   {Charleston}
Mathews, _____   Col. Benjamin   11 RIEQ 205-224   1849
                     Faneul Hunt, Sr. (he died 1854/55)
  (daughter of William Mathews) {Charleston and Georgetown
  District} [Must also see pages 269-281; 296-322]

S.C. Marriages 1749-1867 Implied in S.C. Equity Reports

WOMAN	MAN	VOLUME PAGES	LIVED
Mathews, Ann A.	Benjamin P. Colburn	4 STRO 1-25	1847
(married about 1834) (daughter of William Mathews) {Charleston}			
Mathews, Mary	Rev. Charles Leroy Boyd (to Alabama)	4 STRO 1-25	1848
(daughter of William Mathews)		{Charleston}	
Mathews, Susan B.	Col. Benjamin F. Hunt	4 STRO 1-25	1848
(daughter of William Mathews)		{Charleston}	
Mathis, Jane	Charles B. Guffin	8 RIEQ 79-81	1855
		{Abbeville District}	
Mathis, Mary	Samuel Hill	8 RIEQ 79-81	1855
		{Abbeville District}	
Mathis, Sarah	Thomas M. Morrow	8 RIEQ 79-81	1855
		{Abbeville District}	
Matthews, Ann A.	_____ Colburn	8 RIEQ 166-184	1851
Matthews, Eliza Ann	James M. Staggers	13 RIEQ 142-164	1866
(widow of Samuel P. Matthews)		{Williamsburg}	
Matthews, Susan B.	Col. Benjamin F. Hunt, Jr.	6 RIEQ 183-199	1826
(daughter of William Matthews who died 22 July 1848) {Charleston and			
[See also 8 RIEQ pages 166-184]		Georgetown District}	
May, _____	James Cooner	3 STRO 185-192	1848
(daughter of John May, Sr.)		{Walterborough}	
Maybin, _____	John Chesnut	1 HILL 122-128	1831
(daughter of Andrew Maybin)		{Chester}	
Maybin, _____	John Chesnut	2 HILL 146-152	1833
		{Chester}	
Maybin, _____	_____ Thompson	1 HILL 122-128	1827
(daughter of Andrew Maybin)		{Chester}	
[See also 2 HILL pages 146-152]			
Mayo, Mourning	_____ Floyd	2 McC 137-143	1816
(daughter of John Mayo)			
Mayo, Nancy	James Mayo	2 McC 137-143	1827
(daughter of John Mayo)			
Mayo, Sarah	Albert Beam	2 McC 137-143	1827
(daughter of John Mayo)			
Mazyck, Caroline	Dr. Chas. Desel	RICHEQ 263-282	1831
(daughter of Stephen Mazyck)		{Charleston}	
Mazyck, Jane	George Elfe	1 HILL 242-252	1833
Mazyck, Jane	Arthur O'Hara	RICHEQ 263-282	1831
(daughter of Stephen Mazyck) (her first marriage)			
Mazyck, Margaret	James S. Hopkins	1 HILL 242-252	1824
(marriage settlement 24 February 1824)			

S.C. Marriages 1749-1867 Implied in S.C. Equity Reports

WOMAN	MAN	VOLUME	PAGES	LIVED

Mazyck, Margaret M.　James S. Hopkins　RICHEQ　263-282　1824
　(marriage settlement 24 February 1824)
　(daughter of Stephen Mazyck)　{Charleston}
Mazyck, Susan Smith　William A. Hayne　CHEVES　37-41　1837
　(married 1837) (widow of Stephen Mazyck who died
　November 1832)
Meacham, Margaret　_____ Jones　4 STRO　203-206　1849
　　　　　　　　　　　　　　　　　　{Edgefield}
Meacham, Martha　Josiah Lanham　4 STRO　203-206　1849
　　　　　　　　　　　　　　　　　　{Edgefield}
Meggs, Catharine　J. Speights　3 DESA　139　1794
　(married 1794) (widow of J. Meggs) (she died 1802)
　[In footnotes of 1917 Edition]
Megrath, Ann　John Robertson　1 DESA　445-449　1795
Menude, M. R. C.　Dr. _____ Polony　2 DESA　564-570　1791
　(common-law marriage?) (he died 18 September 1805)
　[Must also see 3 DESA pages 44-46; 74-78] {Charleston}
Messervey, Sophia　Joseph A. Barelli　2 HILL　567-584　1829
　C. (daughter of Capt. Phillip Messervey who
　died 1828) (may have had child only) {Charleston}
　[Must also see 2 RIEQ pages 162-179]
Michau, _____　Thomas Anderson　SPEERS　312-321　1843
　(daughter of Isaac Michau)　{Sumter}
Michau, _____　_____ Buford　3 RIEQ　465-542　1822
　(daughter of Paul Michau)　{Georgetown}
Michau, _____　_____ Perdriau　3 RIEQ　465-542　1822
　(daughter of Paul Michau)　{Georgetown}
Michau, _____　Josiah H. Smoot　SPEERS　312-321　1843
　(daughter of Manassah Michau who died 1805) {Sumter}
　[See also 2 RIEQ pages 285-287]
Michau, Mary M.　Caleb Rembert　SPEERS　312-321　1843
　(daughter of Manassah Michau who died 1805) {Sumter}
　[See also 2 RIEQ pages 285-287]
Micheau, _____　William Buford　RILEY　88-96　1822
　　　　　　　　　　　　　　　　　　{Georgetown}
Micheau, _____　Samuel Perdrieau　RILEY　88-96　1832
　　　　　　　　　　　　　　　　　　{Georgetown}
Middleton, _____　_____ Blake　2 HILL　591-599　1814
　(daughter of Arthur Middleton)
Middleton, _____　Henry Izard　BAILEY　228-240　1813
　　　　　　　　　　{St. James Goose Creek and Charleston}
Middleton, _____　Henry Izard　2 HILL　591-599　1814
　(daughter of Arthur Middleton)
Middleton, _____　Joseph Manigault　2 HILL　591-599　1814
　(daughter of Arthur Middleton)

S.C. Marriages 1749-1867 Implied in S.C. Equity Reports

WOMAN	MAN	VOLUME PAGES	LIVED
Middleton, _____	Richard Quarles	4 DESA 145-148	1810

(daughter of Hugh Middleton who himself was married
four times) {Ninety-Six District}

Middleton, _____ Henry M. Rutledge 2 HILL 591-599 1814
(daughter of Arthur Middleton)
Mikell, _____ Samuel C. Black 13 RIEQ 34-41 1857
(daughter of J. J. Mikell) {Charleston}
Mikell, _____ Archibald John 2 DESA 342-361 1804
Calder (of Edisto Island) (daughter of
Ephraim Mikell) (Calder died 15/20 April 1804)
Mikell, _____ _____ Clark 3 DESA 168-175 1810
(daughter of William Joseph Mikell) {Charleston}
Mikell, Ann Gabriel Seabrook 2 DESA 342-361 1805
(daughter of Ephraim Mikell)
Mikell, Elizabeth William Baynard 2 DESA 342-361 1805
(daughter of Ephraim Mikell)
Mikell, Mary Ann William Seabrook 2 DESA 342-361 1805
(daughter of Ephraim Mikell)
Miller, _____ _____ Ballard 4 RIEQ 358-370 1851
(sister of William Miller of Butts County, Georgia,
who died April 1850) {Lancaster}
Miller, _____ Pleasant H. Glass 4 RIEQ 358-370 1851
(daughter of William Miller of Butts County, Georgia,
who died April 1850) (Glass' second marriage) {Lancaster}
Miller, _____ Job Palmer CHEVES 62-71 1799
(widow of Samuel Miller who died 1789)
(she died 1832) {Charleston}
Miller, Anna William McKenna 4 RIEQ 358-370 1848
(she died 26 February 1848) {Lancaster}
Miller, Emily John Rainsford 4 RIEQ 1-9 1846
(daughter of James Miller) (she was born about 1823)
{Edgefield}
Miller, Mary Thomas R. Anderson 4 RIEQ 1-9 1836
(married 1836) (daughter of James Miller)
(she was born about 1822) {Edgefield}
Miller, Sarah Benjamin Sykes 9 RIEQ 438 1855
Massey
[Referred to in another case] {Lancaster}
Milliken, _____ Francis Thackum 2 HILL 267-277 1835
Minor, Lucy E. Benjamin F. 3 STRO 105-111 1847
Ingraham {Barnwell}
Minor, Lucy E. Benjamin F. Ingram 10 RIEQ 130-138 1847
(married 15 July 1847) (widow) (she died 19
February 1856) {Barnwell}
Minter, Anna Maria John Terry 1 RIEQ 78-91 1807
(daughter of Joseph Minter) (Terry died 1817)
{Ninety-Six District}

S.C. Marriages 1749-1867 Implied in S.C. Equity Reports

WOMAN	MAN	VOLUME PAGES	LIVED

Minter, Elizabeth ____ Clement   1 RIEQ 78-91   1807
 (daughter of Joseph Minter) (she died in Virginia)
                                  {Ninety-Six District}
Minter, Mary   Thomas Yeates   1 RIEQ 78-91   1777
 (daughter of Joseph Minter) (her first marriage)
                                  {Ninety-Six District}
Minter, Mercy   Thomas Jones   1 RIEQ 78-91   1807
 (daughter of Joseph Minter) (her first marriage)
                                  {Ninety-Six District}
Minter, Sarah   Wm. Terry   1 RIEQ 78-91   1807
 (daughter of Joseph Minter)   {Ninety-Six District}
Miscally, Mary Ann William Robinson BAILEY 304-311 1817
 (daughter of Daniel Miscally who died August/
 September 1817) (she died February 1821)
 (Robinson died August 1820)   {Charleston}
Mitchell, ____   William F.   13 RIEQ 9-24   1864
                   De Schamps
 (daughter of Benjamin Mitchell) {Sumter}
Mitchell, Abigail Minor McCoy   12 RIEQ 263-276 1860
 (daughter of Stephen Mitchell)   {Sumter District}
Mitchell, Sarah J. Stephen N. Berry 11 RIEQ 296-322 1855
                                  {Charleston District}
Mitchell, Susannah Christopher Tisdale 12 RIEQ 263-276 1820
 (daughter of Stephen Mitchell)   {Sumter District}
Mitchell, Winney   William McCoy 12 RIEQ 263-276 1860
 (daughter of Stephen Mitchell)   {Sumter District}
Mobley, ____   Leroy Griffin   2 RIEQ 56-58   1841
                                  {Chester}
Moer, Jane   John J. Radford RICHEQ 469-475 1828
 (widow of William Moer)   {Charleston}
Moffatt, Barbara B. Robert C. Grier 5 RIEQ 95-111 1852
 (daughter of William Moffatt who died 15 April 1851)
                                  {Chester}
Moffatt, Martha   William A.   5 RIEQ 95-111   1852
 Mary   Rosborough
 {daughter of William Moffatt who died 15 April 1851)
                                  {Chester}
Montgomery, ____   Jonathan B. Mickle 11 RIEQ 114-134 1851
                                  {Chester}
Moon, Caroline   ____ Cureton   2 STRO 327-334   1848
                                  {Greenville}
Moon, Elizabeth   ____ Fair   2 STRO 327-334   1848
                                  {Greenville}
Moon, Polly   ____ Kilgore   2 STRO 327-334   1848
                                  {Greenville}
Moon, Sarah   David T. Cureton 2 STRO 327-334 1848
                                  {Greenville}

S.C. Marriages 1749-1867 Implied in S.C. Equity Reports

WOMAN	MAN	VOLUME	PAGES	LIVED
Moore, Alice	Merry Bracey	RICE	110-132	1835

(daughter of Isham Moore) (to Mississippi)
{Clarendon County, Sumter District}

Moore, Ann	William J. Wightman	SPEERS	357-372	1837

{Edgefield}

Moore, Anne J. M.	Anthony Butler	RICE	110-132	1804

(daughter of Isham Moore) {Clarendon County, Sumter District}

Moore, Charlotte	____ Weatherford	2 STRO	27-30	1818

{Charleston}

Moore, Harriet	William Tuttle	2 STRO	27-30	1818

(to Georgia) {Charleston}

Moore, Harriet	____ Watson	7 RIEQ	100-105	1839

(daughter of Henry Moore) (she died June 1852)
{Fairfield}

Moore, Mary	Jacob Zimmerman	BAILEY	195-204	1803

(widow) (she died about 1803) (he died about 1803)
{Coosawhatchie}

Moore, Mary Jane	Edward C. Keckley	2 STRO	21-24	1840

(daughter of James Moore) {Charleston}

Moore, Rebecca	Thomas H. Wade	9 RIEQ	362-364	1826

(marriage settlement 12 September 1826)
(she died July 1846) {Richland}

Moore, Sarah	Thomas S. Polk	RICE	110-132	1839

(daughter of Isham Moore) {Clarendon County, Sumter District}

Moore, Tabitha	James Polk	RICE	110-132	1804

(daughter of Isham Moore) {Clarendon County, Sumter District}

Moore. See Moer

Moorman, ____	Reuben Chick	SPEERS	343-350	1840

(daughter of Thomas Moorman) {Union}

Moorman, Jemima	Jethro L. Reid	SPEERS	343-350	1840

(widow of Thomas Moorman) {Union}

Morris, Martha	____ Bellinger	2 RIEQ	30-31	1845

{Union District}

Morrow, Sarah	John B. Bull	11 RIEQ	156-204	1843

(widow) (she died 1857) (he died 6 January 1855)
{Abbeville District}

Morton, Patience McKenzie	____ Marshall	BAILEY	395-397	1831

{Philadelphia, Pennsylvania}

Mosely, ____	Eli Clark	1 RIEQ	396-404	1845

(daughter of John Mosely) {Edgefield}

Moser, Eliza	Dr. William Burgoyne	DUDLEY	133-140	1837

(in New York)
(daughter of Philip Moser formerly of Charleston, lately of Philadelphia)

S.C. Marriages 1749-1867 Implied in S.C. Equity Reports

WOMAN	MAN	VOLUME PAGES	LIVED
Mouzon, Eliza Ann (widow of James L. Mouzon) (Matthews widower)	Samuel P. Matthews	13 RIEQ 142-164 {Williamsburg}	1866
Moye, Elizabeth (daughter of Matthew Moye) (Priester's second marriage) (he died March 1856)	William Priester	12 RIEQ 361-378 {Barnwell}	1828
Moye, Gatsey (daughter of Matthew Moye)	_____ McMillan	12 RIEQ 361-378 {Barnwell}	1828
Moye, Harriet (widow of Matthew Moye)	_____ Rice	12 RIEQ 361-378 {Barnwell}	1863
Muckenfuss, _____ (daughter of Michael Muckenfuss)	_____ Dinckle	1 DESA 109	1784
Murchison, _____ (widow of Kenneth Murchison)	C. H. Durant	3 STRO 159-161 {Orangeburgh}	1849
Murray, Abigail Jenkins (daughter of Joseph James Murray who died 18 July 1818) (Clark married twice) [Must also see pages 80-93]	William M. Clark	CHEVES 129-142 {Charleston}	1815
Murray, Charles (married 1783) (daughter of David Murray who died 29 April 1771) (she died 1804) (Washington died 1791)	Major Thomas Washington (alias Thomas Walsh)	McMULL 157-200 {Beaufort District}	1783
Murray, Charles (daughter of David Murray who died 1770/71 Savannah, Georgia) (Washington died 1791)	Thomas Washington	RILEY 102-112	1783
Murray, Elizabeth Crosskeys (daughter of Joseph James Murray who died 18 July 1818)	Josiah Mikell	CHEVES 80-93	1839
Murray, Jane (widow of John M. Murray)	James Thompson	2 HILL 204-215 {Charleston}	1832
Murray, Margaret	John Seabrook	CHEVES 80-93	1839
Murray, Martha M. (daughter of Joseph J. Murray)	John Hannahan	McMULL 352-357 {Charleston}	1835
Murray, Martha Mary (married 1820/21) (daughter of Joseph James Murray) (Clarke's first marriage) (she died 1821) {Charleston}	William M. Clarke	3 RIEQ 318-341	1821
Murray, Martha Mary (daughter of Joseph James Murray who died 18 July 1818)	John Hanahan	CHEVES 80-93	1839
Murray, Susan (daughter of Joseph James Murray who died 18 July 1818)	James Meggett	CHEVES 80-93	1839
Musgrove, Ann (widow of Edward Musgrove who died 1790)	David Smith	HARPER 175	1824
Myers, _____ (daughter of David Myers)	_____ Clendinen	2 McC 214-269 {Lexington District}	1827

S.C. Marriages 1749-1867 Implied in S.C. Equity Reports

WOMAN	MAN	VOLUME PAGES	LIVED
Myers, _____ (daughter of David Myers)	Robert Clendinen	BAILEY 23-33 {Columbia}	1830
Myers, _____ (daughter of David Myers of Richland District, who died 3 March 1835)	James O'Hanlon	12 RIEQ 196-212 {Richland District}	1835
Myers, Elizabeth (daughter of Col. David Myers)	_____ O'Hanlon	2 RIEQ 321-354 {Richland and Union}	1845
Myers, Magdalina	_____ Theus	2 McC 214-269 {Lexington District}	1804
Myers, Mary (daughter of Col. David Myers)	_____ Clendinen	2 RIEQ 321-354 {Richland and Union}	1835
Myers, Nancy	Joseph D. Allen	2 RIEQ 321-354 {Richland and Union}	1838

(N)

Nail, Sarah (married October 1826) (widow of John Nail)	John Marsh	RICHEQ 115-121 {Edgefield}	1826
Nail, Sarah (married October 1826) (widow of John Nail) [Referred to in another case]	John Marsh	1 RIEQ 24	1826
Naisor, Mary M. (daughter of Philip Naisor)	_____ Brockaway	RICHEQ 449-451 {Charleston}	1799
Nasar, Mary M. (daughter of Philip Nasar)	_____ Brockway	3 DESA 550-553	1805
Neely, Rebecca	Dr. Joel L. Anderson	2 STRO 262-272 {Laurens and Abbeville Districts}	1847
Neilson, Elizabeth (common-law marriage) (wife of John Neilson)	Cornelius Tobin	DUDLEY 161-174 {Barnwell}	1829
Nelson, Elizabeth (common-law marriage) (he died October 1830)	Cornelius Tobin	RILEY 64-76 {Barnwell}	1830
Nelson, Isabella (an orphan)	Capt. John Mayrant	4 DESA 591-611 {Camden}	1791
Nettles, _____ (married 1855) (daughter of Wyatt J. Nettles)	Charles W. Lee	11 RIEQ 574-583 {Sumter}	1855
Nettles, Anna (daughter of Zachariah Nettles) (her first marriage)	Jordan Sanders	10 RIEQ 394-407 {Darlington}	1854
Nettles, Lucy (daughter of Zachariah Nettles)	_____ Smith	10 RIEQ 394-407 {Darlington}	1803
Neyle, _____	John S. Thomas	CHEVES 21-26	1839
Neyle, Caroline	_____ Herbemont	CHEVES 21-26	1839
Neyle, Charlotte	_____ Marshall	CHEVES 21-26	1839

S.C. Marriages 1749-1867 Implied in S.C. Equity Reports

WOMAN	MAN	VOLUME	PAGES	LIVED
Neyle, Harriet	_____ Sollee	CHEVES	21-26	1839
Nichols, Rachel	William Black	RICHEQ	85-109	1791

(common-law marriage) {Newberry and Spartanburg}

Niles, Esther A.	Joseph Cunningham	4 RIEQ	135-151	1841

(marriage settlement 20 July 1841) (he had been
married before) (he died May 1850) {Kershaw}

Norwell, Eleanor	_____ Davis	1 DESA	202-207	1791
Norwell, Isabella	John Mayrant	1 DESA	202-207	1791

(O)

Oats, Elizabeth	George Day	RILEY	162-165	1794

(married 6 February 1794) (she was born about 1777)
(she died 21 April 1804) (he died 29 June 1811)
{Charleston}

Ogletree, Caroline	Wm. P. Beard	3 STRO	149-158	1844

(daughter of Rev. Benjamin S. Ogletree) {Newberry}

Ogletree, Mary	Benj. P. Aughtry	3 STRO	149-158	1844

(daughter of Rev. Benjamin S. Ogletree) {Newberry}

O'Hara, Jane	Geo. Elfe	RICHEQ	263-282	1831

(widow of Arthur O'Hara) {Charleston}

Oliver, Mariah H.	William C. Footman	3 RIEQ	33-60	1832

(from Orangeburg District to Bryan County, Georgia)
{Williamsburg and Orangeburg Districts}

O'Quin, Elizabeth	James L. Spann	1 HILL	324-325	1833

(married 1824) (daughter of Daniel O'Quin, Jr.)
(Spann died 1827) {Sumter}

Omones, Louisa	Hamlin Mallory	McMULL	157-200	1821

(common-law marriage?) (she died 1822)
{Beaufort District}

Omones, Louisa	Hamlin Mallory	RILEY	102-112	1822

(she died 1822)

Osborne, Currency	Gideon H. Hull	2 STRO	174-195	1820

(divorced February 1830, Connecticut)

Oswald, _____	Bethel Dewes	RILEY	38-41	1836

{Beaufort District}

Oswald, Charlotte	B. Dews	RICHEQ	326-352	1817

(daughter of Joseph Oswald) {Beaufort}

Oswald, Martha	J. Scanlan	RICHEQ	326-352	1817

(daughter of Joseph Oswald) {Beaufort}

Oswald, Mary	_____ Freeman	RICHEQ	326-352	1831

{Beaufort}

Oswald, Mary	_____ Freeman	RILEY	38-41	1836

{Beaufort District}

S.C. Marriages 1749-1867 Implied in S.C. Equity Reports

WOMAN	MAN	VOLUME PAGES	LIVED
Oswald, Sarah	William Ricard	RICHEQ 326-352 {Beaufort}	1817
Oswald, Sarah	_____ Rickard	RILEY 38-41 {Beaufort District}	1836
Oswald, Sarah	_____ Slowman	RICHEQ 326-352 {Beaufort}	1831
Oswald, Sarah	_____ Slowman	RILEY 38-41 {Beaufort District}	1836
Oswald, Sarah	James Slowman	2 HILL 504-511 {Beaufort District}	1835
Oswald, Susan (daughter of James Oswald)	T. Skellon	RICHEQ 326-352 {Beaufort}	1817
Owens, Mary W.	J. J. Fogler	2 STRO 289-296	1848

(widow of John A. Owens of Beaufort District, who died 12 December 1830) (she died 21 March 1836) {Barnwell}

Owens, Sarah E.	John E. Tobin	2 STRO 289-296	1848

(daughter of John A. Owens of Beaufort District, who died 12 December 1830) {Barnwell}

(P)

Palmer, _____	_____ Ortner	6 RIEQ 150-154	1853

(daughter of Thomas Palmer who died about 1800) {Union}
[Must also see footnotes of 1917 Edition]

Palmer, Charlotte	Samuel Sumner	6 RIEQ 150-154	1851

[In footnotes of 1917 Edition] {Union}

Palmer, Eliza	James White, Sr.	McMULL 115-125	1821

(married 1821) (daughter of Jesse Palmer) (White's second marriage) {Georgetown}

Palmer, Mary	John Talbird	1 HILL 142-145	1822

(married 1822) (widow of William Palmer) (she died 1825) {Coosawhatchie}

Palmer, Mary	John Talbird	RICHEQ 361-369	1825

(widow) (sister of Talbird's first wife Elizabeth Bell) (Mary Talbird died November 1825) {Beaufort}

Parham, _____	Charles Bogan	6 RIEQ 140-146	1853

{Spartanburg}

Parker, Christiana	_____ Hatcher	4 STRO 179-186	1840

[See also 3 RIEQ page 136 in footnotes of 1917 Edition] {Edgefield}

Parker, Elizabeth (or Tracy)	_____ Barns (Barnes)	4 STRO 179-186 {Edgefield}	1831

[See also 3 RIEQ page 137 in footnotes of 1917 Edition]

S.C. Marriages 1749-1867 Implied in S.C. Equity Reports

WOMAN	MAN	VOLUME PAGES	LIVED
Parris, Eleanor	Henry Cobb	5 RIEQ 450-472	1843
(daughter of Henry Parris who was born 1752/53 and died 27 September 1847)		{Anderson}	
Parris, Elizabeth	_____ Gorden	5 RIEQ 450-472	1843
(daughter of Henry Parris who was born 1752/53 and died 27 September 1847)		{Anderson}	
Parris, Laurania	Rolly Jenkins	5 RIEQ 450-472	1843
(Lauraney) (daughter of Henry Parris who was born 1752/53 and died 27 September 1847)		{Anderson}	
Parris, Mary	James Hickey	5 RIEQ 450-472	1850
(daughter of William Parris of Tennessee)		{Anderson}	
Parris, Mary	Rucker Mauldin	5 RIEQ 450-472	1843
(daughter of Henry Parris who was born 1752/53 and died 27 September 1847)		{Anderson}	
Partain, Nelly	Burdett Etheredge	10 RIEQ 207-216	1855
(common-law marriage)		{Edgefield}	
Paslay, Hannah H.	Daniel Cook	5 RIEQ 351-355	1838
(she died 1850)		{Charleston}	
Patrick, Caroline	W. W. Garvin	10 RIEQ 130-138	1847
		{Barnwell}	
Patrick, Laura	J. J. Wood	10 RIEQ 130-138	1847
(she died 1856)	(he died 1855/56)	{Barnwell}	
Patrick, Lucy E.	_____ Minor	10 RIEQ 130-138	1847
(widow)		{Barnwell}	
Patterson, Barbara S.	John Lucas	4 RIEQ 340-348	1852
(daughter of Anthony Patterson who died 31 May 1850)		{Orangeburg}	
Patterson, Eliza	_____ Wactor	4 RIEQ 340-348	1852
(daughter of Anthony Patterson who died 31 May 1850)		{Orangeburg}	
Patterson, Leah E.	William Cleckley	4 RIEQ 340-348	1852
(daughter of Anthony Patterson who died 31 May 1850)		{Orangeburg}	
Patterson, Margaret	George Crim	4 RIEQ 340-348	1852
(daughter of Anthony Patterson who died 31 May 1850)		{Orangeburg}	
Patterson, Mary	Amos Harris	4 RIEQ 340-348	1844
(daughter of Anthony Patterson who died 31 May 1850) (she died 25 February 1844)		{Orangeburg}	
Patterson, Rachael O.	James Wimbish	4 RIEQ 340-348	1852
(daughter of Anthony Patterson who died 31 May 1850) (to Virginia)		{Orangeburg}	
Pawley, Mary	P. W. Frazier	1 HILL 203-210	1826
(daughter of John Pawley of Georgetown)			
Payne, Catharine	_____ Lark	12 RIEQ 487-497	1857
		{Newberry}	

S.C. Marriages 1749-1867 Implied in S.C. Equity Reports

WOMAN	MAN	VOLUME PAGES	LIVED
Payne, Lucinda (widow of John W. Payne)	William B. Boyd	12 RIEQ 487-497 {Newberry}	1862
Payne, Susan (daughter of Wesley Payne)	Matthew Heldman	8 RIEQ 9-12 {Greenville}	1851
Pearce, Ann (widow?) (she died 1854)	_____ Venning	14 RIEQ 84-89 {Charleston}	1854
Pearson, Dorcas (widow of William Pearson who died 6 December 1783) (Birch died 1808)	Michael Birch	McMULL 279-289 {Sumter}	1783
Pelham, _____ (his first marriage) (separated 1806) (he died 1835)	Richard Dawson	RICE 243-274 {Beaufort District}	1806
Pendarvis, Amanda (daughter of Joshua Pendarvis)	William Wamer	DUDLEY 154-160 {Colleton}	1836
Pendergrass, _____	Peter M. Oliver	3 RIEQ 33-60 {Williamsburg and Orangeburg Districts}	1850
Perdriau, Ann L. (daughter of Peter Perdriau)	_____ Clark	5 RIEQ 20-31 {Sumter}	1842
Perdriau, Ann M.	John China, Jr.	5 RIEQ 20-31 {Sumter}	1842
Perdriau, Hester (daughter of Peter Perdriau)	_____ Ramsey	5 RIEQ 20-31 {Sumter}	1842
Perdriau, Hester	_____ Wells	5 RIEQ 20-31 {Sumter}	1842
Perdriau, Lydia A. (daughter of Peter Perdriau)	_____ Evans	5 RIEQ 20-31 {Sumter}	1842
Perdriau, Mary G.	_____ Barrett	5 RIEQ 20-31 {Sumter}	1842
Perronneau, _____ (daughter of Arthur Perronneau)	Wm Hayne	1 DESA 521-537	1796
Perry, _____ (daughter of Isaac Perry of St. Paul's Parish, who died 1818)	_____ Bass	8 RIEQ 136-144 {Colleton}	1851
Perry, _____ (daughter of Isaac Perry of St. Paul's Parish, who died 1818) (Waring's first marriage) (Waring died December 1852)	Joseph Joor Waring	8 RIEQ 136-144 {Colleton}	1820
Perry, Ann (daughter of James Perry)	_____ Harrison	1 HILL 35-48	1806
Perry, Comfort (widow of Zadock Perry) (she died 1829) (Barber died 1832)	Nathaniel Barber	2 HILL 638-644 {Lancaster}	1798
Perry, Eliza E.	Thomas E. Bass	5 RIEQ 202-220 {Colleton and St. George's Parish}	1824
Perry, Margaret (Peggy) (married about 1800) (daughter of James Perry)	Philemon Starke	1 HILL 35-48	1800

S.C. Marriages 1749-1867 Implied in S.C. Equity Reports

WOMAN	MAN	VOLUME PAGES	LIVED
Perry, Martha	John Sommers	4 STRO 37-58	1809
(daughter of Edward Perry, Sr.)		{Charleston}	
Perry, Mary	John L. Frazer	4 STRO 37-58	1809
(daughter of Edward Perry, Jr.)		{Charleston}	
Perry, Mary E.	Joseph Ioor Waring	5 RIEQ 202-220	1824
		{Colleton and St. George's Parish}	
Perry, Rachel	_____ Logan	1 DESA 271-274	1792
Perry, Sarah	_____ McPherson	4 STRO 37-58	1809
(daugther of Edward Perry, Sr.)		{Charleston}	
Perry, Susannah	Edward Tonge, Sr.	4 STRO 37-58	1822
(daughter of Edward Perry, Sr.) (she died August 1828)			
		{Charleston and St. Bartholomew's Parish}	
Perryclear, Mary	George Kling	BAILEY 42-48	1807
(daughter of Michael Perryclear) (she died 1824)			
(Kling died 1807)		{Walterborough}	
Peters, Mary	Alfred Walter	2 DESA 577-578	1808
Pettus, Hannah M.A.	Thomas Roswell	4 RIEQ 92-105	1845
(daughter of J. D. O. K. Pettus who died 29 October			
1821) (she was born 1817) (of North Carolina) {York}			
Peyre, Mary M.	Samuel Porcher Gaillard	McMULL 358-369	1835
(marriage settlement April 1835) (she died 1839)			
		{Charleston District}	
Peyton, Ann (Nancy)	Capt. Hugh Hutchinson	2 DESA 313-320	1805
Phaelon, _____	Dr. J. G. Houseal	2 McC 423-434	1815
(married 1815) (widow of Major Edward Phaelon who			
died 1810) (she died 1816)			
Phaelon, Ann F.	_____ Brisbane	2 McC 423-434	1827
Phillips, Elizabeth	_____ Nix	3 RIEQ 543-555	1815
(daughter of Stephen Phillips		{Barnwell}	
Phillips, Polly	Alexander Templeton	3 RIEQ 543-555	1847
(daughter of Stephen Phillips) (she died 1847) {Barnwell}			
Pickens, Elizabeth Bonneau	Patrick Noble	13 RIEQ 111-122	1834
(daughter of Ezekiel Pickens of St. Thomas'			
Parish, who died 1813) (she died 1834) {Anderson}			
Pickett, _____	Dr. _____ McCullough	2 STRO 157-165	1825
(married 1825) (widow of James R. Pickett)			
(she died 1826)		{Fairfield District}	
Pickett, Mary Jane	John H. Wilkins	13 RIEQ 366-372	1866
(widow of Phillip H. Pickett who died July 1862)			
		{Chester}	
Pickett, Susannah A.	William K. Simmons	13 RIEQ 366-372 {Chester}	1866
Pierce. See Pearce			
Pinckney, Celestine	Benjamin Huger	2 RIEQ 218-245	1842
(daughter of Thomas Pinckney)			

S.C. Marriages 1749-1867 Implied in S.C. Equity Reports

WOMAN	MAN	VOLUME	PAGES	LIVED

Pinckney, Rosetta   Ralph Stead Izard   2 RIEQ   218-245   1842
    (daughter of Thomas Pinckney)
Platt, Susannah   _____ Swinton   2 McC   440-445   1827
Polock, _____   Lewis Levy   7 RIEQ   20-33   1854
    (daughter of Levi Polock who died 1848) {Columbia, Richland}
Polock, _____   Benjamin Mordecai   7 RIEQ   20-33   1854
    (daughter of Levi Polock who died 1848) {Columbia, Richland}
Pope, Sarah   James David Snowden   RICE   174-198   1816
    (married February 1816) (daughter of Capt. William
    Pope, Sen. of St. Luke's Parish, who died 1823)
    (Snowden of Charleston, died August 1818/19)
                                      {Beaufort District}
Porcher, Jane S.   Theodore S. DuBose   McMULL   358-369   1842
                                      {Charleston District}
Porcher, Martha M.   Isaac M. Dwight   McMULL   358-369   1842
                                      {Charleston District}
Porcher, Sarah B.   States Gist   RICHEQ   209-219   1814
    (married about September 1815) (he died 1822){Charleston}
Porcher, Sarah C.   Lawrence Hext   1 STRO   170-172   1806
    (marriage settlement 15 December 1806) (daughter
    of Peter Porcher)   {Beaufort District}
Porter, _____   David L. Thomson   4 STRO   58-66   1840
    (of Beaufort)   {St. Helena's Parish}
Porter, Elizabeth   Rev. Hugh Frazer   2 HILL   529-542   1796
    Clegg (marriage settlement 1796) (she was born about
    1780) (she died 1797)   {Georgetown}
Porter, Eliza   _____ Brown   SPEERS   496-507   1844
    Cheeseborough (daughter of John Porter, Jr. who
    died 1828)
Porter, Susan Cox   James Haynesworth   HARPER   117-124   1824
Postell, Jane   Alexander Houston   9 RIEQ   85-99   1826
    (she died 26 November 1843) (he was married before)
                                               {Abbeville}
Postell, Joanna   _____ Ingraham   1 McC   94-99   1825
    (daughter of William Postell of Charleston)
Pou, Elizabeth   Lewis Jones, Sen.   1 RIEQ   50-52   1820
    (daughter of William Pou)   {Edgefield}
Poussin, Adele   Thomas W. Price   BAILEY   458-460   1812
    (common-law marriage) (he died 1827) {Charleston}
Powe, _____   William Falconer   4 DESA   86-87   1805
                                             {Cheraws}
Powel, _____   John P. Thompson   4 DESA   162-165   1811
    (widow of James Powel)   {Pinckney District}
Powell, Maria   Elias L. Fraser   2 STRO   250-258   1848
    Louisa (widow of Medicus Powell)   {Barnwell}

S.C. Marriages 1749-1867 Implied in S.C. Equity Reports

WOMAN	MAN	VOLUME PAGES	LIVED
Prevost, Sophie (from Savannah to Barnwell District about 1804, then to Charleston) (separated 10 December 1810) {Charleston District}	Benjamin Jewell	11 RIEQ 296-322	1795
Prevost, Sophie (married 1796 at Savannah) (separated 1810) {Charleston} [In footnotes of 1917 Edition]	Benjamin Jewell	RICHEQ 112-115	1796
Price, Elizabeth (daughter of William Price, Jr.) (she was born 1818-1820) {Charleston}	_____ Toomer	2 RIEQ 412-472	1846
Priester, _____ (daughter of Nicholas Priester, Senr.) {Barnwell}	W. R. Thomas	RICHEQ 26-35	1831
Priester, _____ (daughter of Nicholas Priester, Senr.) {Barnwell}	James Ulmer	RICHEQ 26-35	1831
Priester, Harriet (daughter of William Priester) {Barnwell}	W. M. Hunter	12 RIEQ 361-378	1863
Priester, Rebecca T. (daughter of William Priester) {Barnwell}	Jones M. Williams	12 RIEQ 361-378	1863
Priester, Susannah (daughter of William Priester) {Barnwell}	John C. Holley	12 RIEQ 361-378	1863
Prince, Sarah Dunn (married 1808, Boston, Massachusetts) (his second marriage) (to Charleston 1818/19) (separated 1819-22) (she died 1836, Massachusetts) (he died 1859) {Charleston}	James Smith Colburn	14 RIEQ 176-244	1808
Pringle, Eliza Butler (daughter of James Reid Pringle) {Charleston}	William Ravenel	3 RIEQ 342-360	1851
Pullam, Eliza (daughter of Benjamin Pullam) {Abbeville}	Thomas B. Brooks	4 RIEQ 9-14	1851
Pullam, Mahala (daughter of Benjamin Pullam) {Abbeville}	Matthew H. Bryson	4 RIEQ 9-14	1851
Pullam, Mary (daughter of Benjamin Pullam) {Abbeville}	Lewis Busby	4 RIEQ 9-14	1851
Pullam, Rhoda (daughter of Benjamin Pullam) {Abbeville}	Wm. Sanders	4 RIEQ 9-14	1851
Puryear, Sally (daughter of Reuben A. Puryear) {Richland}	William E. Morgan	9 RIEQ 459-473	1857

(Q)

| Query, Ann Findlay (Finley) [Must also see pages 271-272] | L. B. Baker | 1 RIEQ 296-301 {Charleston District} | 1844 |

S.C. Marriages 1749-1867 Implied in S.C. Equity Reports

WOMAN   MAN   VOLUME   PAGES   LIVED

(R)

Rabb, _____   David Aiken   2 McC   118-126   1827
                                             {Fairfield District}
Rainsford, _____   James Rainsford   DUDLEY   57-71   1833
   (daughter of Thomas Rainsford)   {Edgefield}
   [See also McMULL pages 16-21; 335-343]
Rainsford, Esther   James Rainsford   RICE   343-371   1833
   (daughter of Thomas Rainsford) (she was born
   June 1815)   {Edgefield}
Rainsford, Esther   James Rainsford   SPEERS   385-398   1833
   (married 1833) (daughter of Thomas Rainsford who
   died December 1837)
Rainsford, Mary   Lewis C. Cantelou   SPEERS   385-398   1834
   (daughter of Thomas Rainsford who died December 1837)
Ramsey, Nancy   John H. Joyce   McMULL   236-253   1832
   (married 15 May 1832) (separated 1834) (widow of
   John Ramsey of Edgefield District) (she went to Alabama)
                                             {Greenville}
Read, Caroline   John N. Maffitt   11 RIEQ 285-295   1852
   (married August 1852) (widow of James Withers Read)
   (she died March 1859)   {Charleston}
Read, Caroline   John W. Maffitt   8 RIEQ   145-154   1852
   Laurens (married 2 August 1852) (widow of James
   Withers Read who died June 1851)   {Charleston}
Reeves, Ann   _____ Stewart   1 DESA   500-515   1777
                      (Stuart)
Reid, Jemima   Jesse Maybin   SPEERS   343-350   1840
   (widow of Jethro L. Reid)   {Union}
Reid, Nancy   W. T. Clark   SPEERS   343-350   1840
   (daughter of Jethro L. Reid)   {Union}
Reid, Teresa   _____ Maybin   SPEERS   343-350   1840
   (daughter of Jethro L. Reid)   {Union}
Rhode, Elizabeth   John Connor   2 HILL   41-45   1831
   (widow of Christian Rhode)   {Orangeburgh}
Rhodus, Mary Ann   _____ Brunson   12 RIEQ 104-113   1859
   (daughter of William Rhodus)   {Clarendon}
Rhodus, Rebecca   Benjamin A.   12 RIEQ 104-113   1859
                      Anderson   {Clarendon}
Richardson, _____   James Allen   9 RIEQ   53-57   1837
   (daughter of John Richardson)   {Lancaster}
Richardson, Camilla   _____ Cantey   12 RIEQ 454-486   1859
   F.   {Clarendon District}

172

S.C Marriages 1749-1867 Implied in S.C. Equity Reports

WOMAN	MAN	VOLUME PAGES	LIVED
Richardson, Dorothy ____ Mitchell (daughter of James Burchell Richardson who died 28 April 1836)		DUDLEY 184-201	1826
Richardson, ____ Hermione (daughter of James Burchell Richardson who died 26 April 1836)	John J. Moore	DUDLEY 184-201	1837
Richardson, ____ Margaret C. (daughter of James Burchell Richardson who died 28 April 1836)	John R. Spann	DUDLEY 184-201	1826
Richardson, Mary Matilda (daughter of James Burchell Richardson who died 26 April 1836)	Augustus Fludd	DUDLEY 184-201	1837
Richardson, Mary R. ____ McCord (daughter of Col. ____ Richardson)		5 RIEQ 370-403 {St. Matthew's Parish}	1820
Richardson, Sarah J. C. (daughter of James Burchell Richardson who died 26 April 1836)	____ Moore	DUDLEY 184-201	1826
Richbourg, Mary G.	H. S. Dunlap	HARPER 168-170	1824
Rinaldo, Mary (widow)	John S. Cunningham (he died November 1851)	9 RIEQ 475-482 {Lancaster}	1850
Risher, Harriet Ann	George Warren	CHEVES 44-47 {Walterborough}	1839
Rivers, Ann	____ McCants	3 STRO 225-245 {Charleston}	1839
Rivers, Mary Emily (daughter of George A. C. Rivers of Wadmalaw, who died 6 August 1840) (she was born 17 January 1831)	W. H. Seabrook	9 RIEQ 203-216 {Charleston}	1856
Rives, Agnes (she died November 1850)	James T. Wade	7 RIEQ 353-357 {Charleston}	1833
Rives, Ainsley	Edward Horlbeck	7 RIEQ 353-357 {Charleston}	1850
Rives, Ann Elizabeth	____ Waties	7 RIEQ 353-357 {Charleston}	1850
Rives, Martha	James T. Wade	7 RIEQ 353-357 {Charleston}	1854
Roach, ____ (widow) (she died 1816)	Daniel Henderson	BAILEY 138-141 {York}	1794
Robbs, ____	Thaddeus C. Sims	8 RIEQ 286-290 {Spartanburg}	1855
Robert, ____ (daughter of John Robert)	Richard Bostick	1 STRO 393-420 {Gillisonville}	1815
Robert, Cornelia E. (daughter of John Robert)	____ Riley	2 STRO 86-90 {Charleston}	1833

S.C. Marriages 1749-1867 Implied in S.C. Equity Reports

WOMAN	MAN	VOLUME	PAGES	LIVED

Robert, Elizabeth   Nicholas Cruger   2 STRO   86-90   1847
  Anne (daughter of John Robert) (to Baker County, Georgia)
                                                {Charleston}
Roberts, Elizabeth   Thomas Singleton   2 McC   410-419 1790
  (marriage settlement 25 August 1790) (daughter of
  John Roberts)   {Beaufort District}
Robertson, _____   Edward Collier   1 HILL   370-375 1821
  (married 1821) (widow of George Robertson) {Abbeville}
Robertson, _____   _____ Horn   3 RIEQ   136   1840
  Elizabeth [In footnotes of 1917 Edition] {Edgefield}
Robertson, Helen R. Charles E. Rowand, 4 STRO   37-58   1839
                     Jr. (he died 6 January 1839) {Charleston}
Robinson, _____   James E. Glen   4 DESA   546-550 1816
                                                {Orangeburg}
Robinson, Ann   Hiram Davis   RICHEQ   390-397 1828
  (widow of William Robinson who died 1805) {Union}
Robinson, Maria   John Frederick   4 DESA   546-550 1816
                                                {Orangeburg}
Robinson, Sarah   John Warren   RICHEQ   390-397 1828
  (daughter of William Robinson who died 1805) {Union}
Rochefort. See de Rochefort
Rogers, Mary   _____ Spears   RICHEQ   287-293 1810
                                                {Walterboro}
Rogers, Sarah   Thomas Riggs   RICHEQ   287-293 1810
                                                {Walterboro}
Rogers, Sarah A.   _____ McDonald   7 RIEQ   422-429 1854
  (daughter of William Rogers)   {Spartanburg}
Rossignol, Marie   Guillaume (William) 7 RIEQ   201-218 1810
  Adelaide   Dumont
  (she died 1833)   {Charleston}
Roten, Elizabeth   John James   4 DESA   185-199 1780
  (Routen) (married 6 April 1780) (he died 6 December 1807)
  (of Newberry District)   {Washington District}
Rowand, Martha S.   Alfred R. Drayton   4 STRO   37-58   1849
  (daughter of Charles E. Rowand, Sr.) {Charleston}
  [See also 4 RIEQ page 416 in footnotes of 1917 Edition]
Rowand, Mary E.   Dr. Thomas Y.   4 STRO   37-58   1849
                     Simons   {Charleston}
  (daughter of Charles E. Rowand, Sr.) [See also 4 RIEQ
  pages 416-420, in footnotes of 1917 Edition]
Ruff, _____   William Rutherford BAILEY   7-13   1830
  (daughter of George Ruff who died 1803) {Newberry}
Rugely, Ann   _____ Slaughton   RICHEQ   235-246 1776
                                                {St. Phillip's Parish}
Russell, Alicia H.   Arthur Middleton   DUDLEY   115-123 1832
  (daughter of Nathaniel Russell of Charleston)
                                                {Charleston}

S.C. Marriages 1749-1867 Implied in S.C. Equity Reports

WOMAN	MAN	VOLUME	PAGES	LIVED
Russell, Sarah	____ Dehon	DUDLEY	115-123	1832
(daughter of Nathaniel Russell of Charleston)				
Rutledge, Caroline A.	____ Ball	14 RIEQ	245-270	1858
(daughter of Edward Rutledge)				
Rutledge, Louisa	Rev. ____ Nichols	14 RIEQ	245-270	1858
(daughter of Edward Rutledge)				
Rutledge, Mary	Francis B. Fogg	2 HILL	591-599	1837
(daughter of Henry M. Rutledge)				

(S)

WOMAN	MAN	VOLUME	PAGES	LIVED
Sabb, Ann	Donald Rowe	5 RIEQ	370-403	1809
(widow of William Sabb)		{St. Matthew's Parish}		
Sabb, Ann	James Stewart	5 RIEQ	370-403	1808
(she died 1813)		{St. Matthew's Parish}		
Sabb, Elizabeth	William R. Thompson	5 RIEQ	370-403	1807
(she died November 1838) (he died 1807)				
		{St. Matthew's Parish}		
Sabb, Sarah Frances	James F. Erving	5 RIEQ	370-403	1808
(widow of Thomas Sabb who died 1811)				
		{St. Matthew's Parish}		
Sams, Sarah	Benjamin Mathews	1 DESA	127-135	1785
Sampson, Abigail	Levin L. Levy	3 STRO	197-211	1834
(marriage settlement 12 April 1834) (widow) {Charleston}				
Sanders, Anna	William H. Cannon	10 RIEQ	394-407	1854
(widow of Jordan Sanders) (she died May 1854)				
		{Darlington}		
Sandford, Beatrix	W. Flurry	RICHEQ	357-361	1817
(widow)		{Charleston}		
Sartor, Nancy	Joseph McJunkin	11 RIEQ	527-535	1856
(daughter of William Sartor) (she died 15 January 1856) (McJunkin died 1855)		{Union}		
Sasportas, Zelmire	Edward Peraire	10 REIQ	38-52	1857
		{Charleston District}		
Satterwhite, Jemima	Wiley Glover, Sr.	4 RIEQ	25-38	1803
(daughter of Bartlet Satterwhite who died 21 January 1807) (Glover died 8 February 1806) {Abbeville}				
Saunders, Agness	John Canady	6 RIEQ	103-110	1804
		{Barnwell}		
Savage, Elizabeth	William Branford	2 DESA	115-127	1754
Savage, Elizabeth	Thomas Heyward	2 McC	435-440	1823
Savage, Mary	Joseph Clay	2 McC	435-440	1827
Scarborough, Mary F.	James J. Harlee	9 RIEQ	100-110	1853
		{Marion}		

S.C. Marriages 1749-1867 Implied in S.C. Equity Reports

WOMAN	MAN	VOLUME	PAGES	LIVED

Schinholster, Sarah _____ Sherry   2 McC   60-72   1794
    (widow of John Schinholster who died 1781) {Beech Island}
Schinholster,   Abraham Ardis   2 McC   60-72   1794
    Susannah (daughter of John Schinholster who died 1781)
                                             {Beech Island}
Schmidt, Henrietta   Augustus Benjamin   7 RIEQ 219-229   1829
    Portner   O'Bannon
    (married April 1829)   {Barnwell and Charleston}
Schmidt, Mary   Cicero M. Arnold   7 RIEQ 201-218   1845
    Selena (marriage settlement 2 July 1845)
    (daughter of Dr. John W. Schmidt)   {Charleston}
Scott, _____   Hezekiah Thomson   1 McC   32-42   1825
Scott, Ann   Joseph Shanks   HARPER   5-19   1781
    (married 1781) (daughter of Thomas Scott who died 1782)
    (she died June 1801 in Wales) (Shanks of Great Britain)
Scott, Mary   Armstead Burt, Sen.   9 RIEQ 358-361   1839
    (she died 1857) (he died 1839)   {Edgefield}
Scott, Sarah   Daniel Pepper   HARPER   5-19   1802
    (daughter of Thomas Scott who died 1782) (she died 1802)
Screven, _____   John Posey   1 HILL 252-264   1833
Screven, Ann   John McNish   7 RIEQ 186-200   1829
    (she died 1 October 1851)   {Beaufort District}
    [See also 8 RIEQ pages 112-129]
Screven, Ann   John McNish   4 STRO   66-83   1829
    (in Savannah, Georgia)   {Beaufort District}
Screven, Hannah   George Cogdell   1 DESA 454-458   1792
                      (his first marriage)
Screven, Sarah E.   Dr. Thomas W.   1 HILL 326-334   1824
                      Wright (he died about 1825) {Sumter}
Seabrook, Elizabeth   Rev. Doctor Donald   1 RIEQ 155-186   1820
    Bailey   M'Leod (he died 1820)
    (widow of John Seabrook)   {Charleston District}
Seabrook, Honoria   W. J. McFeely   2 STRO   69-71   1848
    Wilkes (daughter of Thomas Wilkes Seabrook who
    died in Florida)   {Charleston}
Seabrook, Mary   James L. Rose   2 STRO   69-71   1848
    Martha (widow of Thomas Wilkes Seabrook who
    died in Florida)   {Charleston}
Sealy, Eliza Ann   Dutarque Fogartie   BAILEY 510-514   1830
    (widow of David Sealy)   {Charleston}
Sealy, Mary E.   Jacob N. Lord   BAILEY 510-514   1826
    (stepdaughter of David Sealy)   {Charleston}
Seibels, Caroline   Barnet Statham   2 HILL 605-611   1837
    Lamkin   {Edgefield}
Sessions, Esther   Benjamin W. Brown   10 RIEQ 408-411   1855
    Elizabeth   (he died 1855)   {Sumter}

S.C. Marriages 1749-1867 Implied in S.C. Equity Reports

WOMAN	MAN	VOLUME	PAGES	LIVED
Shackelford, Mary (widow of William C. Shackelford)	William C. Lester	2 STRO	51-63 {Charleston District}	1847
Shackelford, Mary Lupton	Thomas Butler	2 STRO	51-63 {Charleston District}	1847
Shackelford, Susan (daughter of William C. Shackelford)	Benjamin W. Rumney	2 STRO	51-63 {Charleston District}	1847
Shackleford, ____	William Mazyck	BAILEY	48-57	1828
Shackleford, Mary (widow of Richard Shackleford)	Richard W. Vanderhorst	BAILEY	48-57	1828
Shaffer, Margaret G. (reference to marriage settlement)	George M. Fairlee	14 RIEQ	146-149 {Marion}	1867
Shanks, Jane	Abraham Dupont	HARPER	5-19	1824
Shannon, Isabella C. (married September 1838)	Elmore Manes	2 RIEQ	404-407 {Marion}	1838
Shannon, Ruth (widow)	____ Durant	2 RIEQ	404-407 {Marion}	1838
Sharpless, Lucretia	David Youngblood (he died 7 July 1791)	2 DESA	295-299	1790
Shaw, Eliza (widow of William D. Shaw) (she died May 1849) (Black died September 1849)	Alexander Black	6 RIEQ	240-248 {Charleston}	1849
Shaw, Eliza (widow of Wm. D. Shaw)	Major Alexander Black	SPEERS	431-438	1825
Shaw, Mary Ann (daughter of David Shaw)	____ Black	6 RIEQ	240-248 {Charleston}	1817
Sherry, Sarah (widow)	John Butler (he died 1818)	2 McC	60-72 {Beech Island}	1800
Shrewsbury, ____ (daughter of Edward Shrewsbury) [Referred to in another case]	Isham Williams	10 RIEQ	137	1793
Shrewsbury, Ann M.	____ Brown	3 STRO	211-224 {Charleston}	1848
Shrewsbury, Eliza (daughter of Edward Shrewsbury who died 1793) (she died 20 October 1844) (he died August 1846) {Charleston}	Isham Williams	3 STRO	211-224	1793
Shrewsbury, Elizabeth K.	John B. Adger	3 STRO	211-224 {Charleston}	1848
Shrewsbury, Louisa	Dr. William Moultrie	3 STRO	211-224 {Charleston}	1848
Shrewsbury, Mary	Thomas Williams	3 STRO	211-224 {Charleston}	1848
Sibley, ____ [In footnotes of 1917 Edition]	James R. Crispin	2 HILL	430-442 {Newberry}	1833

S.C. Marriages 1749-1867 Implied in S.C. Equity Reports

WOMAN	MAN	VOLUME PAGES	LIVED
Sibley, _____ [In footnotes of 1917 Edition]	John Taylor	2 HILL 430-442 {Newberry}	1833
Simmons, Patience P.	Abram F. Lumpkin	13 RIEQ 366-372 {Chester}	1866
Simons, M. E.	_____ Holmes	3 DESA 149-154 {Charleston}	1810
Simons, Rebecca (widow of Samuel B. Simons)	_____ Wilson	2 McC 385-395	1827
Simons, Sarah (marriage contract 18 March 1817) (widow of Charles Dewar Simons) (she died 30 June 1841) {Charleston}	Edward Gamage	3 RIEQ 271-281	1817
Simons, Sarah M. C.	_____ Pyron	SPEERS 134-142 {Charleston}	1829
Simpson, Laura (married 1811)	Nathaniel Wade	2 McC 130-136	1811
Sims, _____ (daughter of Col. Reuben Sims who died 1844) {Union}	A. R. Aughtery	4 STRO 103-122	1842
Sims, _____	Josey Gordon	2 McC 151-167	1827
Sims, _____ (daughter of Col. Reuben Sims who died 1844) {Union}	Dr. Milton Goudelock	4 STRO 103-122	1842
Sims, _____ (married 1825) (daughter of Reuben Sims) {Union}	John S. Sarter	RICHEQ 122-141	1825
Sims, _____ (daughter of Col. Reuben Sims who died 1844) {Union}	John P. Sartor	4 STRO 103-122	1842
Sims, _____	John Warden	2 McC 73-77	1827
Sims, Amelia (daughter of Nathan Sims of Abbeville) (Griffin died 1799) (to Lincoln County, Georgia) {Abbeville}	Richard Griffin	2 RIEQ 99-114	1784
Sims, Ann	J. C. Caldwell	4 RIEQ 168-197 {Union}	1850
Sims, Frances (daughter of Charles Sims)	Thomas M'Daniel	HARPER 108-116	1785
Sims, Patsey (daughter of Reuben Sims)	John P. Sarter	2 HILL 121-140 {Union}	1832
Singletary, Celia Ann (married May 1855) (daughter of Daniel M. Singletary) (she was born about 1834) {St. James Goose Creek}	Wade J. Markley	11 RIEQ 393-404	1855
Singleton, Ann (daughter of Matthew Singleton of St. Mark's Parish, who died 1784) (Moore died 1803/04) {Clarendon County, Sumter District}	Isham Moore	RICE 110-132	1784
Singleton, E.	R. Bostick	2 McC 410-419 {Beaufort District}	1827

S.C. Marriages 1749-1867 Implied in S.C. Equity Reports

WOMAN	MAN	VOLUME PAGES	LIVED
Singleton, Mary Martha (separated 6 March 1817) (daughter of John Singleton) (McRa died 19 May 1847)	Powell McRa	3 RIEQ 96-111 {Kershaw}	1817
Singleton, Videau M.	_____ De Veaux	1 STRO 283-294 {Charleston}	1834
Singleton, Videau Marion (daughter of Richard Singleton)	Robert Marion De Veaux	9 RIEQ 535-571 {Sumter District}	1849
Sinkler, Ann Cantey (married 10 May 1791) (daughter of James Sinkler who died 20 November 1800)	James B. Richardson	2 DESA 127-140	1791
Sinkler, Elizabeth	_____ DuBose	1 RIEQ 141-154 {Colleton}	1791
Sinkler, Jane (she died 5 December 1842)	_____ Glover	1 RIEQ 141-154 {Colleton}	1791
Skeen, _____ (widow) (married 1842)	Francis G. Haseldon	10 RIEQ 53-63 {Charleston}	1842
Skinner, Elizabeth A. (married 1807) (widow of George Skinner who died 1801)	Alexander Collins	BAILEY 74-77 {Georgetown}	1807
Skirving, _____ (daughter of James Skirving)	_____ Postell	1 DESA 158-159	1780
Skirving, _____ (daughter of James Skirving)	O. B. Smith	1 DESA 158-159	1780
Skirving, _____ (daughter of Col. James Skirving) (Smith died January 1796)	Philip Smith	BAILEY 244-267 {Charleston}	1791
Skrine, Mary S. M. (she died 1837)	_____ Hardwicke	3 RIEQ 262-271 {Georgetown}	1833
Sleigh, M.	_____ Liddle	2 DESA 295-299	1805
Sligh, Catharine	Uriah Wicker (he died 1808)	1 HILL 376-382 {Newberry}	1808
Smart, Maria (daughter of James Smart)	_____ Johnson	McMULL 345-348 {Beaufort}	1842
Smith, _____ (daughter of John Smith of New York) (Bradshaw died 1828)	James Bradshaw	1 HILL 140-142	1833
Smith, _____ (daughter of Thomas Smith)	Hon. John F. Grimke	1 McC 119-148	1825
Smith, _____ (daughter of Jesse Smith who died about 1826)	Isaac Hardee	1 RIEQ 130-140 {Horry District}	1845
Smith, _____ (daughter of Henry Smith)	J. E. Poyas	1 DESA 156-157	1780
Smith, _____	John E. Poyas	2 DESA 65-66	1788
Smith, _____ (daughter of Thomas Smith)	_____ Rutledge	1 McC 119-148	1806

S.C. Marriages 1749-1867 Implied in S.C. Equity Reports

WOMAN	MAN	VOLUME	PAGES	LIVED
Smith, _____	Archer Smith	2 DESA	124	1802

(daughter of George Smith who died 17 June 1784)
[In footnotes of 1917 Edition]

Smith, _____	George Smith	3 RIEQ	465-542	1807

(daughter of Josiah Smith) (George Smith died
September 1818) (lived in Charleston) {Georgetown}

Smith, _____	William Tygart	9 RIEQ	46-52	1856
		{Union}		
Smith, Ann	_____ Gibbes	1 McC	119-148	1825

(daughter of Peter Smith)

Smith, Ann	_____ Purcell	1 HILL	193-203	1821
		{Charleston}		
Smith, Ann L.	Major Thomas Fraser	3 DESA	393-417	1782

(marriage settlement 6 November 1782) {Colleton District}

Smith, Charlotte	Thomas W. Price	BAILEY	240-267	1791

(married 1791) (deed of separation 31 December 1812)
(daughter of Philip Smith)   {Charleston}

Smith, Charlotte	Thomas W. Price	3 DESA	165-168	1811

(daughter of Philip Smith)   {Charleston District}

Smith, Elizabeth	_____ Buler	3 RIEQ	244-256	1831

(daughter of Samuel Smith who died 1815) {Beaufort}

Smith, Judith	Major James Ladson	RICHEQ	315-320	1778

(married 1778)   {Charleston}

Smith, Mary	Dr. _____ Dupont	3 RIEQ	244-256	1831

(daughter of Samuel Smith who died 1815) {Beaufort}

Smith, Mary	John F. Grimke	1 DESA	366-382	1794

(daughter of Thomas Smith)

Smith, Mary	William Jones	BAILEY	244-267	1811

(daughter of Philip Smith)   {Charleston}

Smith, Mary	William Jones	3 DESA	165-168	1811

(stepdaughter of Philip Smith)   {Charleston District}

Smith, Nancy	George James	2 McC	143-150	1797

(daughter of Samuel Smith of North Carolina)

Smith, Nancy	_____ Mew	3 RIEQ	244-256	1831

(daughter of Samuel Smith who died 1815) {Beaufort}

Smith, Rebecca	William Hornsby	10 RIEQ	475-483	1838

(in Wayne County, Georgia) (he died September 1855)
                                              {Beaufort}

Smith, S. E.(or A.)	Charles T. Brown	2 HILL	558-566	1824

(daughter of George Smith) {Georgetown and Charleston}

Smith, Sarah E.	Charles T. Brown	3 RIEQ	465-542	1819

(daughter of George Smith)   {Georgetown}

Smith, Susannah	Col. Barnard Elliott	2 DESA	299-304	1778

(daughter of Benjamin Smith) (Elliott died October 1778)

Smyth, Eliza Ashley	_____ Bauxbaum	1 McC	301-310	1826

S.C. Marriages 1749-1867 Implied in S.C. Equity Reports

WOMAN	MAN	VOLUME	PAGES	LIVED
Smyth, Nancy	James Patterson	McMULL	459-475	1827
(daughter of Robert Smyth)		{Abbeville}		
Snelgrove, Dolly	____ Lester	4 DESA	274-304	1812
(daughter of Henry Snelgrove)				
Snelgrove, Eliza	____ Gregorie	4 DESA	274-304	1812
(daughter of Henry Snelgrove)				
Snelgrove, Hannah	____ Turner	4 DESA	274-304	1812
(daughter of Henry Snelgrove)				
Snelgrove, Mary	____ Livingston	4 DESA	274-304	1812
(daughter of Henry Snelgrove)				
Snelgrove, Rebecca	____ Kelly	4 DESA	274-304	1812
(daughter of Henry Snelgrove)				
Snell, Catharina	Charles Rottenbury	4 DESA	268-273	1812
(widow)		{Orangeburg}		
Snell, Catharina	John Stroman	4 DESA	268-273	1812
		{Orangeburg}		
Snider, Ann	Littleberry Varn	9 RIEQ	303-310	1847
(stepdaughter of John Snider of St. Bartholomew's Parish)		{Colleton District}		
Snider, Laura	James G. Varn	9 RIEQ	303-310	1847
(stepdaughter of John Snider of St. Bartholomew's Parish)		{Colleton District}		
Snoddy, Elizabeth	____ Sims	1 STRO	84-89	1846
(widow of Andrew Snoddy who died November 1841)		{Spartanburg}		
Snowden, Sarah	Maj. George J. Logan (married February/March 1820)	RICE	174-198	1820
(widow of James David Snowden) (she died August 1822)		{Beaufort District}		
Sommers, Henrietta	____ Rowand	4 RIEQ	416-420	1852
[In footnotes of 1917 Edition]		{Charleston}		
Sommers, Henrietta	Charles E. Rowand, Sr.	4 STRO	37-58	1838
		{Charleston}		
(daughter of John Sommers) (she died 1 April 1838)				
Sommers, Henrietta	Charles Edward Rowand, Sr.	3 RIEQ	281-304	1838
(she died April 1838)		{Charleston}		
Sommers, Mary	____ Buist	3 RIEQ	281-304	1848
		{Charleston}		
Sommers, Mary	____ Buist	4 RIEQ	416-420	1852
[In footnotes of 1917 Edition] [See also pages 421-445; 496-504]		{Charleston}		
Sommers, Mary	Rev. George Buist	4 STRO	37-58	1845
(daughter of John Sommers) (she died 1 April 1845)		{Charleston}		

S.C. Marriages 1749-1867 Implied in S.C. Equity Reports

WOMAN	MAN	VOLUME PAGES	LIVED

Sommers, Susan B.   William McDow   3 RIEQ   281-304   1819
   (married about 1819) (widow of James D. Sommers
   who died 1817-19) (she died about 1831) {Charleston}
Sommers, Susan B.   William McDow   4 STRO   37-58   1820
   (widow of James D. Sommers) (McDow died 1839)
                                  {Charleston and Colleton Districts}
Spann, Caroline M.   William Rice   13 RIEQ   59-103   1849
   (daughter of Charles Spann, Jr. who died 1834)
                                           {Sumter District}
Spann, McConico   James L. Haynsworth 12 RIEQ   114-123   1860
   Gulielma (daughter of William Spann) {Sumter District}
Spann, Mary   Henry Haynsworth   12 RIEQ   114-123   1844
   Elizabeth Britton (she died 1 June 1846)
                                           {Sumter District}
Spears, Eliza T.   Samuel B. Davis   RICHEQ   287-293   1828
   (she was born about 1803) (she died January 1828)
                                           {Walterboro}
Spears, Sarah Ann   Samuel Harvin   RICHEQ   287-293   1828
   (she was born about 1797) (she died March 1828)
                                           {Walterboro}
Spencer, Mary V.   _____ Godfrey   BAILEY   468-479   1818
   (widow of Captain John Vesey Spencer) {Charleston}
Spierin, _____   John J. Alexander   BAILEY   223-225   1830
                                           {Georgetown}
Spiva, _____   _____ Davis   9 RIEQ   434-439   1846
   (daughter of David Spiva)   {Union District}
Staggers, Venus   _____ Blakely   14 RIEQ   90-104   1867
                                           {Williamsburg}
Stairley, P.   William Rabe   McMULL   22-26   1839
   (married March 1839) (widow of George Stairley)
                                           {Greenville District}
Stanley, _____   Maj. John Compty   4 DESA   486-504   1799
Stanyarne, Edith   _____ Mathews   1 DESA   127-135   1772
   (daughter of J. Stanyarne)
Stanyarne, _____   John Wilson   2 HILL   550-553   1804
   Elizabeth (daughter of William Stanyarne who
   died 5 May 1783) (she died 1804)   {Charleston}
Stanyarne, Jane   _____ Simmons   1 DESA   127-135   1772
   (daughter of J. Stanyarne)
Stanyarne, Mary   Charles Freer   2 HILL   550-553   1811
   (daughter of William Stanyarne who died 5 May 1783)
   (she died 1811)   {Charleston}
Stanyarne, Mary   _____ M'Gillivray   1 DESA   127-133   1785
   (daughter of J. Stanyarne)
Starke, _____   _____ Picket   4 DESA   92-94   1810
   (widow of Reuben Starke)

S.C. Marriages 1749-1867 Implied in S.C. Equity Reports

WOMAN	MAN	VOLUME PAGES	LIVED
Starke, Jane	Elijah Hinson	1 HILL 35-48	1829

Caroline (married January 1829) (daughter of Philemon Starke) [See also 2 HILL pages 351-360]

| Stephens, _____ | Joseph Oswald | RICHEQ 326-352 | 1813 |

(daughter of George Stephens who died 7 February 1817)
{Beaufort}

| Stephens, _____ | William Oswald | RICHEQ 326-352 | 1813 |

(daughter of George Stephens who died 7 February 1817)
(Oswald of St. Helena)   {Beaufort}

| Stephens, Martha | _____ Jenkins | RICHEQ 326-352 | 1813 |

(daughter of George Stephens who died 7
February 1817)   {Beaufort}

| Stevens, _____ | _____ Oswald | 2 HILL 504-511 | 1835 |

(daughter of George Stevens)   {Beaufort District}

| Stewart, Ann | Dr. James Carson | 1 DESA 500-515 | 1777 |

(Stuart) (widow) (she died 18 May 1780)

| Stewart, Ann | William L. Lewis | 5 RIEQ 370-403 | 1831 |

(daughter of James Stewart) (she died 11 December 1831)
{St. Matthew's Parish}

| Stewart, Ann | Wm. Porter | 3 DESA 135-148 | 1803 |

(daughter of Thomas Stewart who died 16 September 1788)
{Charleston}

| Stewart, Martha M. | Henry W. Barnes | 1 RIEQ 396-404 | 1824 |

(daughter of Alexander Stewart who died 25
October 1824) (Barnes died September 1840) {Edgefield}

| Stewart, Mary | Patrick Byrne | 3 DESA 135-148 | 1792 |

(married 8 March 1792) (widow of Thomas Stewart who
died 16 September 1788) (she died 8 March 1803)

| Stewart, Prudence Harriet | Dr. Leander Z. Williamson | 10 RIEQ 323-328 | 1841 |

(daughter of John Stewart who died 1857) {Lancaster}

| Stewart, Rebecca A. | John Mosely | 1 RIEQ 396-404 | 1825 |

(daughter of Alexander Stewart who died 25
October 1824) (she died 18 November 1825) {Edgefield}

| Stobo, Ann | R. H. Peyton | 2 DESA 375-380 | 1806 |

(widow of J. Stobo of St. Paul's Parish)

| Stone, _____ | _____ McNeil | RICHEQ 397-399 | 1832 |

(widow of Daniel Stone who died 9 January 1822)
(she married at least three times)   {Marion}

| Stone, Susannah | Benjamin Franklin | HARPER 243-255 | 1810 |

(he died January 1820) {Clarendon and Sumter Counties}

| Stovall, Jane | Stephen Stovall | 2 RIEQ 99-114 | 1845 |

(widow of Lewis Stovall) (in Lincoln County, Georgia)   {Abbeville}

| Stribling, Sarah | Clement Mitchell | 2 McC 16-22 | 1827 |

S.C. Marriages 1749-1867 Implied in S.C. Equity Reports

WOMAN	MAN	VOLUME PAGES	LIVED
Stringfellow, _____	John Canady	6 RIEQ 103-110	1851
(common-law marriage)		{Barnwell}	
Strong, Susan A.	_____ Knox	7 RIEQ 117-124	1845
(daughter of Robert Strong who died 19 September 1845)			
		{Williamsburg}	
Stuart, Maria	_____ Johnson	6 RIEQ 95	n.d.
(daughter of James Stuart) [Referred to in another case]			
Stuckey, _____	Wm. Peebles	1 HILL 308-311	1833
		{Sumter}	
Sullivan, _____	Ezekiel Rowland	4 DESA 518-522	1814
(daughter of James Sullivan)		{Washington District}	
Summers, _____	Henry Ruff	4 DESA 529-532	1814
		{Washington District}	
Summers, Mary	David Deas	BAILEY 283-304	1822
(daughter of Humphrey Summers) (Deas died 1822)			
		{Charleston}	
Surr, Lydia	Benjamin Adams	11 RIEQ 264-268	1859
(widow) (reference to marriage settlement) {Charleston}			
Swan, Elizabeth	_____ Spencer	1 McC 227-233	1801
		{Virginia}	
Swan, Judith	Thomas Swan	1 McC 227-233	1826
(marriage contract 24 October 1801 in Virginia)			
(widow of Thomas Thompson Swan) (Thomas Swan was			
married before)			
Swindersine,	William J. Berrie	BAILEY 304-311	1817
Elizabeth (daughter of Andrew Swindersine who died			
November 1802)		{Charleston}	
Swinton, Maria	_____ Bonneau	2 McC 440-445	1827
(daughter of Hugh Swinton)			

(T)

Talbird, Sarah	_____ Henry	BAILEY 535-566	1830
(daughter of John Talbird)		{Beaufort District}	
[Must also see RICHEQ pages 361-369]			
Tamplet, Elizabeth	Thomas Cambridge	7 RIEQ 358-374	1789
		{Charleston}	
Tamplet, Mary	William Sergeant	7 RIEQ 358-374	1789
		{Charleston}	
Tate, _____	Alexander D. Hunter	3 STRO 136-149	1842
(daughter of Enos Tate)		{Abbeville}	
Taylor, _____	_____ Brackit	4 DESA 167-175	1810
(daughter of John Taylor)		{Abbeville}	
Taylor, _____	Allen Nesbitt	4 DESA 167-175	1810
(daughter of Walter Taylor)		{Abbeville}	

S.C. Marriages 1749-1867 Implied in S.C. Equity Reports

WOMAN	MAN	VOLUME PAGES	LIVED
Taylor, _____ (daughter of William Taylor)	_____ White	5 RIEQ 426-434 {Williamsburg}	1821
Taylor, _____ (widow of Henry Taylor)	G. A. Wilkins	8 RIEQ 291-297 {Beaufort District}	1846
Taylor, Floride (married 6 May 1802) [See also pages 419-422]	Thomas H. Jervey	2 DESA 221-226	1802
Taylor, Maria Bonneau (daughter of William Taylor) (she died April/May 1852)	Thomas China	5 RIEQ 426-434 {Williamsburg}	1852
Taylor, Mary S. (daughter of William M. Taylor)	_____ Darby	1 RIEQ 155-186 {Charleston District}	1832
Taylor, Sarah (widow)	John Dill	1 DESA 237-244	1791
Teasdale, _____	Edward Mathews	3 DESA 25-28	1809
Teasdale. See Tisdale			
Templeton, _____ (daughter of Alexander Templeton)	_____ Walker	3 RIEQ 543-555 {Barnwell}	1847
Teulon, Anna	_____ Sheppard	7 RIEQ 84-94 {Abbeville District}	1852
Teulon, Elizabeth	_____ Brown	7 RIEQ 84-94 {Abbeville District}	1852
Teulon, Mary	William Beasley	7 RIEQ 84-94 {Abbeville District}	1852
Teulon, Rebecca	_____ Stillman	7 RIEQ 84-94 {Abbeville District}	1852
Tewlune, Mary	William Beasley	6 RIEQ 408-433 {Abbeville}	1852
Thayer, Anna Maria	_____ Holmes	10 RIEQ 484-494 {Charleston}	1850
Thayer, Caroline S.	_____ Gibbes	10 RIEQ 484-494 {Charleston}	1850
Thomas, _____	John Aitkin	RICE 73-79 {Colleton District}	1837
Thomas, _____ Ashby (to Chickasaw County, Mississippi) (daughter of D. Thomas) {Union District} [Must also see footnotes in 1917 Edition]	Stephen Jordan	7 RIEQ 430-449	1843
Thomas, _____ (marriage settlement 10 May 1792) (daughter of Edward Thomas) (Heriot died November 1807)	William Heriot	4 DESA 227-242 {Georgetown}	1792
Thomas, Sarah J. (widow)	John Fant	11 RIEQ 527-535 {Union}	1858
Thompson, Anna (daughter of John Linton Thompson)	William H. Sinkler	5 RIEQ 370-403 {St. Matthew's Parish}	1848
Thompson, Caroline (daughter of William R. Thompson)	John B. Lewis	5 RIEQ 370-403 {St. Matthew's Parish}	1843

S.C. Marriages 1749-1867 Implied in S.C. Equity Reports

WOMAN	MAN	VOLUME	PAGES	LIVED

Thompson, Charlotte   Derril Hart   5 RIEQ   370-403   1839
  (her first marriage) (daughter of William R.
  Thompson)   {St. Matthew's Parish}
Thompson, Elizabeth   Dr. Hugh McBurney   3 RIEQ   257-262   1850
  (widow of James Booth Thompson who died March 1799)
                        {St. Bartholomew's Parish and Colleton}
Thompson, Margaret   Dr. Artemas T.   5 RIEQ   370-403   1848
               Darby
  (daughter of John Linton Thompson) {St. Matthew's Parish}
Thompson, Mary   A. B. Darbey   5 RIEQ   370-403   1848
  Eugenia (daughter of William R. Thompson)
                                         {St. Matthew's Parish}
Thomson, Charlotte   Joshua Player   2 DESA   264-271   1801
  E. (marriage settlement 31 December 1801)
Threewits, _____   Capt. _____ Thomas   4 DESA   560-578   1815
Tillman, _____   James Miller   4 RIEQ   1-9   1824
  (his first marriage) (she died 17 January 1824)
  (he died 29 March 1847)   {Edgefield}
Tims, Caroline   _____ Gordon   1 HILL   51-59   1833
  (daughter of Amos Tims)   {Chester}
Tisdale, Ann   Myles Burke   1 McC   551-557   1826
  (widow of John Tisdale)
Tisdale.   See Teasdale
Tobin, Mary   James Murphy   DUDLEY   161-174   1829
  (in County Kilkenny, Ireland)   {Barnwell}
Tomlinson, _____   Culpepper R.   11 RIEQ 52-72   1856
               Watkins (Wadkins) (daughter of
  Thomas Tomlinson, Sr.) (in Stanley County, North
  Carolina)   {Chesterfield District}
Tompkins, Elizabeth   John Rochell   1 STRO   114-128   1827
  (married 1827) (widow of Samuel Tompkins)
  (she died 1842)   {Edgefield}
Tompkins, Sarah   John Crawford   4 DESA   176-183   1800
  (daughter of Stephen Tompkins, Sr.)   {Edgefield}
Tonge, Ann   _____ Gist   4 STRO   37-58   1828
  (widow of Edward Tonge who died 1809) {Charleston}
Toomer, Sabina   _____ Hall   2 HILL   27-34   1833
  (widow)
Trescot, Caroline   William E. Smith   1 RIEQ   123-130   1845
  (daughter of Doctor John Sen Trescot) {Charleston}
Trescot, Caroline   Charles Follin   1 RIEQ   123-130   1833
  C. (widow of Doctor John Sen Trescot who died
  1820) (she died 1833, New Orleans)   {Charleston}
Tucker, _____   D. Reeves   5 RIEQ   150-155   1852
                                         {Barnwell}

S.C. Marriages 1749-1867 Implied in S.C. Equity Reports

WOMAN	MAN	VOLUME PAGES	LIVED
Tucker, Ann (Nancy) (common-law marriage) (of Newberry District) {Washington District}	John James	4 DESA 185-199	1800
Tucker, Elizabeth	_____ Shearman	BAILEY 351-359 {Charleston}	1814
Tucker, Elizabeth (common-law marriage)	Isaac Waight	BAILEY 351-359 {John's Island}	1814
Tucker, Martha (also known as Waight) (daughter of Isaac Waight of John's Island) [See also 2 HILL pages 26-27]	Justus Angel	BAILEY 351-359 {Charleston}	1814
Turner, _____	Joseph Price	1 HILL 445-465 {Spartanburgh}	1818
Tyler, _____	George Pooser	1 McC 18-22	1825
Tyler, _____ (widow of Henry Tyler who died 1815)	William Riley	1 McC 18-22	1815
Tyler, Ann (daughter of William Tyler)	James Simmons	1 McC 18-22	1825
Tyler, Elizabeth (daughter of William Tyler)	John Sanford	1 McC 18-22	1825

(U)

Userry, Elizabeth (daughter of Thomas Userry of Montgomery County, North Carolina, who died 12 May 1828) {Newberry}	Williamson Baker	RICHEQ 191-197	1828

(V)

Vanderhorst, Harriet (daughter of Arnoldus Vanderhorst) {Charleston}	Elias Horry	DUDLEY 145-154	1810
Vanderhorst, Jane Dawson (he died 3 October 1823) (daughter of Arnoldus Vanderhorst) (she died 5 December 1823) {Charleston}	Lawrence Monk	DUDLEY 145-154	1823
Vanderhorst, Maria (daughter of Arnoldus Vanderhorst) {Charleston}	Dr. _____ Simmons	DUDLEY 145-154	1810
Vanderhorst, Sarah C. (widow of Elias Vanderhorst) (she died November 1845) {Charleston District}	William Cartwright Shackelford	2 STRO 51-63	1845

S.C. Marriages 1749-1867 Implied in S.C. Equity Reports

WOMAN	MAN	VOLUME	PAGES	LIVED

Varlin, Ann   Berkly Ferguson   DUDLEY 224-229   1810
   (she died 1832) (he died about 1827) {Colleton and
   Beaufort Districts}
Verdier, _____   _____ Fraysse   12 RIEQ 138-146   1858
   (sister of Simon Verdier)   {Colleton District}
Vernon, Ann   Claudius P. Hicks   RICHEQ 5-23   1816
   (to Mississippi)   {Darlington}
Vickory, Nancy   _____ Davis   4 RIEQ 16-22   1825
   (daughter of William Vickory who died 1804)
   (she died 1825)   {Abbeville}
Vickory, Ruth   _____ Hunter   4 RIEQ 16-22   1825
   (daughter of William Vickory who died 1804) {Abbeville}
Viers, Sarah   Timothy Bunch   3 DESA 273-296   1795
   (widow of Maurice Viers)
Villeponteaux, Mary Gideon Faucheraud 1 DESA 366-382   1751

(W)

Wadlington, _____   Jefferson L.   HARPER 224-242   1824
                     Edmonds
Wadlington, _____   Jefferson L.   1 HILL 288-296   1833
                     Edmonds   {Newberry and Union}
Wagner, Maria Thomas J. Legare   2 STRO 1-13   1845
   Louisa (daughter of Effingham Wagner) {Charleston}
Waight, Martha   Justus Angel   BAILEY 351-359   1814
   (also known as Tucker) (daughter of Isaac Waight of
   John's Island) [See also 2 HILL pages 26-27] {Charleston}
Waight, Sarah M.   B. Stiles   2 DESA 66-79   1802
   (widow of Abraham Waight)
Wakefield, Emily   E. G. Thomas   RILEY   279   1831
   [Referred to in another case]
Walfe, Elizabeth   Otis Edgerton   DUDLEY 179-183   1824
   (married 16 December 1824) (daughter of Jacob Walfe)
   (she was born about 1804) (Edgerton died August 1830)
                                      {Barnwell}
Walker, Mary E.   Edward Thomas   7 RIEQ 230-247   1832
   (marriage agreement 3 April 1832) (widow of Legrand
   Guerry Walker who died 26 March 1829) (she died 1836)
   (Thomas died December 1851)   {Georgetown District}
Wallace, Elizabeth   David Boozer   1 HILL 393-396   1827
   (widow of Howell Wallace who died 1822)
   (she died 1831)   {Newberry}
Wallace, Elizabeth   Robert McCollough 1 RIEQ 426-449   1827
   (marriage settlement 23 February 1827) {Union District}

S.C. Marriages 1749-1867 Implied in S.C. Equity Reports

WOMAN	MAN	VOLUME	PAGES	LIVED

Waller, _____   Harmon Cox   6 RIEQ   275-283   1842
                                                                            {Horry}
Ward, _____   Frederick W. Sollee   7 RIEQ   34-53   1848
    (daughter of Richard Ward) (Sollee was born 19 May 1827)
                                                                            {Greenville}
Ware, Elizabeth   Robert Garrett   2 STRO   272-284   1801
    (daughter of Henry Ware)   {Edgefield}
Waring, Amelia   James D. Mitchell   RICE   389-409   1809
Dorothy V. (marriage settlement 27 February 1809)
    (daughter of Thomas Waring, Senr.)   {Charleston}
Washington, Louisa   _____ Omones   McMULL   157-200   1819
    (she died 1822)   {Beaufort District}
Washington, Louisa   _____ Omones   RILEY   102-112   1822
    (daughter of Thomas Washington) (she died 1822)
Waters, Mary B.   Phillip Schoppert   6 RIEQ   83-87   1853
    (daughter of Philemon Berry Waters)   {Newberry}
Waters, Sarah   William Sheppard   6 RIEQ   83-87   1813
    (widow of Philemon Berry Waters)   {Newberry}
Waties, Catharine   Col. Orlando S.   10 RIEQ   86-109   1852
                      Rees (he died April 1852)
    (she died 22 January 1855)   {Sumter}
Watson, Ann   _____ Robertson   3 STRO   1-15   1837
    (widow)   {Fairfield District}
Watson, Eliza   Joseph Kennedy   3 STRO   1-15   1837
    (married 1837) (daughter of Hardaway D. Watson)
                                                                       {Fairfield District}
Watson, Eliza A.   Joseph Kennedy   7 RIEQ   100-105   1854
                                                                          {Fairfield}
Watson, Sarah   Thomas Stitt   3 STRO   1-15   1837
                     (Stith)
    (daughter of Hardaway D. Watson)   {Fairfield District}
Watson, Sarah S.   Thomas Stitt   7 RIEQ   100-105   1854
                                                                       {Fairfield}
Webb, Ann   Joseph Glover   2 DESA   482-509   1777
    (married April 1777) (widow of Benjamin Webb who
    died 18 February 1776)   {St. Bartholomew's Parish}
Webb, Jane   _____ Josey   9 RIEQ   369-375   1828
    (married about 1828) (widow of John Webb, Sr.)
    (Josey died about 1832)   {Kershaw}
Webb, Louisa   Thomas G. Duke   5 RIEQ   121-128   1820
    (married 23 June 1820, Fairfield District)
    (divorced October 1825, Georgia) (he went to Chambers
    County, Alabama and married again)   {Lexington}
Webb, Morning   John Dickson   5 RIEQ   121-128   1820
    (daughter of Joseph Webb of Fairfield, who died
    January 1820) (she died February 1848) {Lexington}

S.C. Marriages 1749-1867 Implied in S.C. Equity Reports

WOMAN	MAN	VOLUME	PAGES	LIVED
Webb, Morning	_____ McKnight	5 RIEQ	121-128	1820
(daughter of Joseph Webb of Fairfield, who died January 1820)		{Lexington}		
Welch, Catharine	_____ Wedeman	SPEERS	256-263	1843
		{Newberry}		
Welch, Catharine	_____ Wideman	2 STRO	348	n.d.
[Referred to in another case]				
Wells, Hannah	William Elms	3 DESA	155-164	1794
(widow of Matthew Wells) (Elms died January 1794)		{Charleston}		
Wells, Hester	_____ Harvin	5 RIEQ	20-31	1842
		{Sumter}		
Wells, Lydia A.	_____ Tindall	5 RIEQ	20-31	1842
		{Sumter}		
Wells, Martha P.	_____ Tindall	5 RIEQ	20-31	1842
		{Sumter}		
Wells, Mary E.	_____ Linam	5 RIEQ	20-31	1842
		{Sumter}		
Wells, Mary E.	Hamilton Raiford	RICE	243-274	1838
	(in Georgia)	{Beaufort District}		
West, _____	John L. Westmoreland	9 RIEQ	418-419	1857
		{Greenville}		
West, Lucy B.	James Reese	5 RIEQ	531-579	1796
(widow of John West) (to Columbus, Georgia)		{Edgefield District}		
Whaley, _____	J. R. Mathews	3 DESA	80-84	1805
(widow of Thomas Whaley who died 28 October 1805)		{Charleston District}		
Whaley, Elizabeth	Griffin Coleman, Jr	2 STRO	334-341	1837
(married 1837) (he was born 1819)		{Marion}		
Whatley, Helen Ann	Dr. Thomas Batty	2 HILL	605-611	1837
		{Edgefield}		
Wheeler, Susan	Thomas Hargroves	2 HILL	222-228	1834
(widow of William Wheeler who died July 1829)		{Charleston District}		
White, _____	J. S. Bartlett	8 RIEQ	271-285	1847
(daughter of Leonard White)		{Sumter}		
White, _____	Rev. J. L. Bartlett	13 RIEQ	269-338	1854
(daughter of Leonard White who died May 1853)		{Sumter District}		
White, _____	Thomas M. Dick	13 RIEQ	269-338	1854
(daughter of Leonard White who died May 1853)		{Sumter District}		
White, _____	Thomas W. Dick	8 RIEQ	271-285	1847
(daughter of Leonard White)		{Sumter}		

S.C. Marriages 1749-1867 Implied in S.C. Equity Reports

WOMAN	MAN	VOLUME PAGES	LIVED
White, _____	James W. Frazier	2 RIEQ 99-114	1845
(daughter of William White) (in Lincoln County, Georgia) {Abbeville}			
White, Charlotte	J. P. Bossard	9 RIEQ 483-499	1829
(daughter of Joseph B. White of Sumter District, who died 31 December 1852) {Sumter District}			
White, Eliza Margaret	Samuel Hale	9 RIEQ 483-499	1853
(daughter of Joseph B. White of Sumter District, who died 31 December 1852) {Sumter District}			
White, Jane (widow)	_____ Wrenn	4 DESA 405-421 {Camden}	1812
White, Mary Ann	William M. DeLorme	9 RIEQ 483-499	1829
(daughter of Joseph B. White of Sumter District, who died 31 December 1852) {Sumter District}			
White, Sarah Ann	Valentine Richardson	McMULL 115-125	1840
(daughter of James White, Sr.)		{Georgetown}	
Whitlock, Eliza	_____ Durham	13 RIEQ 165-171 {Union}	1866
Whitlock, Ellinor	_____ Black	13 RIEQ 165-171 {Union}	1866
Whitlock, Melissa	_____ Harlan	13 RIEQ 165-171 {Union}	1866
Wicker, _____	John Riddlehoover	1 HILL 376-382 {Newberry)}	1832
Wicker, Catharine	John P. Kinard	1 HILL 376-382	1826
(widow of Uriah Wicker) (she died 1826) (Kinard died 1828)		{Newberry}	
Wigg, Ann	James H. Cuthbert	2 HILL 228-235 {Coosawhatchie}	1798
Wigg, Jane Hay	John B. Barnwell, Senr.	2 HILL 228-235	1798
(she died 1817)		{Coosawhatchie}	
Wightman, Elizabeth (common-law marriage)	_____ Bath	DUDLEY 212-224 {Charleston}	1779
Wightman, Sarah	Jacob R. Valk	DUDLEY 212-224 {Charleston}	1838
Wightman, Sarah	Jacob R. Valk	10 RIEQ 518-533 {Charleston}	1838
Wilbourne, _____	William Newman	1 HILL 10-14	1831
Wilbourne, _____	William Webb	1 HILL 10-14	1831
(daughter of William Wilbourne)			
Wilkinson, _____	Christopher Jenkins	HARPER 72-88 {Charleston}	1824
Wilkinson, Sarah	William Clement	HARPER 72-88	1799
(married 1799) (Clement was born about 1778) (he died 1820) {St. Paul's Parish, Charleston}			

S.C. Marriages 1749-1867 Implied in S.C. Equity Reports

WOMAN	MAN	VOLUME PAGES	LIVED

Willard, Jane H.   William Matheuman   RICE   198-242   1817
    (married 1817) (widow of Prentiss Willard)
    (she died 16 September 1817)   {Beaufort District}
Willard, Mindwell   Joseph Goodhue   RICE   198-242   1835
    (widow)   {Beaufort District}
Williams, _____   James Caldwell   BAILEY   175-179   1830
    (daughter of Washington Williams)   {Laurens District}
Williams, Drucilla   J. B. Floyd   8 RIEQ   248-258   1850
    (married 1850)   {Newberry}
Williams, Lucy B.   John West   5 RIEQ   531-579   1790
    (married April 1790) (her first marriage) (daughter
    of Thomas Williams of Brunswick County, Virginia,
    who died January 1787)   {Edgefield District}
Williams, Rachel   Lewis Holloway   5 RIEQ   531-579   1787
    (married December 1787) (widow of Thomas Williams
    of Brunswick County, Virginia, who died January 1787)
    (she died 10 December 1847) (Holloway died 1814)
    {Edgefield District}
Williman, Eliza   Gilbert Davidson   4 RIEQ   475-496   1813
    (daughter of Christopher Williman)   {Charleston}
Williman, Harriet   _____ Jough   4 RIEQ   475-496   1850
    D. (or E.) (daughter of Christopher Williman)
    {Charleston}
Williman, Margaret   _____ Bethune   4 RIEQ   475-496   1813
    (daughter of Christopher Williman)   {Charleston}
Williman, Mary   _____ Peters   4 RIEQ   475-496   1813
    (daughter of Christopher Williman)   {Charleston}
Willison, Harriet   James Dellet   CHEVES   213-232   1838
    (in Claibourn County, Alabama)   {Edgefield District}
Willson, Sarah   Isaac Carr   1 McC   60-91   1825
    (daughter of Thomas Willson of Georgetown)
Wilson, _____   John Blakely   2 McC   1-11   1827
Wilson, Ann   James Jacks   1 DESA   543-557   1797
    (widow of George Wilson)
Wilson, Eleanor   Keating Simons   1 DESA   401-409   1790
    (widow of John Wilson who died 1790; marriage Wilson's
    settlement 1 January 1789, recorded 16 August 1790)
Wilson, Mary   William Hays   1 McC   233-242   1826
    {Laurens District}
Wilson, Mary   _____ Lowrey   2 DESA   66-79   1783
Winckler, Elizabeth   _____ Vaigneur   2 DESA   640-646   1808
    {Beaufort District}
Winckler, Margaret   David Strobhart   2 DESA   640-646   1808
    {Beaufort District}
Winckler, Mary Jane   William John Kirk   2 DESA   640-646   1808
    (widow of Nicholas Winckler, Jun. who died March 1802)
    {Beaufort District}

S.C. Marriages 1749-1867 Implied in S.C. Equity Reports

WOMAN	MAN	VOLUME	PAGES	LIVED
Winfrey, Judith	Robert Lamar	4 DESA	617-645	1806
(did not marry; had child only)		{Edgefield District}		
Wirtemburgh, ____	James H. Marshburn	BAILEY	334-342	1826
		{Charleston}		
Wise, Jane Ann	____ Ball	4 DESA	330-350	1800
(separation agreement 1800) (daughter of Major Samuel Wise who died 1779) (she died 1808) {Richland District}				
Wise, Jane Ann	____ Butler	4 DESA	330-350	1808
(daughter of Major Samuel Wise who died 1779)				
(she died 1808)		{Richland District}		
Wise, Jane Ann	____ Campbell	4 DESA	330-350	1808
(she died 1808) (daughter of Major Samuel Wise who died 1779)		{Richland District}		
Withers, Ann	George Wilson	1 DESA	543-557	1789
(married 1789) (he died 1791)				
Withers, Mary	John Harleston Read, Sr.	8 RIEQ	145-154	1811
(marriage settlement 18 July 1811) (she died May 1817)				
		{Charleston and Georgetown District}		
Withers, Matilda Ann	Joseph S. Bossard	3 STRO	76-78	1849
		{Columbia}		
Withers, Sarah C.	Elias Vanderhorst	2 STRO	51-63	1829
(her first marriage) (daughter of Richard Withers)				
		{Charleston District}		
Wolfe. See Walfe				
Wonderly, Anna Barbara (or Mary Barbara)	Nicholas Winckler, Sen.	2 DESA	640-646	1768
(common-law marriage) (widow of David Wonderly) [See also BAILEY page 196]		{Beaufort District}		
Wood, Laura Ann	James E. Spear	9 RIEQ	184-202	1840
(marriage settlement 11 November 1840, Savannah, Georgia) (she died 16 September 1851) {Charleston}				
Woodberry, Mary	Richard Shackleford	BAILEY	48-57	1828
Woodward, Eliza	____ Britton	5 RIEQ	187-202	1852
(widow of William T. Woodward)		{Charleston}		
Wragg, ____	Milward Pogson	3 DESA	31-38	1809
		{Charleston District}		
Wragg, ____	W. L. Smith	3 DESA	31-38	1809
		{Charleston District}		
Wragg, Henrietta	M. Pogson	2 HILL	180-184	1805
(marriage contract 6 February 1805)		{Charleston}		
Wright, ____	Daniel J. Beacham	2 McC	185-206	1825
		{Laurens}		
Wright, ____	Tobias Cook	2 McC	185-206	1825
		{Laurens}		
Wright, ____	Henry Paisley	2 McC	185-206	1825
		{Laurens}		

S.C. Marriages 1749-1867 Implied in S.C. Equity Reports

WOMAN	MAN	VOLUME	PAGES	LIVED
Wright, _____	Elijah Watson	2 McC	185-206	1825
		{Laurens}		
Wright, Patience C.	Reuben Ligon	2 McC	185-206	1825
(widow of Samuel Wright who died 1808) {Laurens}				
Wurtz, _____	Wm Bartlett	2 HILL	171-180	1833
		{Charleston}		

(Y)

Yeates, _____	Jedediah Cook	1 RIEQ	78-91	1807
(daughter of Thomas Yeates)		{Ninety-Six District}		
Yeates, _____	Green Jackson	1 RIEQ	78-91	1807
(daughter of Thomas Yeates)		{Ninety-Six District}		
Yeates, Mary	John Elam	1 RIEQ	78-91	1780
(married 16 November 1780) (widow of Thomas Yeates) (she was born 8 June 1756) (she died 1841)				
(Elam widower) (he died 1824)		{Ninety-Six District}		
Yeldell, Mary	James F. Burton	9 RIEQ	9-18	1854
(daughter of James Yeldell)		{Edgefield}		
Young, _____	Peter Porcher	1 STRO	170-172	1806
		{Beaufort District}		
Young, Elizabeth	William Tyler	1 McC	18-22	1792
(she died July 1813) (his first marriage)				
Young, Mary	William Giles	RICE	315-329	1827
(marriage settlement 29 April 1827/29) (she died 1833)				
		{Abbeville District}		
Young, Mary	Stephen Mazyck	RICHEQ	263-282	1796
(daughter of Thomas Young)		{Charleston}		
Young, Sarah	James Naylor	1 HILL	383-387	1833
(widow) (he of Maryland) (he had divorced 14 February 1820, Maryland) (South Carolina marriage declared null and void)		{Laurens}		
Youngblood, _____	P. Hyrne	2 DESA	294-299	1790
Youngblood, _____	William Norton	1 STRO	122-128	1839
(daughter of William Youngblood)		{York}		
Youngblood, _____	J. H. Suggs	1 STRO	122-128	1845
		{York}		
Youngblood, _____	William Williams	1 STRO	122-128	1846
(daughter of William Youngblood)		{York}		
Youngblood, Elizabeth	William Wilder	1 STRO	122-128	1844
		{York}		
Youngblood, Emily C.	_____ Thomasson	1 STRO	122-128	1845
		{York}		
Youngblood, Jane	W. S. Wood	1 STRO	122-128	1845
		{York}		

S.C. Marriages 1749-1867 Implied in S.C. Equity Reports

WOMAN	MAN	VOLUME	PAGES	LIVED
Youngblood, Lucretia (married March 1795) (she died August 1799)	Daniel Munro (widow of David Youngblood)	2 DESA	294-299	1795

(Z)

Zimmerman, Harriet (daughter of Jacob Zimmerman)	_____ Jones	BAILEY {Coosawhatchie}	195-204	1821

SUBINDEX

THIS BOOK IS SELF-INDEXED.
THIS INDEX IS TO OTHER NAMED INDIVIDUALS IN THE ADDITIONAL
NOTATIONS CONTAINED IN SOME OF THE REFERENCES.

Abney, John, 86,102
Adams, Ephraim, 68,102
Adams, James, 23,102
Adams, N., 48,102
Adams, Shockley, 37,60,102
Adamson, John, 17,24,102
Addison, Allen B., 64,102
Addison, James, 81,102
Adger, William, 8,102
Albergottie, Anthony, 15,102
Albergottie, William J., 16, 102
Allen, Josiah, 79,103
Allen, Josiah G., 22,103
Allen, Mathew, 21,103
Allen, Matthew, 20,94,103
Anderson, Allen, 74,103
Anderson, Silas, 10,103
Arnett, John, 10,14,67,104
Ashe, John, 55,104
Ashe, Richard C., 34,42,72,104
Askew, Dr. ___, 2,21,104,105
Askew, Seth, 38,62,105
Atchison, John, 11,105

Badger, Nathaniel, 39,105
Bailey, Henry, 27,76,105
Baird, Archibald, 98,105
Baker, Robert L., 91,105
Baker, William, 33,105
Ball, John, 89,106
Ball, Samuel, 81,105
Ballard, Thomas, 15,106
Ballentine, Dougal, 39,106
Barber, John M., 48,106
Barkley, Robert, 6,106
Barksdale, George, 62,106
Barksdale, Joseph, 80,106
Barksdale, Thomas, 8,27,46,60, 70,83,106,107
Barnett, Jorial, 52,81,107
Barnwell, J. J., 24,107
Barnwell, John Berners, 98, 107

Baynard, William, 60,107
Beale, John, 86,92,107
Beale, Othniel, 12,107
Beasley, Thomas, 98,107
Beaty, James, 16,51,107
Beazley, W. B., 53,107
Bell, Thomas, 6,61,69,88,108
Bennett, Peter, 93,108
Benson, Joshua, 11,108
Birch, Michael, 7,108
Bird, Arthur, 7,42,69,108
Bird, Peter, 69,99,108
Black, William, 32,109
Blackburne, William, 15,45,109
Blake, Edward, 74,109
Blewer, John G., 19,39,41,75, 109
Blount, Stephen W., 81,109
Bobo, Barron, 61,66,109
Bond, John P., 6,22,43,109, 110
Bonds, William, 43,110
Booker, Bird, 44,110
Bookter, Jacob, 5,110
Boone, John, 31,110
Boulware, Thomas, 69,110
Bowers, Edward, 77,110
Bowler, J. H., 46,111
Bowman, George, 21,29,81,82, 111
Boyd, Samuel, 21,51,111
Boyer, Jacob H., 80,99,111
Boyle, John, 81,111
Bradley, Dr. ___, 59,111
Bradley, Dr. James, 59,111
Brailsford, Robert, 59,111
Branford, William, 45,111
Bratton, Dr. William, 29,36, 111,112
Brice, William, 25,87,112
Britton, Henry, 11,112
Brooks, Col. Z. S., 8,112
Brown, Bartlett, 14,112
Brown, Charles J., 41,112,113

SUBINDEX

Brown, Colonel Tarlton, 39, 112
Brown, Cornelius, 26,112
Brown, Frederick, 97,112
Brown, William, 55,112
Broxson, Henry, 9,83,113
Brummet, Daniel, 54,113
Brummet, William, 70,113
Bruton, George, 24,40,113
Buist, Rev. George, 52,113
Burgess, James A., 65,113
Burke, Dr. Michael, 44,51,113
Burton, William, 74,91,113
Byers, William, 71,114
Byrd, Joseph, 12,32,114

Cabeen, Thomas, 42,91,114
Caldwell, John M., 31,114
Calhoun, Downes, 6,114
Campbell, Dr. Robert, 83,114
Canady, John, 20,115
Cannon, Daniel, 25,55,115
Cannon, Russell, 26,115
Cantey, Charles, 83,115
Carn, Frederick, 76,115
Carr, John, 23,115
Carr, Dr. William, 74,115
Carroll, Thomas, 33,115
Carson, James, 12,99,116
Cason, William, 55,116
Caston, Samuel, 98,116
Cates, Aaron, 94,116
Cattell, William, 10,116
Cave, David, 9,52,67,116
Champion, Jacob, 3,116
Channing, Walter, 4,5,70,116
Chaplin, Benjamin, 1,117
Cheves, Hon. Langdon, 40,45, 56,117
Chick, Burwill, 16,29,43,90, 117
China, Thomas, 51,61,117
Chitty, Charles C., 80,117
Clark, William M., 38,117
Clarke, William, M., 39,96,117
Clarkson, John, 49,117
Clifton, James, 56,64,118
Cloud, William, 14,118

Coachman, James, 25,72,118
Coate, Henry, 55,118
Coburn, John, 99,118
Cogdell, George, 50,72,118
Cogdell, John, 5,27,118
Coiel, Alston, 89,119
Colburn, James B., 44,119
Cole, John, 3,119
Coleman, Charles, 9,119
Collier, John, 65,96,119
Collins, George W., 28,119
Collins, J., 82,119
Collins, Jonah, 99,119
Compty, Maj. John, 58,119
Connoly, Richard, 66,119
Connors, Charles P., 4,119
Conyers, Straud, 2,120
Cook, Daniel, 3,8,67,99,120
Cooper, George, 36,120
Corbett, Thomas, 53,120
Cornwell, Eli, 25,120
Craddock, Edmund, 17,80,120
Crocker, Solomon, 56,120
Croft, Edward, 70,85,120,121
Crosswhite, Jacob, 22,78,121
Crosswhite, William, 86,121
Cunningham, John S., 5,57,121
Cunningham, Joseph, 22,121
Curtis, Thomas, 3,121
Cuttino, Wm., 85,121

Dantzler, David, 72,122
Dart, Thomas L., 92,122
Davenport, Jonathan, 42,59, 79,100,122
David, Benjamin, 71,122
Davis, Col. Jonathan, 33,122
Davis, Elnathan, 73,122
Dawson, Lawrence Monk, 2,123
Dawson, Richard, 58,61,89,96, 123
Day, George, 8,123
Dean, John, 10,53,69,94,123
Deas, John, 75,123
De Graffenreid, Allen, 8,56, 124
Delk, Newit, 42,124
Delk, Newitt, 42,124

SUBINDEX

Dennis, John, 22,23,124
Dennis, William J., 24,124
De Veaux, Robert Marion, 20, 64,124
De Veaux, Stephen Gabriel, 45,124
Dinkins, Gilbert, 43,124,125
Dinkins, John, 77,84,125
Dixon, John, 70,125
Donald, Alexander, 36,125
Donnelly, Patrick, 26,125
Downs, Jonathan, 2,125
Dragaud, Pierre, 1,125
Drayton, Glen, 67,125
Drayton, John, 9,125
Drayton, Thomas, 37,125
Dugan, Col. Thomas, 66,126
Dugan, John, 82,125
Dugan, Park, 23,125
Duke, Moses, 27,108
Dumont, Guillaume (William), 80,126
Dunlap, James, 25,68,100,126
Dunlap, Rev. David Ellison, 87,126
Dupree, James, 57,126
Durr, Jacob, 76,126

Edgerton, Otis, 66,127
Edings, Joseph, 81,127
Edings, William, 16,32,96,127
Ellerbe, Capt. William, 15,19, 28,86,127,128
Elliott, Charles, 7,95,128
Elliott, Col. Barnard, 15,128
Elliott, Samuel, 25,128
Elliott, Thomas Law, 28,128
Ellis, John, 82,128
Ellison, Robert, 26,128
Elms, William, 46,128
Ernest, Henry, 55,129
Evans, Cadwell, 1,129
Evans, John, 43,63,97,129
Ewing, Adam, 49,129
Exum, William, 72,129

Fair, Isaac, 2,20,129

Falconer, William, 45,129
Faucheraud, Gideon, 37,130
Felder, Henry, 2,51,65,130
Felder, Samuel J., 12,29,130
Fennel, Cullen, 55,130
Ferguson, Charles, 28,79,130
Finch, Edward, 21,131
Finklea, Hugh, 50,131
Flanagan, Dr. Reuben, 36,131
Footman, William C., 58,131
Ford, John, 57,131
Foreman, Benjamin, 13,131
Foreman, Isaac, 86,131
Fraser, Dr. James, 77,132
Fraser, J. B., 8,24,131,132
Fraser, John B., 8,131
Frazier, Benjamin, 35,132
Freer, Charles, 99,132
Freer, John, 77,132
Fretwell, William, 13,18,51, 64,81,132
Fripp, Isaac Perry, 32,132
Fripp, William P., 32,132

Gadsden, Thomas, 55,133
Gaillard, Capt. Peter, 87,133
Gallagher, John, 1,71,133
Gallman, Benjamin, 79,133
Garden, Alexander, 63,133
Gardner, Robert, 39,68,133
Garrett, Stephen, 64,133
Garvin, James M., 20,134
Geiger, Harmon, 84,134
Gervais, Rev. Paul T., 63,67, 77,93,134
Gilbert, Caleb, 90,134
Gilbert, Mrs. Caleb, 82
Gilbert, Jesse, 49,134
Gillam, Robert, 95,134
Gillett, Dr. Elijah, 19,42, 72,134,135
Gillett, Elijah, 19,135
Gillison, Samuel R., 53,135
Givens, John, 16,135
Glenn, James, 15,135
Glover, Andrew, 66,135
Glover, Col. Wilson, 45,135
Glover, Wiley, 40,55,135

SUBINDEX

Godard, Rene, 3,94,135,136
Godbold, General _____, 28,40, 136
Godbold, General Thomas, 29, 40,136
Goodwyn, Major James, 8,136
Gourley, Joseph, 39,136
Graves, Admiral _____, 92,137
Graves, Admiral Richard, 19, 74,92,93,137
Graves, Samuel C., 17,18,137
Graves, Samuel Colleton, 17, 18,136,137
Gray, John, 81,137
Gray, Robert, 25,69,137
Green, Col. _____, 35,137
Green, Richard G., 84,137
Griffin, Richard, 14,15,21,54, 59,87,94,138
Guess, John, 61,138
Gunnels, William C., 50,53,138

Haigood, William, 96,138
Hall, Ainsley, 20,139
Hall, Andrew, 62,139
Hall, David, 5,139
Hall, Thomas, 21,139
Hall, William, 23,139
Hall, Z., 31,139
Hamilton, Paul, 59,139
Hamlin, E., 79,139
Hamner, George B., 48,53,68, 74,94,96,139,140
Hancock, Simon, 20,37,140
Harleston, Col. John, 20,75, 79,140
Harleston, John, 20,38,75,79, 140
Harley, William J., 53,140
Harris, John, 11,15,25,44,65, 80,140,141
Harrison, Edward, 66,141
Hart, Daniel, 40,141
Hart, Derril, 36,141
Harter, Henry, 34,141
Haseldon, John, 28,64,141
Hay, Col. Frederick J., 33,141
Heath, Frederick, 46,141

Henderson, David, 54,142
Henderson, General Wm., 89, 142
Henry, George, 3,100,142
Henry, James Edward, 29,142
Herbemont, Nicholas, 8,142
Herron, William H., 88,100, 142
Hesse, Daniel, 30,142
Heyward, Daniel, 10,21,35,38, 142
Heyward, James, 5,143
Heyward, John, 35,142
Heyward, William, 22,142
Hicks, Claudius P., 98,143
Higginbottom, James, 52,143
Hill, Jonathan, 35,143
Hodges, Gen. George W., 87, 143
Hodges, Richard, 47,143
Holland, John, 63,143
Holman, Conrad, 66,101,143
Holman, James C., 99,101,143
Hoof, James D., 44,48,143,144
Hoover, John, 48,144
Hopkins, George W., 35,89,144
Horger, Jacob, 85,144
Horry, Elias, 24,32,144
Horry, Elias Lynch, 53,60,144
Houston, Alexander, 69,144
Howard, Richard, 56,144
Huger, Hon. Daniel Elliott, 47,60,144,145
Hughson, John, 32,145
Hull, Gideon H., 11,53,145
Hunt, Col. Benjamin F., 65, 145
Hunter, Andrew, 11,145
Hurst, Robert, 58,145
Hutchinson, Mathias, 26,30, 97,145

Inabinit, James, 33,146
Irby, Charles, 54,146
Izard, Ralph, 71,85,146

Jackson, Thomas, 44,146

SUBINDEX

Jaffray, J., 15,146
James, George, 37,38,42,146, 147
James, John, 3,34,66,147
James, Philip, 51,147
Jenkins, John H., 36,147
Jenkins, Joseph John, 35,147
Jenkins, Micah, 34,147
Jeter, William, 61,71,98,147, 148
Jewell, Benjamin, 1,63,64,77, 87,148
Johnson, Col. Wm., 33,90,148
Johnson, James, 10,148
Johnson, Thomas N., 33,148
Jones, Thomas, 69,149

Kennedy, Robert, 1,6,149
Kennerly, Joseph, 30,149
Kimbrough, John, 7,149
Kinard, John M., 28,149
Kinard, Martin, 41,149
King, John, 98,149
Kittles, Jacob C., 9,149

Laborde, Peter, 26,150
Lacoste, Charles Gregorie Arnauld, 37,150
Ladson, Major James, 6,150
Ladson, Thomas, 40,150
Lamb, Alexander, 54,150
Lane, William S., 46,150
Langley, Christopher, 15,150
Lattimer, Benjamin, 28,150
Laurens, Col. John, 41,150
Laurens, Edward R., 53,150
Laurens, Henry, 47,151
Lawton, Winborn, 46,151
Leake, George, 9,11,18,151
Lee, Andrew, 26,151
Lee, Eleazar, 87,151
Lewis, Jesse, 73,152
Lewis, John, 47,59,151
Lewis, Samuel, 81,151
Lewis, William, 71,151,152
Lewis, William L., 19,152
Lindsay, Patrick, 99,152

Lloyd, John, 83,152
Long, Robert, 97,152
Long, William, 29,60,98,152
Lothrop, Seth, 59,73,152
Lowndes, Thomas, 52,152
Lowrey, James M., 9,153
Lushington, R., 31,153
Lyles, Col. Aromanos, 64,153

McBee, Elijah, 77,153
McCullough, Hans, 11,154
McDaniel, James, 70,154
McDonald, Adam, 48,154
McDonald, Middleton, 11,154
McDonald, Wm. M., 59,154
McDow, James, 22,33,34,154
McDow, John J., 1,154
McJunkin, Joseph, 23,29,49, 90,99,155
McKenzie, Daniel W., 16,17, 93,155
McLennan, John, 95,155
McLure, William, 29,33,59,78, 156
McMullen, Hugh, 17,100,156
McNish, Charles L., 63,156
McNish, Charles Lycurgus, 63, 156
McPherson, General John, 73, 156
McPherson, James E., 95,156
McWilliams, Samuel, 58,157
M'Connico, William, 20,153
M'Culloch, Hance, 12,153
M'Daniel, Charles, 65,154
M'Daniel, Thomas, 26,154
M'Dowall, Captain Alexander, 71,154
M'Dowell, Patrick, 14,154
M'Leod, Rev. Doctor Donald, 97,155
M'Pherson, Gen. John, 73,156

Mackey, Thomas, 83,157
Manning, Mealy, 7,157
Manning, William L., 86,157
Martin, George, 37,157

SUBINDEX

Martin, Robert, 1,157
Martin, William O., 88,157
Massey, George, 20,34,38,157
Massey, James R., 22,157
Mathewes, Wm., 46,157
Mathews, William, 9,19,46,157, 158
Matthews, Samuel P., 86,158
Matthews, William, 46,158
May, John, 20,158
Maybin, Andrew, 16,90,158
Mayo, John, 6,30,62,158
Mazyck, Samuel, 44,158
Mazyck, Stephen, 24,41,68,158, 159
Meggs, J., 86,159
Mellard, Elisha, 83
Messervey, Capt. Phillip, 5, 159
Michau, Isaac, 2,159
Michau, Manassah, 76,85,159
Michau, Paul, 12,70,159
Middleton, Arthur, 7,47,60,79, 159,160
Middleton, Hugh, 74,160
Mikell, Ephraim, 6,13,81,160
Mikell, J. J., 7,160
Mikell, William Joseph, 17,160
Miller, James, 2,75,160
Miller, Samuel, 69,160
Miller, William, 4,35,160
Minter, Joseph, 18,50,89,100, 160,161
Miscally, Daniel, 78,161
Mitchell, Benjamin, 24,161
Mitchell, Stephen, 57,91,161
Moer, William, 74,161
Moffatt, William, 37,78,161
Moore, Henry, 95,162
Moore, Isham, 9,13,71,72,162
Moore, James, 51,162
Moorman, Thomas, 16,76,162
Mosely, John, 17,162
Moser, Philip, 12,162
Mouzon, James L., 62,163
Moye, Matthew, 59,73,76,163
Muckenfuss, Michael, 25,163
Murchison, Kenneth, 26,163
Murray, David, 95,163

Murray, John M., 90,163
Murray, Joseph J., 39,163
Murray, Joseph James, 17,39, 62,63,163
Musgrove, Edward, 84,163
Myers, Col. David, 18,68,164
Myers, David, 18,68,163,164

Nail, John, 61,164
Naisor, Philip, 10,164
Nasar, Philip, 10,164
Neilson, John, 91,164
Nettles, Wyatt, J., 53,164
Nettles, Zachariah, 80,84,164

Ogletree, Rev. Benjamin S., 3,6,165
O'Hara, Arthur, 28,165
O'Quin, Daniel, 85,165
Oswald, James, 83,166
Oswald, Joseph, 24,80,165
Owens, John A., 30,91,166

Palmer, Jesse, 97,166
Palmer, Thomas, 68,166
Palmer, William, 88,166
Parris, Henry, 18,36,49,62, 167
Parris, William, 42,167
Patterson, Anthony, 21,40,55, 93,99,167
Pawley, John, 32,167
Payne, John W., 9,168
Payne, Wesley, 41,168
Pearson, William, 7,168
Pendarvis, Joshua, 94,168
Perdriau, Peter, 17,28,75,168
Perronneau, Arthur, 41,168
Perry, Edward, 31,59,85,91,169
Perry, Isaac, 5,95,168
Perry, James, 40,86,168
Perry, Zadock, 4,168
Perryclear, Michael, 52,169
Pettus, J. D. O. K., 78,169
Phaelon, Major Edward, 45,169
Phillips, Stephen, 67,89,169

SUBINDEX

Pickens, Ezekiel, 67,169
Pickett, James R., 57,169
Pickett, Phillip H., 97,169
Pinckney, Thomas, 45,47,169,
    170
Polock, Levi, 54,65,170
Pope, Capt. William, 85,170
Porcher, Peter, 42,170
Porter, John, 10,170
Postell, William, 47,170
Pou, William, 50,170
Powel, James, 90,170
Powell, Medicus, 31,170
Price, William, 91,171
Priester, Nicholas, 90,92,171
Priester, William, 44,46,98,
    171
Pringle, James Reid, 75,171
Pullam, Benjamin, 10,11,13,80,
    171
Puryear, Reuben A., 65,171

Rainsford, Thomas, 15,75,172
Ramsey, John, 50,172
Read, James Withers, 60,172
Reid, Jethro L., 17,62,172
Rhode, Christian, 19,172
Rhodus, William, 11,172
Richardson, Col. _____, 56,
    173
Richardson, James Burchell,
    30,64,65,86,173
Richardson, John, 1,172
Rivers, George A. C., 81,173
Robert, John, 9,21,77,173,174
Roberts, John, 83,174
Robertson, George, 19,174
Robinson, William, 23,95,174
Rogers, William, 57,174
Rowand, Charles E., 25,83,174
Ruff, George, 79,174
Russell, Nathaniel, 24,63,174,
    175
Rutledge, Edward, 4,67,175
Rutledge, Henry M., 30,175

Sabb, Thomas, 28,175

Sabb, William, 78,175
Sanders, Jordan, 15,175
Sartor, William, 58,175
Satterwhite, Bartlet, 35,175
Schinholster, John, 2,82,176
Schmidt, Dr. John W., 3,176
Scott, Thomas, 70,82,176
Seabrook, John, 59,176
Seabrook, Thomas Wilkes, 57,
    78,176
Sealy, David, 30,55,176
Shackelford, William C., 54,
    79,177
Shackleford, Richard, 92,177
Shaw, David, 7,177
Shaw, William D., 7,177
Shaw, Wm. D., 7,177
Shrewsbury, Edward, 98,177
Simons, Charles Dewar, 33,178
Simons, Samuel B., 98,178
Sims, Charles, 57,178
Sims, Nathan, 37,178
Sims, Col. Reuben, 3,36,80,178
Sims, Reuben, 80,178
Singletary, Daniel M., 61,178
Singleton, John, 60,179
Singleton, Matthew, 65,178
Singleton, Richard, 24,179
Sinkler, James, 77,179
Skinner, George, 19,179
Skirving, Col. James, 84,179
Skirving, James, 72,84,179
Smart, James, 49,179
Smith, Benjamin, 28,180
Smith, George, 11,84,180
Smith, Henry, 72,179
Smith, Jesse, 39,179
Smith, John, 10,179
Smith, Josiah, 84,180
Smith, Peter, 34,180
Smith, Philip, 50,73,180
Smith, Samuel, 12,26,48,63,180
Smith, Thomas, 37,79,179,180
Smyth, Robert, 69,181
Snelgrove, Henry, 37,51,54,
    55,92,181
Snider, John, 93,181
Snoddy, Andrew, 83,181
Snowden, James David, 55,181

SUBINDEX

Sommers, James D., 57,182
Sommers, John, 12,78,181
Spann, Charles, 76,182
Spann, William, 41,182
Spencer, Captain John Vesey, 35,182
Spiva, David, 23,182
Stairley, George, 74,182
Stanyarne, J., 57,62,79,82, 154,182
Stanyarne, William, 32,98,182
Starke, Philemon, 43,183
Starke, Reuben, 71,182
Stephens, George, 48,68,183
Stevens, George, 68,183
Stewart, Alexander, 5,65,183
Stewart, James, 54,183
Stewart, John, 98,183
Stewart, Thomas, 13,72,183
Stobo, J., 71,183
Stone, Daniel, 59,183
Stovall, Lewis, 87,183
Strong, Robert, 52,184
Stuart, James, 49,184
Sullivan, James, 78,184
Summers, Humphrey, 23,184
Swan, Thomas Thompson, 88,184
Swindersine, Andrew, 7,184
Swinton, Hugh, 8,184

Talbird, John, 41,184
Tate, Enos, 46,184
Taylor, Henry, 97,185
Taylor, John, 9,184
Taylor, Walter, 67,184
Taylor, William, 16,97,185
Taylor, William M., 22,185
Templeton, Alexander, 94,185
Thomas, D., 3,185
Thomas, Edward, 42,185
Thompson, James Booth, 56,186
Thompson, John Linton, 22,83, 185,186
Thompson, William R., 22,40, 54,185,186
Tims, Amos, 36,186
Tisdale, John, 13,186
Tomlinson, Thomas, 95,186

Tompkins, Samuel, 78,186
Tompkins, Stephen, 21,186
Tonge, Edward, 34,186
Trescott, Doctor John Sen, 30,85,186
Tyler, Henry, 77,187
Tyler, William, 80,82,187

Userry, Thomas, 4,187

Vanderhorst, Arnoldus, 23,45, 82,187
Vanderhorst, Elias, 82,187
Verdier, Simon, 31,188
Vickory, William, 23,46,188
Viers, Maurice, 12,188

Wagner, Effingham, 54,188
Waight, Abraham, 87,188
Waight, Isaac, 2,187,188
Walfe, Jacob, 27,188
Walsh, Thomas, 95,163
Walker, Legrand Guerry, 90, 188
Wallace, Howell, 9,188
Ward, Richard, 85,189
Ware, Henry, 34,189
Waring, Thomas, 64,189
Washington, Thomas, 68,189
Waters, Philemon Berry, 80, 82,189
Watson, Hardaway D., 51,87,189
Webb, Benjamin, 35,189
Webb, John, 50,189
Webb, Joseph, 25,58,189,190
Wells, Matthew, 28,190
West, John, 76,190
Whaley, Thomas, 62,190
Wheeler, William, 39,190
White, James, 77,191
White, Joseph B., 9,24,38,191
White, Leonard, 5,25,190
White, William, 32,191
Wicker, Uriah, 51,191
Wilbourne, William, 96,191
Willard, Prentiss, 62,192

SUBINDEX

Williams, Thomas, 44,96,192
Williams, Washington, 14,192
Williman, Christopher, 7,23,
    50,70,192
Willson, Thomas, 15,192
Wilson, George, 48,192
Wilson, John, 83,192
Winckler, Nicholas, 52,192
Wise, Major Samuel, 4,13,14,
    193
Withers, Richard, 92,193
Wonderly, David, 99,193
Woodward, William T., 10,193
Wright, Samuel, 54,194

Yeates, Thomas, 20,27,48,194
Yeldell, James, 13,194
Young, Thomas, 62,194
Youngblood, David, 66,195
Youngblood, William, 67,98,194

Zimmerman, Jacob, 50,195